The Coincidence of Novembers

The Coincidence
of Novembers

*Writings from a life of public service
by Sir Patrick Nairne*

Edited by Sandy Nairne

unbound

First published in 2020

Unbound
6th Floor Mutual House, 70 Conduit Street, London W1S 2GF

www.unbound.com

Text Design by Ellipsis, Glasgow
The text is set in Sabon, designed by Jan Tschichold and released in 1967

A CIP record for this book is available from the British Library

ISBN 978-1-78352-830-1 (hardback)
ISBN 978-1-78352-831-8 (ebook)

Printed in Great Britain by CPI Group, UK

1 3 5 7 9 8 6 4 2

CONTENTS

When our family was younger, my wife and I lived near the famous Hampton Court Maze – not the most difficult of mazes, but less easy than it looked. I can see now my children dashing excitedly into it – as many of us dash into life when we are young, full of hope and confidence that we shall get what we want and find what we are looking for.

Our life in this world has something of the character of a maze. We are soon touched by doubt and a sense of failure as we begin to learn how easy it is to take the wrong turning or to mistake the path. Occasionally we are disturbed by the confident cries, or the plaintive shouts, of others on the far side of the yew hedges. We know that we must keep going or we shall be lost. And as we struggle on, we realise that, if we could only get above the dark maze – if we could rise just a short way above it – we could see the right path and the turnings we must take.

From 'Christian Faith and the Public Service',
University Sermon given by Patrick Nairne at the University Church
of St Mary the Virgin, Oxford, 30 October 1983

FOREWORD

by Peter Hennessy

It was Pat Nairne's friend and Civil Service contemporary, Ian Bancroft, who caught the motive power of that generation of civil servants who made the transition from the battle scapes of North Africa, Western Europe and the North Atlantic to the corridors of Whitehall once the war was over. We were, said Bancroft, forty years later as his cohort moved into retirement, the intake who 'began their official lives believing that everything was achievable'. Pat was a shining member of the group of men and women brought into the Civil Service by what were called the 'reconstruction competitions' run by the Civil Service Commission. Pat's was a public life shaped and sculpted by the notion of Crown Service, both military and civil, starting with the Seaforth Highlanders during the Second World War and through a range of government departments in the peace. It was one of the great bonuses of my professional life, as the young man who wrote about Whitehall for *The Times* in the late 1970s and early 1980s, that I got to know him.

Like most of his contemporaries, Pat steered by the stars bequeathed by the Second World War and the early Cold War. The Beveridge Report of 1942, the Education Act 1944, the Full Employment White Paper the same year and the National Health Service Act 1946 gave them that social and economic blueprint, and the NATO treaty of 1949 their politico-military one. Mix in the process of turning the Empire into a Commonwealth and you capture the shared purpose and promise of which Ian Bancroft spoke.

Pat, as I came to appreciate as a young reporter, brought a special personal duty of care to all this, allied to a striking precision with thought translated into words, and words transmitted to the page in especially beautiful writing – a hand so distinctive that I could instantly recognise it in the files in the National Archives from Operation Zebra (the Admiralty's contingency plan for mitigating the 1948 Dock Strike) onwards when I began my historical research into the Attlee government. His sense of beauty and purpose also found expression on paper in his landscape watercolours.

From our very first conversation in 1975, when Pat was administering the EEC Referendum of that year for the Cabinet Office and was authorised to speak to me, I appreciated his gift for context and explanation. Looking back, Pat was on the inside track of so many policies and events that punctuated the post-war years – those seemingly endless defence reviews, that perpetual disrupter the European Question, the maintenance of the UK as a nuclear weapons state, civil contingency planning and, finally, as permanent secretary at the Department of Health and Social Security, the sustenance of the great engine rooms of the welfare state at a time of high inflation and industrial strife. All of them were stress points – under increasing strain after the oil price shocks of 1973–74 and the succession of sterling crises before and later. Pat worried – but he never despaired – he continued to abide by the 1940s ideals supported by his deep love of his country. He also sustained excellent relationships with his ministers and his time as private secretary to Denis Healey as Secretary of State for Defence was one of *the* great partnerships (*see Appendix 1*).

Pat's post-Whitehall life was rich in public service too. His membership of the Franks Committee into the causes of the Falklands War meant his being touched, yet again, by one of the great hiatus moments of post-war British history. He also flourished as Master of St Catherine's College, Oxford with his special gift for personal as well as collegiate relationships.

The Pat Nairne I knew comes alive in the pages that follow. His breadth of interests shines through (he was truly a broad-gauge man) as does his humanity. I relished every conversation I had with Pat – and I miss him.

May 2019

Peter Hennessy is an award-winning writer and historian with a special interest in the history of government. He has worked as a journalist and leader writer for many years and was Whitehall correspondent for The Times *between 1974 and 1982. In 1992 he was appointed as Attlee Professor of Contemporary British History at Queen Mary, University of London. He was created a cross-bench member of the House of Lords, as Lord Hennessy of Nympsfield, in November 2010.*

INTRODUCTION

by Sandy Nairne – Father and Son

Tuesday 15 August 2006. My eighty-fifth birthday. Oh dear. 'At my back I always hear / Time's winged chariot hurrying near'*

I may not always see my father, but I often hear him nearby. I hear his soft but insistent voice – an occasional slur on the r's, but an otherwise clear intonation and his slightly old-fashioned Home Counties' accent. The sound of his voice remains intertwined with his written words: the carefully chosen phrases, his precise punctuation and spacing of text.

I can picture him writing. Indeed, my father sitting at his desk in his study at South Lodge (our family home in Surrey) is an early and persistent childhood memory. He might turn around as I enter, or signal for me to come in while he finishes some dictation or completes a letter or postcard in his fine italic hand. I wait, and then he gives me his attention. Or when, even younger, I am looking up at his study window from the yard at South Lodge (on a Sunday afternoon for instance), I see him with his head down, focused on the papers spread across his desk.

Somewhat against himself, he would sometimes quote the well-known line from Logan Pearsall Smith: 'People say that life is the

---

* From Patrick Nairne's 'Pain Diary 2', 2006–2010, 15 August 2006; quotation from Andrew Marvell's 'To His Coy Mistress', published 1681.

Patrick Nairne, South Lodge, Christmas Card, 1955.

thing, but I prefer reading.' He did read a lot – and enjoyed cross-words from a very young age – which gave him a lifelong love of words and writing but always linked to his interests in art, history and people.

———

To ask what kind of a father he was is to open up many questions about a father–son relationship spanning sixty years. He couldn't be there when I was born because in June 1953 he was confined to the Benenden Sanatorium in Kent, being treated for tuberculosis, while my mother was staying near Winchester with her parents-in-law. Nor could we celebrate my sixtieth birthday together as he had died just days before, aged nearly ninety-two. But pretty much everything in between involved my love and respect for an out-standing though modest man and immensely supportive father, whom I admired and adored. Words already feel inadequate.

In the practical aspects of parenting my mother was, of course, closer than my father. In child-rearing and domestic matters –

certainly cooking, meals and clothes – she had absolute command. On a visit much later to Yew Tree (the home in Chilson near Charlbury purchased by my parents in 1982) my father suggested as we were leaving that we might collect some windfall cooking apples to take home (probably fearing, as he would with a glut of damsons, that they would otherwise appear at the supper table for the foreseeable future). Immediately my mother jumped in with: '*You* are not in charge of apples,' now an oft-repeated family catchphrase.

I don't have a single memory of my father ever being involved in discipline. He must have had a view; certainly when my misbehaviour caused me to be 'locked in the cupboard' – a kind of utility room at South Lodge for tools and odds and ends – until I had calmed down. But my father was there if I needed him, and his twinkling eye and broad smile were always encouraging. I may have accepted when young that his time was rationed. Even now I feel slightly guilty when I think how many summer regattas my parents attended through the years of school rowing.

Nairne family at South Lodge, 1964.

I learned much from being a third child, growing up in a noisy, argumentative family melee with two brilliant and bossy elder sisters, Kathy and Fiona. By the time I was eight my twin brothers, James and Andrew, had arrived, and soon after my youngest sister, Margaret, was born, making the full set of six, three of each. Together with my parents we could dance an eightsome reel; though the only time I remember us trying, it ended in some disarray.

Trim but not tall, my father was still a man to look up to. In my teenage years, I became increasingly aware of the importance of his role and status as a senior civil servant. In 1970 he came to lecture to the sixth form at Radley College and I listened with rapt attention as he described coordinating the responses to the *Torrey Canyon* oil-spill disaster of 1967. There were occasional events linked to his work. To stand at the Admiralty or Cabinet Office windows to watch the Trooping of the Colour was a great thing. I might, as a child, have wanted a father who would play football with me, but I don't remember pining for this.

However, as an adolescent I had acquired a father who would on occasion take me to exhibitions – including into private galleries in Cork Street, ignoring any off-putting looks from someone sitting at the desk – and encouraged me to join him when painting at weekends or on holiday. His incredibly skilful handling of watercolours was somewhat intimidating – controlling the wetness of the rough paper and working with subtle colours to create beautiful landscapes – so I picked up a pen to draw instead. This way I could still claim my time with him.

As a child, my knowledge of my father was simply the *experience* of him. As I grew older there were a few rites of passage. Although he offered no general discussion of sex – that I remember – before I went away to boarding school, he gave a gentle warning to be wary of older boys. Later I asked him what career he thought I should follow. He was a bit nonplussed but explained that as no one in the family had ever made any serious money (being vicars, solicitors or other low-key professionals), maybe I should consider going into business. I asked him how I might pursue this and he said he thought 'there are some quite interesting people in merchant banking'. Only years later did I register the significance of his implication that what really mattered was *who* you worked with: the crucial thing being to have intellectual stimulation in your working day wherever you were employed.

Much later, being aware that my parents had managed to support all six of us through private education, I asked him if he felt he had missed anything by not having more money for himself. He paused, then said, 'I might really have liked a better gramophone.'

It took me many years to get out of my head that I ought, like him, to have a *proper* professional career. It was hard not to be affected at some level by having a father who was running significant elements of the country, particularly when, after many years in Defence and then organising Britain's first referendum (in 1975, on Europe), he was switched to become permanent secretary looking after health and social security. It helped that he took such an equitable interest in what each of his children was doing. He never offered career advice again. Gradually I moved (through the Arts Council, two stints at the Tate and to direct the National Portrait Gallery) to become part of 'the establishment' – just working in a different section.

Our connection grew through making and looking at art but also through links with the same school (both of us being fortunate to study at a private boarding school, Radley College, where Peter Way, my housemaster, had been a contemporary of his) and a college at Oxford (University College). Later it was a delight to attend a couple of dinners at Univ that included three generations: my father, my son Kit and myself.

There were occasional professional overlaps involving discussions of art and health and the family connection with the Seafarers Hospital Society. My great-great-grandfather, Captain Alexander Nairne, was a founding trustee in the 1820s and I took my father's place on the general committee when he became

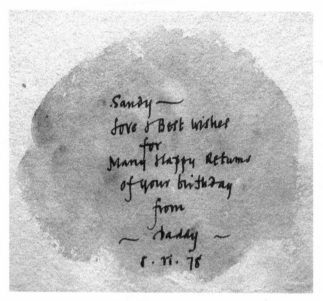

Birthday card, 1978.

President.* I was interested in family history and his Scottishness, though by my twenties I knew he enjoyed a Beethoven arrangement of Scottish tunes while I might choose to listen to unaccompanied singers from the Western Isles.

When younger, you know little of what goes into the making of your parents. Now I know more. Working through his papers since his death and editing his writings, I've explored parts of my father's work I knew less about and have been touched and impressed by his intelligence and diligence. The effort he made to fashion himself, in the best sense, emerges in his own account of his early schooldays. And this, like his wartime and post-war texts, links to an idea briefly pursued: that he might become a writer. His letters,

---

* The Seafarers Hospital Society was originally named the Seamen's Hospital Society and had the use of the Napoleonic hulk ships the *Grampus* and the *Dreadnought*. In 1870 it came ashore as the Dreadnought Seamen's Hospital, Greenwich, and was involved in various initiatives including the founding of the Albert Dock Hospital and the Hospital for Tropical Diseases. Today the Society supports the Dreadnought Unit at Guy's and St Thomas' Hospital as well as giving grants and promoting the health and welfare of seafarers and their dependants.

mostly in his italic hand, testify to his great ability to draft concisely and engagingly.* He was understandably bothered about any wilful misreading of what he had written: for instance by commentators on the conclusions of the Franks Report on the Falklands conflict. He had drafted much of the final text, and he cared very much about what each word was intended to convey.

———

After he had completed his tenure as Master of St Catherine's College, Oxford, in 1988, I repeatedly, probably boringly, urged my father to write about his life and about the passion for public service that his life exemplified. He told me that he was starting to write but didn't offer draft chapters for me to read. He worked from the intermittent diaries he kept – he always encouraged his children and grandchildren to keep diaries themselves – and his excellent memory. I realised the process might run against his Civil Service instinct to be discreet, though he was latterly a campaigner for freedom of information and might have regarded his own accounts as an intriguing historical source. This process coincided with other requests made to him to be a 'participant witness', from researchers wanting to understand about the navy after the Second World War or the handling of strategic defence issues or reform of the Civil Service or managing Health Service resources or inviting him to record (as he did) his memories of the North African campaign on the occasion of the fiftieth anniversary of the battle of El Alamein in 1992.

The speakers at his Service of Thanksgiving and the obituaries in 2013 neatly summarised what he had accomplished.† *The Times*

———

* Alongside the autobiographical writings left by my father (which form most of this book) are his many handwritten letters and postcards, as well as painted birthday cards, with carefully crafted words and italic script – all from a pre-email world.
† At the Thanksgiving Service in the University Church of St Mary the Virgin, Oxford, on 17 October 2013, Lord Wilson referred to 'this talented Renaissance man who shone in so many spheres'.

Painting at Lane End, Bembridge, Isle of Wight, early 1960s.

received an unusually large number of additional comments from readers. Many of these catalogued my father's achievements in public life but equally reflected a man who cared about other people: who remembered names and faces; who asked questions of them; who was unfailingly kind and generous in his day-to-day life.

When I prepared my own contribution to the Service of Thanksgiving, I found it especially hard to pin down my father's wit and sense of humour. I made reference to his catchphrases within the family: wryly amused ripostes such as 'Take your hands off that ham' or 'Liberty Hall' when someone was asking for something excessive. Andrew Motion described nicely how:

> I see him now as I saw him first, at what must have been Sunday lunch, round a crowded table, with the sun shining in, and the window behind him giving a half-view of the garden of South Lodge . . . He's smiling: that amused three-quarters smile. He's listening and observing, as if he finds all this kerfuffle loveable and necessary but at the same time extraordinary and slightly farcical. His eyes are twinkling. He's laughing – that sudden and unexpected-sounding bark of laughter.

There was the raised eyebrow as well as a broad smile. Having 'a detached sense of the ridiculous' was how he referred to it himself. Inevitably, the two official painted portraits (by Andrew Festing for the University of Essex and Tom Phillips for St Catherine's College) show a figure somewhat sterner than ever encountered in life. He had idiosyncrasies: porridge every morning with salt and never sugar; a routine of morning fitness exercises, which he once showed me and from which my own daily exercises are derived. His friend, Jan Morris, in a postcard from the 1980s, refers to his 'whistlephobia' (an aversion to people whistling loudly) which I never heard from anyone else, but may have been true. How little we know.

———

Reading his own accounts of parts of his life, there is some self-consciousness in relation to the earlier years and various things he seems to avoid. Little mention is made of his elder brother Sandy or Sandy's death, aged seventeen, of peritonitis following acute appendicitis in July 1937. The impact of this is hard to imagine. The nearest we get is in 'The Colonel's Tale':

> They [*his mother and father*] suffered together the sudden tragic death in 1937 of my elder brother, Sandy; I can scarcely bear to read my mother's few sentences in her diary. It was an acutely painful experience for us all but my father never felt able to talk about it to me. I would probably have felt embarrassed if he had.

Suddenly Pat (as he was known in the family and to friends, although he was called Paddy in his army days) was no longer the second of four but the eldest of three boys.* The loss was not discussed in the family, the sterner elements of a Scottish and military

---

* The four Nairne brothers: John Alastair (Sandy), 1920–1937, Patrick Dalmahoy, 1921–2013, James Kemp, born 1923, and David Colin, 1929–1998.

stiff upper lip prevailing.* But perhaps Sandy's death contributed to my father's lifelong sense of anxiety? This must have intensified through wartime service, and he makes reference to the terrible random loss of friends and colleagues. In a 1949 letter to his close friend Christopher Fyfe, he writes (probably only half-joking):

> I am often shocked that serenity should be so skin-deep. Blister my knee and the spectre of death marches at my side; give me a touch of flu and malignant melancholia shrivels my smile. I laugh at such weakness (and when pushed to it, conceal it); but why should it exist? I feel myself to be a very happy man, blessed ten thousand times. And yet always in one's spiritual veins there runs this dark bitter stream of pessimism. Perhaps it is essential, if one is to reach out a finger length towards attaining a state of grace. I would also argue that it is necessary nourishment for a state of happiness.

The war precipitated claustrophobia. Though not disabling, it meant he wanted to sit at the end of a row in the theatre and was uncomfortable if boxed in at a dinner. Anxiety – not depression – may have reinforced his determination to be well-ordered, planning ahead whenever he could. The many surviving stacks of neatly written and typed notes for public talks are testimony to his meticulous preparation. He was always tidy and well-dressed, with shoes shined (by him, every Sunday afternoon). The carefully chosen ties and a handkerchief in his top pocket were not just a hangover from school or army. Even into his nineties, when severely disabled, he ensured that he was properly presentable – clean-shaven on all occasions. He regarded shaving as a positive and therapeutic daily ritual.

Any anxiety was invisible to those who met him, to whom he showed charm, warmth and an unassuming confidence. And it was generally well hidden from his children. I little appreciated that his habit of working at weekends and in the evening stemmed both

---

* My father's younger brother James commented much later how this lack of acknowledgement was strange – tragedy masked by social decorum – but was simply accepted at the time.

from his scrupulous attention to detail and a desire to 'keep up'. He talked later in life about feeling 'behind' when he started in the Civil Service in 1947 and then from suffering the impact of two severe bouts of tuberculosis (in 1950 and 1953) which took him away from work and home for long periods. In a farewell letter of August 1967, Denis Healey (whom he served as private secretary for two and a half years) teased him by saying, 'If you have one failing, it is being over-conscientious' (*see Appendix 1*). However true, I am struck by his ability to focus at work on an amazing range of detail while commanding larger strategic issues. He also – always – contributed wonderfully to family life, kept up with most aspects of contemporary politics and culture, and stayed in touch with numerous friends.

———

My father's determination, stoicism and strong but critical Christian faith helped overcome his anxiousness, together with his fundamental bond with my mother. From falling in love in Oxford in the summer of 1947 to their wedding in September 1948, finding

Penny and Pat Nairne at South Lodge, 1962.

somewhere to live in London and then the birth of a first child in 1949, marriage and family became the crucial counterpoint to work and were central to his life. And the love and respect between my parents made them role models for their children and grand-children. Symbolic of their mutual respect was the fact that over sixty-five years they each stuck firmly to their own choice of tea: every day making a pot of Indian tea for my mother and another of China tea for my father.

The writings that follow (unlike private correspondence) do not offer much about their love and companionship. A complementary record exists in our mother's regular and delightful contributions to a correspondence club (named 'Phoenix') in which she chron-icled, over sixty years, the details of family life with six children and her contributions to the church, the local community and initiatives such as Sure Start.

———

When my niece Jo, daughter of my sister Fiona, gave birth to Ruby in 2015 – who would have been our parents' first great-grandchild – Kit remarked, 'And so it starts.' And I feel fascinated and fatal-istic about generational change. 'How soon our children make us die' is Dom Moraes' way of expressing the consciousness of play-ing one's part within a generational scheme.* At the time my father was very ill in 2013, I was thinking a great deal about change and retiring from my own job. I was conscious of how the phases of his life had divided between time in the Civil Service, time in vari-ous important public roles over the next decade or so and then time spent advising and writing (though interrupted by increasing physical disabilities, charted in a 'Pain Diary' that his doctors asked him to keep). The last time I saw him he was sitting up in bed in Banbury General Hospital, weakened but still with us. As my wife

---

* A phrase from the poem, 'For My Son', by Dom Moraes, quoted on p. 237 of *My Son's Father*, Secker & Warburg, 1968. I am, however, cheered every morning by brushing my hair with my great-grandfather's hairbrush.

Lisa and I left the ward with our daughter Ellie, I turned to look back to him. He gave a small wave, and smiled.

———

After my mother's death in December 2014 and since leaving the National Portrait Gallery in 2015, I have explored my father's life through sorting his papers and earlier family material. This was important for me and for my brothers and sisters and our children. I realised that his ideas and glimpses of his life might also interest those who never met him, and the idea of this book emerged.

The book is a selection from what my father wrote about himself and his life – his upbringing, education, work and ideas – most of which he intended for circulation or publication, together with a selection of his watercolours. His 1989 sermon 'The Sin of Pride' follows as a prologue and offers an introduction to his thinking, but otherwise pieces are arranged in broadly and sometimes overlapping chronological sections. Some were written at the time and others as reflections looking back, and some are taken from lectures or reports on important topics, with various styles included without my editorial correction. A few pieces focus on national policy issues, such as defence, health or the conduct of referendums, the last of which has a particular resonance since the 2016 European Referendum. Some pieces, such as 'Franks and the Falklands' and 'A Monitor in Hong Kong', appear to have been written with history in mind, while others, like 'A Christian in the Public Service' or 'The Perfect Pastime of Painting', have a more intimate sense of exploration. These matters engaged him differently at different points in his life.

A Chronology summarises the events of his life and the Bibliography includes a full list of his professional writings. My father's papers (now housed at the Churchill Archives Centre, Cambridge) contain many other texts from lectures and talks that I haven't selected for this volume; private diaries, scrapbooks and personal letters also survive. Included in this book are those writings that I felt to be personally or historically revealing, or simply poignant. Some of it is in close focus; other parts are broadly brushed. One longer piece of writing, to which my father gave the significant title of 'The Coincidence of Novembers' has been divided to fit the rough chronology. At the start of each section I have chosen a quotation from the commonplace book that he compiled and numbered from 1946 and which provides a snapshot of his reading.

The Coincidence of Novembers

The Sin of Pride

Excerpt from the Oxford University Sermon, given by Patrick Nairne in the University Church of St Mary the Virgin, 19 November 1989*

> Whom am I trying to convince now, human beings or God? Am I trying to please human beings? If I were still doing that, I should not be a servant of Christ.
>
> St Paul's letter to the Galatians, Chapter 1, verse 10

Can established truths take on a different aspect in each generation? Is pride quite the sin that it was? If it is, should it still be the first of the Deadly Sins? And why should it be regarded as lethal? Those questions confront us because pride, with a potential for sin, is subtle and perplexing in the forms it can take. And our increasing understanding of psychology in this century makes us more sensitive to its different facets.

At first sight, it appears so simple. There is *proper* pride, which we can respect; there is a *pernicious* pride, which can be like a cancer in the soul; there is a pride which reflects no more than *excessive self-esteem.*

I received a letter last year from the mother of a young RAF officer who had left St Catherine's College three years earlier and

---

* This annual sermon on the sin of pride was founded in 1684 by the Revd William Master, one-time fellow of Merton College, Oxford, and he offered each speaker a choice from twelve texts that accompany his benefaction.

had recently been killed in an aircraft accident. She wrote of her pride in him: 'He was a most respectful and loving boy who, in his short life, achieved everything, academically and physically, that he set out to do and finally gave the ultimate sacrifice.' Her pride sustained her in her grief. Proper pride, which is outgoing, rightly enriches the memories of many people each Remembrance Sunday.

Pernicious pride is turned inwards; it can corrode or embitter, for example, the relationships within families or between neighbours. It is not unknown for those who have quarrelled or felt themselves slighted or betrayed to be unwilling or unable to speak to each other for many years, allowing pride to block the way for the love of Christ and Christian forgiveness.

On the other hand, excessive self-esteem or vainglory can often be laughed away as the harmless vice of those with admirable virtues to offset it. Pooh-Bah in *The Mikado* or Malvolio in *Twelfth Night* were men of substance as well as figures of fun. The biographer Philip Ziegler opened his life of Lord Mountbatten of Burma by describing him as a man '. . . who for his own amusement, rarely took up any book unless it was one of genealogy, more especially one relating to his own forebears. Mountbatten would relax over the tapestry of his ancestry, enumerating the generations that divided him from the Emperor Charlemagne. His studies . . . gratified that pride in family that was one of the most prominent of his characteristics.'*

We smile with indulgence at the pride of a gardener in the best of rose beds or of a fisherman in the size of the catch. We recognise the pride of St Paul as he writes of the extent of the sufferings he has endured. All this is straightforward and may not be inconsistent with service to Christ.

But pride can be more complex. In the summer of 1988 St Catherine's had a second tragedy – the suicide of a second-year undergraduate. The undergraduate had appeared cheerful and easy-going, described by friends as the life and soul of any party.

---

* Philip Ziegler, *Mountbatten: The Official Biography*, HarperCollins, London, 1985, p. 21.

We were all deceived. Only after death did it emerge that, unknown to everyone in the college, the undergraduate had sought and received counselling because of acute feelings of inadequacy aggravated by a personal sense of the pointlessness of life and the prospects it offered after Oxford. It was Mark Twain who remarked at the turn of the last century: 'When people do not respect us, we are sharply offended; yet deep down in his private heart no man much respects himself.' There was no simple explanation for the undergraduate's tragic and unexpected death; but it appeared at the time that pride – in the shape of self-respect, and of a reluctance to admit any weakness to friends – was at the heart of unresolved inner conflicts.

Pride, and a consequent unwillingness to admit or accept any weakness, can be a cause of much wider conflicts. Last year I visited Israel and stood one morning on the massive outcrop of Masada 1,200 feet above the Dead Sea – a place symbolic of the pride of the Jewish people. A ceremony was taking place – one of many such ceremonies on that spot – to mark the commitment of a group of young Israelis to serve their country in the tradition of the self-sacrificing courage shown against the Romans at Masada by a Jewish garrison in AD 72. Nations should, of course, take pride in their own history; but, as the last hundred years have painfully shown, they also need to recognise the complexity of a proud nationalism that can promote aggression and foster irreconcilable international conflict.

A comparable pride in the achievements of the past and the present can be found closer to home, and closer to the bone . . . A former Master of my own undergraduate college, when he suggested as a junior fellow that the college might adopt in some matter the practice of another college, was sharply rebuked by the senior fellow: 'We on this side of the High Street, young man, are not interested in what happens in a college on the other side . . .'

But, if pride can be parochial in the worst sense, it can also be a stimulus to endeavour in the best. A month ago I attended a reunion in Caithness of my own battalion of the Seaforth Highlanders, one of the units of the Highland Division in the Second

World War. Over a hundred men and women had come together to renew the comradeship of the war years and to remember those who died on the long march from Alamein in the Western Desert to Cuxhaven in Germany. The Scots have never been backward in expressing their pride, as shown in their unashamed toast: 'Here's to us – Who's like us?' Under stress of war we shared something of the spirit of the young Israelis at Masada. But it was pride in our own battalion and in ourselves which sustained our morale – our courage and endurance – in the face of the enemy and far from home.

If William Master was disturbed by the pride of the Puritans and the autocracy of the Lord Protector, he would have been much more disturbed today by the sin of pride at its darkest – the godless pride of the communist regimes across the world with their repressive imposition of a party political system and their contempt for human rights; and he would have rejoiced at the promise of perestroika, the recent events in Berlin and Eastern Europe, and the remarkable revival of the Church in Russia. He might have deplored the political priority of seeking 'to convince' or 'to please human beings', which is inherent in the practices of our Western democracy, but he would also have applauded the impact on its political parties of the sometimes humiliating power of the ballot box.

And might he also have reflected, as I believe that we should reflect, that the deadliest, the most insidious, pride may be found today, not in any direct challenge to God, but in a widespread pride – a contemporary strain of hubris in society – that rests on a belief in man's self-sufficiency and on a rejection of the claims of the spirit? It is a pride which is deaf to God's word and blind to the light of Christ's redeeming power, unwilling or unable to accept in faith the mystery of divine love.

Pride is at the very centre of our being. It can strengthen our lives as Christians and so enrich our service to Christ; but it can also imprison us in our own self-centredness or self-righteousness and cut us off from God. It can lead us into the other Deadly Sins; but it can also give us a self-respect that preserves us from committing them.

We must humbly pray for God's help in understanding pride and in using it aright. We should never take pride in our humility, and we should always be humble in our pride. May our prayer be the prayer of John Donne: 'O Lord, never suffer us to think that we can stand by ourselves, and not need thee.'

I end with words from a sermon of John Henry Newman which place pride in ourselves in true perspective: 'We are not our own, any more than what we possess is our own. We did not make ourselves; we cannot be supreme over ourselves. We cannot be our own masters. We are God's property by creation, by redemption, by regeneration . . . Is it not our happiness thus to view the matter? Is it any happiness, or any comfort, to consider that we are our own? It may be thought so by the young and prosperous . . . But as time goes on, they, as all men, will find that independence was not made for man – that it is an unnatural state – may do for a while, but will not carry us on safely to the end . . .'*

* John Henry Newman, 'Sermon 6', Remembrance of Part Mercies, www.newman.org

FAMILY AND SCHOOL: 1921–1939

Introduction

Moreover, to be happy takes a complete lifetime. For one swallow does not a summer make, nor does one fine day; and similarly, one day or a brief period of happiness does not make a man supremely blessed and happy.

Aristotle, *Ethics*

Commonplace book, entry no. 276

In 1940, just before his nineteenth birthday, after one term at Oxford and before joining the army, my father wrote:

> *Saturday 13 July 1940* – 5.45 p.m. I meant to start writing this – diary I suppose you'd call it – two days ago, but it's always difficult to get down to Literary things – all forms of writing are hard work ... Very few don't have literary aspirations and some inspirations, but then, as H. Nicolson says in *Small Talk*, very few get beyond writing the first chapter or even choosing the title – that describes me – I'm certain to be idle about keeping this up.*

He was never idle and was always writing something – but diaries came and went. A few had been attempted earlier but during the war and through much of his Civil Service career, he was simply too busy. He wrote while recuperating from wartime

---

* Harold Nicolson, *Small Talk*, Constable, London, 1937.

injuries and illness, and later while away from work in 1950 and 1953 because of TB, and of course when retired. Most entries are in his italic hand, taken up in 1948 following encounters with Alfred Fairbank and Arthur Osley, who were both working in the Admiralty at that time [*see Chapter 26: Handwriting for Life*]. Letters were written to friends and to his parents (to his mother every week until she died), but a different, more knowing kind of writing emerges when he sets down parts of his life as a record.

However secure at home, his early school years were not straightforward and when he says of Hordle House in 'The Beginning' that 'It failed to enrich the spirit', one senses some degree of understatement. Occasionally my father and I played golf and I was aware of the 'lost' sporting interest which had been so important to him. But when he writes about it here, some of his concern is with navigating peer-group school pressures: an indication perhaps of his growing self-determination.

'The Colonel's Tale', by contrast, is based on having time, much later, to read his mother's diaries from the period of his childhood and to explore more about his father. This depiction of my grandfather (and the many letters with affectionate exchanges between them) contrasts with my own childhood impression of him, when he appeared somewhat fearsome and gruff. This view was reinforced through stories told by my father and his younger brother James, such as the tale of the Dundee cake, which we will come to later.

Scottish restraint in their very middle-class but somewhat austere upbringing was considerable. But despite my grandfather being unemployed between the wars, there was enough money in the family to send all four sons to board at private schools. My father's elder brother Sandy had narrowly escaped drowning when canoeing off Winspit Point in Dorset in August 1935,* but died from appendicitis and peritonitis in July 1937. The impact of this loss

---

* *Tragedy at Winspit*, published in 2016 by residents of Worth Matravers, tells the story of the death of Alastair Johnstone, with whom Sandy Nairne was out at sea in a double canoe when they got into difficulties; a memorial stone at Winspit was rededicated in August 2016.

must have been terrible; and not something he felt able to write about. He was helped both by being a boarding pupil at Radley College – which he refers to as being turned into 'a stimulating and civilised environment' by John Wilkes, the new warden – and by the support of those who became lifelong friends.*

SN

---

* Notable among these life-long Radley friends is Peter Way, with whom my father kept in touch throughout his life. As well as being Social Tutor for Andrew Motion and myself – Radley being where we met when I was thirteen – Peter was the English master who greatly encouraged Andrew's development as a writer.

I

The Beginning: Hordle House

Written while recuperating from tuberculosis in 1950

I was fascinated by the humming of telegraph wires. I still am. On my way to the Shawford Kindergarten on hot summer afternoons I used to stop by the first telegraph post on the road crossing the golf course and look up enthralled at the wires humming and throbbing against the blue sky. I must have been seven or eight years old and already I was too bullied by my conscience to dawdle for long. But there was something about those wires that would never let me go in a hurry. Their humming had the quality of haunting romance which would stimulate and disturb me when I put my ear to what I was told was the roar of the sea in the curled sea shell on the night-nursery mantelpiece or when I stopped to listen to the feverish high-pitched murmuring of insects in the overgrown rides of the New Forest during butterfly expeditions; only more so. When some-one first mentioned the music of the spheres and tried to explain, I had an immediate mental impression of that recurring scene by the telegraph post: the limitless expanse of blue sky, the harebells and wild thyme on the banks of the road and the fascinating hum in my ears. Time has crystallised it in my memory as the epitome of a golden age before I was sent away to school.

The years were not really so golden. I was born on 15 August 1921 when my father [Charles Sylvester Nairne] was still serving in the Seaforth Highlanders. In January 1925 he retired from the regiment and between then and the end of 1927 we moved house eight times. It was an anxious time for my parents: they had to decide on somewhere to settle and my father was, at the same time, trying to secure a job which would suit him. At that stage I had two brothers, Sandy a year older, James three years younger, so we must have been something of a handful to move about. We journeyed by stages from Belfast to Hampshire by way of Ayrshire and Edinburgh and I have only disconnected visual memories to record the passage: 'a host of golden daffodils' passionately admired at the age of three in the grounds of Culzean Castle; an Ayrshire thatched cottage ablaze in the early morning because its owner had smoked carelessly in bed; pigs, dangerously I thought, lolling along the lanes of the New Forest near Burley; a cousin being led away to be sick at a picnic near Lymington. The thought of one isolated incident amuses me now. We are in Edinburgh and I am four; I am resting on my bed in the afternoon, curtains drawn, when my mother suddenly interrupts to look for something in the room. She is in a hurry and cannot find it: 'Damn!'

Charles Sylvester Nairne, Compton Down, linocut for Christmas card.

Did I make any comment? Or laugh? Perhaps it was just that I was looking on. She turns on me with a sudden fierce intensity and adds: 'That's a bad word. That's a word you must never say.'

I am surprised; I have never heard the word before and it would never have occurred to me to say it. But now it is engraved in my mind forever.

In November 1927 we made our final move into the house which my parents had built on the northern slope of Compton Down, looking towards Winchester three and a half miles away. I would have expected the new home to make a lasting impression on me. We had lived close enough while it was being built and had often been taken to see the builders at work and to inspect progress on Sundays; but I can recall nothing but the discussions about what its name should be. This struck me as a most important problem and it was a relief when 'Plover Hill' – how I wished I had been the one to think of it – was finally agreed upon.

My parents could not have chosen a better place than Compton in which to bring up their children. The village itself was astride a lane in the valley below the Downs which ran westwards from Southampton to the Romsey roads; it had an ancient church in whose churchyard my elder brother was to be buried at the age of seventeen, an immense eighteenth-century rectory in which the rector could not afford to live and at the end of the lane an old farmhouse with a most handsome garden, a goldfish pond and, what meant most to us boys, a ripe selection of plum and apple trees in the autumn. There was no shop and no public house: these were at Shawford, a village on the north-east side of the golf course, divided from Compton by the main road from Winchester to Southampton.

The best feature of the district was the Downs. These were partly cultivated, partly given over to grazing, but mostly rough and open with brambles and yew trees, as wild as when the sons of Charles I rode across them, hurrying to the coast from the Battle of Worcester. From its position on their crest, Plover Hill had a view whose natural design I have never seen bettered. Due north and steeply below it lay Compton, beautifully and snugly wrapped

Charles Sylvester Nairne, Winchester Cathedral, linocut, 1930s.

in elms and beech trees. Above and beyond Compton there were three vast fields, bordered on their eastern edge by a thick finger of fir trees, enclosing the road to Winchester and pointing at the elegant shape of Winchester Cathedral which, whether a deep grey silhouette on misty days or gleaming white like a crystal palace in the sunshine, was a constant astonishment to the eye with its size. And to the north-eastwards, dominating the landscape, was St Catherine's Hill – 'hills' to generations of Wykehamists. This landscape was always bluntly referred to as 'The View'. It gave Plover Hill its character.

The advantages of Compton were more than aesthetic. The Downs had dells for picnics, woods to explore and trees to climb. The Shawford golf course gave me the most absorbing interest of my schooldays. We had many neighbours in similar houses with similar tennis courts and gardens for the summer and similar Christmas parties in the winter. And Winchester, beloved by me for its bookshops alone, was less than half an hour away on a bicycle. The material environment was, in short, perfect for an uninhibited, commonplace, happy childhood.

But when we started living at Plover Hill, my environment was strictly limited by the rule of the nursery. My general impression of life between the ages of six and nine consists of nursery meals, visits after tea to the drawing room and compulsory walks beside the pram along the only sort of roads on which prams could be satisfactorily pushed. I do not think that I was rebellious: I always took things very much as they came. I was never however the least attracted by the predicament of Peter Pan, and was later to feel nothing but contempt for those who have seriously reckoned their schooldays as the happiest of their life. Before I went to school the limitations of the nursery had fully persuaded me of the strategic advantages of going there; and a year or two at school left me in no doubt that the adult existence of my parents was far preferable to my own.

The experience of growing older has not disappointed me. I have only to look at myself at any age in the family photograph album to feel acutely thankful that I am my present age. My inclination has always been – and I suppose that this goes for most people – to concentrate on keeping my eye on the ball of the present in

Pat at Happisburgh, Norfolk, 1931, aged ten.

order to hit it squarely into the future in the direction I intended. Youth and good fortune contribute most to this outlook, but also the absence – in my earliest years anyway – of much past to dwell upon. I was happy enough: and the best evidence of a happy child-hood is that there is no evidence.

No evidence at least in one's own memory. That is the main difficulty in digging up one's own past: one can easily trace the general layout, but, without such landmarks as tragedy or excite-ment may provide, one is at a loss where to thrust the spade in beneath the surface. One seeks to relive the years, but it can be as difficult to enter one's own mind of twenty years ago as it is for a historian to enter the mind of a Pitt or a Fox 200 years ago. I can look at myself and my existence now as if they made up a piece of woven tweed and I can recognise the threads of different character or colour which have gone to make the present texture and pattern. What I cannot do is see the cloth as a whole at each stage of its weaving. I try hard. I stare at the face of the small boy standing in the preparatory school cricket team photograph, but cannot get behind it. His hopes, fears, pleasures, disappointments were intensely real at the time, often far more powerful than any joys and anxieties can be now. But time has buried most and diminished the rest.

Hordle House 1st cricket XI, Pat standing, second from right.

Perhaps frustration has made me too sweeping. Some memories are left, and, if isolated, these are as vivid as green oases in the desert sands. The snow of Christmas day, 1927, when the Cadells failed to reach us by car from Oxford: has snow ever fallen as thick and suddenly again?* The summer of 1929 when my youngest brother, David, was born and James and I were packed off to the Isle of Wight by steamer from Southampton: has there ever been an August of greater heat? And that sky behind the telegraph post on the road across the golf course: no sky has ever been bluer.

———

The spirit of competition was the main motivating force of my early life: I pay tribute to its persistent potency, for I always resented it. I was an anxious and unsure competitor, loathing the prospect of each succeeding competition; loathing because I cared. It would matter desperately whether I did well or badly and I have the deepest impression of struggling from my earliest days to maintain an undeserved reputation for doing well.

But why struggle? At the start, there is a natural instinct at work: a desire to please, often appease, others. I turned out to be bright; or so I had heard 'them' say. I could not let the brightness turn out to be a flash in the pan after all. It was clear that success at work or games meant so much even to undemanding parents. They too are players in the competitive game. 'My eldest, I'm afraid, failed his Common Entrance again' is not an agreeable rejoinder to the neighbour's remark that his boy has just won a scholarship. More important perhaps at the time, success was the surest currency with which popularity could be bought from one's contemporaries. One must make some contribution to the Schoolboy Community: though the capacity for making runs or scoring

* The Cadells were my father's uncle and aunt. Agnes Aimée Kemp, known as Dolly, elder sister to my father's mother, married Sir Patrick Cadell, administrator and historian of colonial India, and for many years they lived near Oxford at Frilford Heath.

goals was worth the most, the ability to play the mouth organ or do someone else's Latin prep for him counted for something.

In time however it became more and more a desire to satisfy oneself; and the screw of this compulsion was gradually tightened as I grew older. I doubt whether I care less now about the opinion of other people than I did when I was younger: I am certain that I care more about the opinion of myself.

My preparatory school, Hordle House, was near Milford-on-Sea and I started my first term there in September 1930. The sea was a splendid asset. Small boys have an unquenchable passion for bathing; in the summer term we would bathe most days after the beginning of June and a picnic on the beach was, I remember, a regular routine on Friday afternoons, when we would watch the weekly Union-Castle liner sailing down the Solent as the climax of our day. Even Sunday walks, anathema to us, were less tedious when conducted along the edge of the cliff as far as Barton-on-Sea golf course or, when winter seas were breaking, along the flotsam-strewn, shingly shore.

But its situation was not the school's only advantage. Apart from the normal amenities such as playing fields, tennis courts and car-pentry shop, there were grounds with paths suitable for bicycling and sandy banks and overgrown woodland where 'houses' could be dug or built. As the school had been in existence for only a few years, the classrooms and dormitories were bright with new paint and furniture, even though the house itself was old. What had impressed my parents the most, however, were the personalities of the headmaster and his wife. The Revd Ernest and Mrs Whately-Smith must have been in their forties; they had had considerable experience of preparatory schools before setting up on their own at Milford-on-Sea and they had sons of their own. It was evident at first sight that they were kind people with a sense of humour and an understanding of boys. All in all, Hordle House appeared to be a place at which boys would be happy. I was happy.

This mattered. Nine is an early age at which to start life away from home and misery may kill all the advantages of the expend-iture. But the purpose of a happy atmosphere is to provide the background for learning. Did I learn anything? When I got to Radley College I was surprised to find the large number of preparatory schools from which boys came. From all accounts these schools, which seemed to grow on the south coast of England as profusely as sea pinks, were, with a few notable exceptions, much of a muchness. They all appeared to produce about the same number of the idle and the hardworking, the good and the bad games players; and, though I fancy that Hordle House was better off than many in this respect, their amenities were more or less the same. However, the intellectual pretensions at Hordle House were low; it was not in the masters to make them otherwise.

Preparatory schools cannot normally afford to attract men with good university degrees as permanent members of staff. To offset this however, headmasters may often be excellent teachers themselves, capable of setting a high intellectual tone for all the masters who work with them. Mr Whately-Smith was not one of these. He was a competent and conscientious teacher of mathematics, but he had a limited imagination, little culture and none of the enthusiasm for intellectual things which all good schoolmasters should be able to communicate. He was a clergyman, though not to notice, and his Scripture lessons were balefully dull. His prestige with the boys rested on a pleasant but irresistibly firm manner, reinforced by the report, possibly mythical, that he had once been invited to keep wicket for Hampshire. I have the friendliest memories of him: reading aloud Sapper and E. Phillips Oppenheim on Sunday evenings, taking the swimmers for a bathe before breakfast on Sundays, supervising the building of a vast bonfire for Guy Fawkes Night, doing *The Times* crossword with me at lunch when I sat next to him as head prefect.* He was a man to inspire loyalty.

The masters under him were on the whole no less pleasant and easy-going; and their scholarship was as limited. One had jogged round the world in the Merchant Navy: fifteen years later he was

---

* Cyril McNeile was a soldier and author who used the pseudonym of Sapper; his most famous creation was *Bulldog Drummond*, published in 1920. Edward Phillips Oppenheim was a writer of many thrillers and short stories.

to be murdered by bandits on a rubber estate in Malaya. Another only stayed long enough, before joining the Sudan Police, to leave behind a well-established reputation for individual and cunningly contrived punishments. A third, after five or six carefree years, went on the stock exchange where he rapidly prospered while a fourth, who could not have been more than nineteen, was always known to be casting about for more congenial and remunerative employment and ultimately was killed as a test pilot before the war. These masters set the tone of the place; and a high-spirited, irresponsible tone it was. They had no vocation to teach and the effect of their loud animal spirits was to make the task harder for those who took their profession more seriously.

The latter were represented by an older set. There was a middle-aged man who taught Latin with admittedly a lazy lack of inspiration and left to be headmaster of a grammar school in Sheffield. What I remember most clearly about him are the backs of his hands, as he bent over one's desk to correct Latin sentences: they looked exactly like the skin of the sausages we had for breakfast on Sundays. After I had been a year at Hordle House, a master arrived to teach history and French who, with the reputation of being an international hurdler to fortify his authority, insisted on standards of application and accuracy which caused a widespread sense of grievance. His blunt announcement on entry, 'Dates this morning', would fill the backsliding members of the class with a most wholesome feeling of anxiety. Not least, there was the school's only mistress, a prim, small, kind-hearted woman of sterling qualities and an elegant round handwriting which was a model to her pupils; she had great patience and a fat Sealyham terrier called Jane.

There were never more than six or seven members of the staff at one time and it was the influence of the younger that prevailed. It was not just that their light-hearted consciences allowed them, for example, to entertain junior forms with reminiscences from their own schooldays or read the stories of P. G. Wodehouse aloud to the top set who were meant to be doing Greek, but something more pervasive. They had been brought up in their own public schools during the heyday of 'bloodism' in which the physical standards of sport were triumphant over things of the mind and spirit. They had more-over grown up in the restless, rootless years following the First World War, which they had just missed; they were typical representatives of the Jazz Age. At the same time, they had little of the detachment, that capacity for seeing the individual merits in every boy, which marks the wise schoolmaster. A boy who worked hard was a 'swot' to them no less than to his contemporaries and one who had no talent for games, a 'wet'. They would have considered a boy an oddity if he preferred Beethoven to Irving Berlin or knew more about books than Bradman.* In their assessment of boys, it was proficiency on the playing field, not in the classroom that counted.

Am I making too much of this? I seek to show the character of the gods whom we had to placate and the rules of the temple in which we had to serve. Hordle House was a strange foreign land to me. I had picked up a little of it from brother Sandy, who, being a year older, had already spent three terms there, returning to the nursery with the swagger of a soldier home from the wars; but, as in war itself, the greater part can only be learned by one's own experience. I had no ideas of my own about how life should be lived; I aimed to adapt myself as quickly as possible to the climate of opinion that prevailed. If an interest in sport was the thing, I was not to be outdone in keenness; if collecting cigarette cards or the manipulation of a yo-yo were the craze, then I would be no exception to it. Assiduity at work apparently went down badly and I took care not to look too assiduous. It seemed incomparably important to be good at games: I set myself to do my best.

But I was not good at games; and competition in these could not fail to be a struggle. Although I was neither tall nor tough, the trouble was not primarily a failure in either physique or determin-ation. What I lacked was a good eye, and without this no one will ever be trained into a first-class ball games player. It was my poor natural aptitude for the quick coordination of hands and feet which led me to take golf so seriously.

---

* The Australian cricketer Sir Donald 'Don' Bradman was the outstanding batsman of the interwar period, and arguably one of the greatest cricketers of any time.

I should like to remember when I was first bitten with golf. It had certainly become important to me by the time I was eleven; there was a crescendo of enthusiasm throughout my Radley years; and only now, living in London and married to a wife who does not play, am I free from the infection, though not immune, I feel sure, from relapse. There are great advantages in golf for the poor games player: one can practise it alone for as long as daylight lasts; and patient assiduity is rewarded to an extent which it can be in few other games. I came to spend more and more of the holidays on the Shawford golf course, sometimes with brother Sandy as my partner, occasionally with one of my parents doing duty as an opponent, but usually by myself.

Gradually I improved. But I never became a first-class player; my official handicap was never lower than eight. I believe that I took the game too seriously: one will never beat bogey out of a book. What is more, I never had the advantage of living near a good course nor of regular games with players better than myself. But apart from a thousand happy hours, what I got from my fanatical passion for golf was, in some measure, the qualities of character which the game stimulates. Golf is the game of self-help: a determination not to admit defeat until the last putt is in, self-reliance which recognises that no one is responsible for one's mistakes but oneself, and patient serenity when things go wrong; these are the qualities it cultivates.

But who am I to say that they have flowered in me? One other thing, however, that golf gave me for certain: a fillip to my morale in the petty world of sport at school. When others talked cricket, I could turn the conversation to golf; I could counter the prospects at Henley with speculations about the Open Championship. Better still, although I was never up to much myself, I usually found that I could beat most of my contemporaries once I had lured them on to a golf course.

I was never so bad at school games that the playing fields were a misery. I was not going to give up trying; no one could have persuaded me that it did not really matter much: it so clearly did. One Easter holiday a year or two later I had lessons from a good-natured Hampshire cricket professional in the grounds of Wolvesey Castle. It was probably due to them however that I was successful in getting my colours in the Hordle House 1st XI the following summer term. I rather fancied myself as a bowler and, with no tricks to offer but conscientious efforts to keep a steady good length, took four or five wickets in several matches. I recall that in the fathers' match at half-term I bowled the best cricketer amongst the fathers with a full toss and was gratified to hear him explaining that he had been yorked.

But if my performance on the pitch was poor, I did my best to make up for it with my keenness for everybody and everything connected with the game. I knew the county and the England record of most professional cricketers; and it was a perpetual disappointment that I lived in Hampshire whose performance in the County Championship was so regularly mediocre. The Commonwealth side visiting England each summer had become as essential a feature of life as plum pudding at Christmas; and when I was bowling at the nets, it was not a matter of short, plump Nairne, but Fleetwood Smith, irrespectively of height, or Martindale, irrespectively of pace, who bowled.*

This enthusiasm, so genuine and at the same time so artificial, was – indeed is – an important element in the competition of life. It is the expression of what amounts to a rule of society: if one cannot perform, at least be able to preach; if one must be only an onlooker, be sure that one proves the truth of the onlooker's own proverb that he sees most of the game. Usually in fact it is not those who are practising artists of assured success who are heard to talk the most about techniques and tendencies in their own craft.

Similarly, Hordle House society fed upon sporting talk; and it is not the only society which I have known to do so. Indeed, I have never been free of it except at home and, to a large extent, at Oxford. Today at the Admiralty I am always with people to whom rugger, rowing or cricket are major interests in life and I

---

* Chuck Fleetwood-Smith was an Australian spin bowler and Manny Martindale a West Indian fast bowler – both played in Test matches in the 1930s.

find myself taking as much trouble as I did fifteen years ago to have some opinion about, for example, what leg spinner England should try or the disadvantages of the County rugger championship. And yet, talk apart, for a short time in 1935 I was sincerely keen on playing cricket and it was a pity that that was not to last. One summer at Radley disillusioned me. Cricket became once again a game, a compulsory game, which provided no excitement and little exercise. I have not now played it for twelve years.

I had some small talent for rugger. Like running, however, it was not a game which depends entirely on a good quick eye: I had only to be sufficiently energetic and determined to achieve some competence. I soon learned that to tackle low was by itself a means of grace and a hope of glory; and this was something that anybody could make himself do. I greatly enjoyed rugger at both Hordle House and Radley and consequently found those terms the happiest in which it was played.

I also played soccer for Hordle House, but I fancy that I did not enjoy myself in the winter term of 1934. My place was on the left wing, a wretched position for a fellow who was distinctly limited to doing the little he could with his right foot. One vivid memory comes back. Eleven muddy small boys are walking slowly off their end of the pitch after the final whistle; the November dusk accentuates the gloom of their defeat by a rival preparatory school. I am one of them and the captain of our side suddenly turns savagely to me: 'You might have tried.'

Preparatory schools are simple, turbulent, primitive societies composed of creatures who cannot but be conscious of the physical things of life. Bicycling as fast as one could go down a stretch of path, remaining as long as one could in the sea on a hot afternoon, scoring tries against a rugger side one could easily defeat, eating one's fill at the Christmas dinner on the evening before the end of the winter term: these were the joys to which one looked forward. And honour, fair play, loyalty and, above all, physical endeavour were the main moral concepts of life rather as they appear to have been for the romantic heroes of medieval ballads or, more significantly, of popular school stories.

We read about Greyfriars, St Dominic's and the rest as if we were studying a textbook on which our professions depended, and, though we often sneered at them outwardly, inwardly we absorbed and accepted much of their morality and spirit. We pieced together from them moreover a pattern of existence: this, we half believed, was the way of life should be lived, the way indeed it most likely was lived at the public schools for which we were destined and about which we could never find out very much even from our brothers.

The fact is that small boys are reactionary and very conservative at that. They do not yet know much and they cling autocratically and stubbornly among themselves to what they do know. I never knew, for instance, even the officers' mess of a highland regiment to be so contemptuous and intolerant of those who showed any signs of having intellectual and artistic tastes. As I have implied earlier, such values were encouraged by the masters, for, broadly, the junior masters at least fully shared them. I do not entirely condemn these values. They were clean and healthy and their intolerance never led to concentrated bullying: we were undeniably a contented school during my time there. But it was wrong that the intellectual and spiritual side of our education should have suffered as a result; and there was no reason for it except the personality of the headmaster and the character of the staff he employed. Besides, less athletic values, so to speak, would have suited me better: I would have found the competitive strain less intense.

I was, I suppose, a success at Hordle House. I certainly thought myself so when I left. I had kept my end up on the playing fields. I had worked my way up to the top form in under three years and, after an unimpressive trial run at Winchester at the age of twelve, had come third on the scholarship list at Radley in March 1935. In my last term I was head prefect. And yet at the end of it all I have a feeling of dissatisfaction, of unfulfilment. I am not sure how conscious I was of this at the age of fourteen: I certainly could not help being aware of the uncongenial atmosphere, however keenly I tried to acclimatise myself to it. And I have never looked back to a sentimental stock of memories. Radley, Oxford, the Seaforth High-landers: they have all secured my affections for ever. But not Hordle House: it contributed its threads to the weaving of the piece of tweed and that is all. I know why. It failed to enrich the spirit.

Pat with John Gere, summer 1935.*

---

* John Gere became an art historian and a distinguished keeper of prints and drawings at the British Museum.

2

The Colonel's Tale

Written in 1996

'Only cads wear carnations at weddings'

Such was my father's greeting outside the College Lodge, recorded in my diary for Saturday, 24 June 1946. Back at 'Univ' – University College, Oxford – after the end of the 1939–45 war. I was attending the wedding of a Univ friend being married in the University Church – the reception, I imagine, in the College Hall. It was the end of the summer term and my father had called with the family car to take home some of my possessions.

My father did not grow carnations; I do not suppose that he knew much about them. He did not belong to the world of carnations and camellias, champagne and claret. But he would have claimed to know about cads – men, as he saw it, who abandoned their wife for another woman, or who were untrustworthy with money, or who displayed bad taste in what they wore. I can hear my father speaking: 'You have only got to meet chaps like that to know what they are like.'

Early in life he had had experience of such people. When he was in his sixties, he wrote a brief account of his school years, describing his unhappiness as a younger boy at Haileybury College. He was shocked by the low standard of honesty and behaviour of his contemporaries: 'It was only years afterwards that I realised that

The Nairne family at Baldock rectory, 1898. Charles Sylvester Nairne,
second from left.

many of my companions were cads. Not all by any means, but
there were enough cads at Haileybury in my day to merit the
description of "a rough shop" – as one of my friends put it some
years later.'

Good behaviour, conforming to the accepted conventions of
their social class, was of prime importance to my parents – perhaps
somewhat to excess. As a regular army officer and the son of an
Anglican clergyman, my father was ingrained with a disposition
for conformity.* Even a period of study at the Slade School of Art
and his friendship with artists did little or nothing to diminish it
– perhaps the reverse. His influence left me inclined to fuss all my
life about whether I was correctly dressed and behaving in the
'right' way. Parental influence at work, though the army left its
mark on me too.

---

* Revd John Domett Nairne, Patrick's grandfather, born 1846, served as vicar of
Baldock, Hertfordshire, from 1893 to 1921.

It was more or less by default that my father had joined the army and was commissioned in the Seaforth Highlanders. Unsatisfactory progress as a boy at Haileybury had led to his being moved from the classical to the modern side – a decision he had resented because he had not been consulted. He did not wish to be articled to his uncle's firm of solicitors, Baker & Nairne, and in his own words 'the fact that I was on the modern side suggested the army'. As he was thought unlikely to pass into Sandhurst, he sought a commission in the militia, for which no examination was required. Since a qualification for a regular commission was four periods of militia training, he wished to undertake his first training period as soon as possible. At the time of his application, in 1899, the only militia unit whose annual training was still to come was that of the Seaforth Highlanders at Fort George on the Moray Firth near Inverness – arranged for the month of September, since this particularly suited many of the rank and file who were fishermen from the Island of Lewis.

Charles Sylvester Nairne, Seaforth Highlander, c.1905.

So, assisted by the family connection of his uncle and god-father, Lieut. General Sir Charles Nairne, well known to the then Commander-in-Chief of Scotland, my father secured a commission in the Seaforth Highlanders. At the age of nineteen he spent the first month of his military career under training at Fort George. The militia unit was commanded by Colonel Sir Hector Munro of Foulis, described by my father as 'a charming and gentle county-magnate . . . nothing of a soldier but everyone liked him'. The men impressed him more than the officers – the former from the West Coast, many speaking only Gaelic, with 'beautiful manners and soft voices', the latter given to a scale of drinking which disgusted my father who had never tasted whisky.

He wrote: 'I think I was always sober. Had I been drunk I might have enjoyed myself more . . . I thought – if the army is all like this I shan't like it.'

I cannot remember him ever drinking whisky, regarding it, together with brandy, as a resource in the cupboard for moments of acute stress. Not surprisingly, however, Scottish regiments have a special regard for whisky, as the people of Devon and Somerset are likely to have for cider. My mother was shocked by the way in which strong drink could ruin the careers of some young officers. She would do her best to ration sweet eating by my brothers and myself, not because of the risk to health or teeth, but because she believed that an addiction to sweets might lead inexorably to an addiction to drink. When I joined the regiment as a subaltern, also at the age of nineteen, I found that I was frequently expected to drink whisky on Monday evenings in the Sergeants' Mess. My reaction was the same as my father's had been.

Two months after the militia training, war broke out with the Boers in South Africa; the militia units were required for active service, and my father was summoned back to Fort George from his parents' home in Baldock. By early 1900 he had completed what amounted to four months of qualifying training; as a result of the wartime need for more officers, no formal military examination was required and, having received good personal reports, my father was given a regular commission in April 1900. Thus began twenty-five years as a regular army officer.

Charles Sylvester Nairne,
drawings, 1916.

My own commissioning into the Seaforth Highlanders forty-one years later was equally quick and easy – and for a similar reason. In the early years of the 1939–45 war, with the serious setbacks of 1940, the army urgently needed more officers. In spring 1941, at the end of a four-month training course, I 'passed out' successfully and, supported by the nomination of the colonel of the regiment, I was posted as a second lieutenant in the Seaforth Highlanders to the same Fort George Depot which my father had joined forty-two years earlier – to be welcomed by several senior officers who had served under him.

It was an easy introduction to a regimental 'family' to which, like my father, I have remained deeply attached ever since. But, with the war over in the autumn of 1945, and not attracted by the suggestion that I might seek a regular commission, I welcomed an early release from the army and a return to my college at Oxford.

My father's experience on leaving the regiment was different and much more painful. It is impossible to judge how much of this was due to misfortune in a difficult post-war period and how much to

Edith Dalmahoy Nairne, 19 April 1923, by Charles Sylvester Nairne, watercolour.

his own character and capabilities. In the early 1920s, as second in command of the Seaforth Battalion in Northern Ireland, he must have had good hopes for the post-war years ahead. But they were not to be realised.

My mother kept a diary for many years of her life. The daily entries were exceptionally brief – usually no more than a note of what she had been doing or what had been happening. The weather might be mentioned, but rarely her feelings.

Tuesday, 14 October 1924: Lovely day after mist. Jimmy [*as my mother called my father*] didn't come home to lunch. Met him. General Cameron has recommended him for 'deferred promotion'. It is a great blow, for it has nothing to do with his personal record, but it will mean India in two years.

Three weeks later:

Saturday, 8 November: J heard from War Office that they won't give him promotion at all. Feel the bottom has fallen out of our world.

Three days later my mother wrote: 'Heard that Hopkinson is going to command. That's nicer than having an outsider and he is nice.'

Lieut. Colonel Hopkinson DSO, MC had had a particularly distinguished war record; he could hardly have been overlooked for promotion. As it happened, seventeen years later, 'Hoppie' (as he was known) was commanding the 1st Moray Battalion, Home Guard, to which I was appointed temporary adjutant after the retired officer serving as adjutant broke his arm when drunk outside a bar in Elgin. I found the white-haired old man friendly but inarticulate. For what guidance I needed I had to rely on the second in command, General Sir Douglas Baird, who had been ADC to Field Marshal Lord Haig ('Don't take notes when I speak to you. Haig never allowed me to take notes') and later Commander-in-Chief in India.

After her marriage in 1919 my mother had accompanied my father to India where he was serving with the regiment, and where my elder brother, Alastair (known as Sandy), was born in 1920.

Five years later, with a family of three small boys, she was unwilling to contemplate India again – even if my father had been ready to return there in the hope that promotion would eventually follow. He began to look elsewhere in the army, and General Cameron supported his application for the post of Commandant of the Boys School at Dunblane.

But on 13 December 1924 my mother wrote: 'The man who has Dunblane is a VC. What bad luck to be up against that!'

The War Office informed my father that he was to go on half pay at the beginning of February the following year. As Christmas Day 1924 approached, Sandy and I became ill with temperatures of over 100. We were moved into my mother's room, and she fell ill herself with a severe cold. On 29 December my father sailed

Alastair (Sandy) and Pat, Rush Park, near Belfast, 1923.

from Belfast to visit the War Office on (my mother recorded) a 'terribly stormy' night. She saw the New Year in without him.

On the last page of her diary for 1924 she wrote: 'Here ends the year in misery.'

There had been, and were to be, other tragedies in her life, but this was a particularly dark and dispiriting moment.

There is no evidence in the diary of any serious discussion about whether or not my father should retire from the army and make a new career in civilian life. On 1 January 1925 my mother wrote rather bitterly: 'The W. Office won't offer him anything of course – except abroad.' She quickly recognised the financial consequences of retirement. My father's retired pay would reduce their income by half; they would have to find a cheaper place in which to live; and, as my mother put it, 'we shall only be able to keep 1 nurse and 1 general servant' in place of the four they had in Belfast. It seems doubtful whether they realised how difficult it would be for my father to find a job. The War Office initially retired him in the rank of major; but his strong protest at the unfairness of this in the light of his wartime service in command led to the granting of the rank of lieutenant colonel. This may or may not have been helpful in the search for a job, but it gave him a respectable status for the rest of his life.

His rank did not apparently carry any weight with the future Lord Reith, the young creator and first director general of the BBC. My father was shortlisted for the post of managing director of the BBC in Glasgow.

My mother's diary for 16 February 1925:

had interview with Mr Reith in Glasgow, managing director of the BBC. He gave him an interview of fifty mins. A most extraordinary man, only about thirty-five and 6 ft. 6. He was manager of Beardmores.* He questioned Jimmy on every subject and was almost impudent sometimes. Jimmy is so honest and wouldn't tell a lie about anything which heaps of people would have. Reith obviously didn't

---

* William Beardmore & Co. was a large-scale engineering and shipbuilding company on Clydeside.

think there really was no reason for his not getting command of the regiment. He thought he was hiding something. This unfairness in the Services is not done in business and they don't understand it.

My father gave up any hope of the appointment when he had heard nothing by mid-March. By then he was pursuing other possibilities, though without success. My mother's cousins, the Haldanes, had encouraged him to put his name forward for the post of secretary of the Wingfield Morris Hospital in Oxford, but he was not shortlisted for interview.* He was, however, interviewed for the appointment of secretary to the Church Emigration Society. On his return from London on 17 March my mother wrote:

He hasn't of course got the Emigration job. He is very sick about his interview, held by the Bp of London and a lot of stiff frumps and one or two men. They obviously looked as if they had been told that he was not the man to vote for. The Bp's questions were childish and the whole interview struck him as just a matter of form to give a backing to the man they meant to choose all along. Anyway J. doesn't think he could have stuck that crowd.

There appeared, at first sight, to be a better chance of success when a new secretary was being sought for the Consumptive Hospital at Hindhead, a branch of the Seamen's Hospital Society. My great-uncle Sir Perceval Nairne had been, for many years, chairman of the Society, and my father's elder brother, my uncle Cyril, was on the management committee. The family name may have actually been a disadvantage, and, as my mother foresaw, the post was considered 'a plum for a naval man'. An officer of the paymaster branch was selected: 'They made out that being a soldier one couldn't understand sailors.'

---

* The Edinburgh family of Haldane, including the lawyer, philosopher and politician, Richard Burdon Haldane, 1st Viscount Haldane, were linked by marriage to my grandmother's family, the Kemps.

They were probably right – though my father's appointment would have extended the historic family connection with the Seamen's Hospital Society. After I had been a few years at the Admiralty, I was elected a member of the management committee, joining my uncle, who was treasurer, and a group of those who were, or had been, naval officers or in the shipping industry. I felt it right to leave the committee on becoming permanent secretary of the Department of Health and Social Security and in 1982 I was elected President of the Society.*

There was to be one more application before my father abandoned the hunt. And after that he never did try again. There is a brief reference later in the diary to the post of bursar at a Cambridge college but it evidently came to nothing. So he had no regular paid employment until, twelve years later, he was invited to teach drawing and painting at Winchester College for the period of the 1939–45 war.

It was a bleak prospect. My mother's diary does not mention money directly; money was not then a subject for social conversation. She was never strong on financial matters and, while never extravagant, she found it a struggle to keep personal accounts of her own and the household expenditure. My father had only a small army pension (not in his day index-linked); he had little or no expectations from his father and mother, living in retirement at Hatfield after twenty-seven years in the rectory at Baldock; and it is unlikely that my mother could contribute since, while her father seemed to have been comfortably off, her widowed mother was to live – requiring a nurse in her last years – until the 1940s. My father certainly needed salaried employment if he could get it. He had sons to bring up and took it for granted that he should keep up, however modestly, the social standards expected of a retired army officer.

So why did he fail to get a job? I never asked him or my mother about those disappointing post-war years. But the general prospects

---

* The family association has continued and I have been a trustee since 1984. The Society no longer has responsibility for a TB hospital at Hindhead.

of employment were not good at the time: in 1921 unemployment had reached a peak of two million, and there were many stories of men, with distinguished war records, unable to find work and reduced to poverty. The social conventions of the time restricted the range of jobs which men like my father would have been ready to consider as the posts he applied for clearly illustrated. Some twenty-five years as an infantry officer had not qualified him for many jobs in civilian life, and the army did not then offer any kind of resettlement training at the stage of retirement.

Finally, and significantly, there were his own character and background. Study the Nairne family trees of the nineteenth and early twentieth century: no one in business can be found. There is an impressive array of soldiers, sailors, lawyers and ordained members of the church. My mother's diary referred to my father's honesty in words that implied a failure to sell himself in interviews – a serious weakness when the competition was stiff for such suitable appointments as were available. He once acknowledged to me his own diffidence – an uncertainty about his capabilities. His school years may have contributed to that; perhaps also his role in the 1914–18 war – which, through no fault of his, had not been for him what people today call 'a good war' in terms of battle experience and personal decorations. In the circumstances it is not surprising that my parents chose to make the best of it with what resources they had.

They decided to leave Scotland and to live near Winchester – not too far from their parents in Hatfield and London, and near an old friend, Harriet Wilson, widow of my father's regimental friend, Robert Wilson, who had been killed in the war. Their decision had the support and encouragement of the family and their friends. And my father did not settle for a life devoted to leisure; he set about keeping himself busy in retirement, and by the end of the 1920s he also had the responsibilities imposed by four young sons.

He was a good father. Sixty years ago nobody studied, wrote or talked about fatherhood or good parenting in the way that people do now. Single mothers (not a term that was used) would normally be widows; there were at least as many war widows in the interwar years as there are single mothers today. Single fathers, almost certainly widowers, would usually marry again as soon as they decently could. So my father took entirely for granted his duties towards his children. He, and also my mother, had been brought up by good parents as members of large families (six children, as Penny and I were to have, in both families). As is often the case, the character of their own upbringing was reflected in their kindness and devotion towards their own children. There was little or no money to spare – no scope for spoiling the young. The loud bark, when required, of a retired colonel, but quiet firmness rather than a sharp bite. No open displays of emotion or affection towards us; nor that I can remember between themselves. Love, in any form, may not have been a taboo subject, but nor was it a matter for free and easy discussion within the family. What mattered – and what I took entirely for granted – was that my father and mother stayed together, evidently devoted to each other, though without any outward show of it. With rare exceptions my father was always at home; when my brothers and I were away from home, both parents had time to write to us and did so.

Tea at Plover Hill was a symbol of family stability – punctually every day at 4.30 p.m. in the dining room; blinds down against the summer sun; my mother's unrivalled home-made fruit cake; my father making the China tea from a kettle by the fireplace. In short, we enjoyed the inestimable blessing of a secure family life – the most important basis for 'good enough' parenting, yesterday no less than today. Although I doubt if my father would have seen it this way, it was for my brothers and myself a valuable benefit to which his failure to secure employment contributed.

How then did he spend his days? Not, I think, a great deal of the time in the company of his children – though during the later years of the 1920s, when we were constantly moving, we must have often been with him.

Plover Hill, on Compton Down, became our family home from 1927 until 1975. We were children of the nursery, like those of

Plover Hill, Compton Down, near Winchester, 1930s.

other middle-class families at the time, occupying ourselves under a nanny's eye, out for a walk with the pram, down to the drawing room after tea for what is now called 'quality time' with our parents. I cannot recall my father getting down on his knees to take the lead in doing a jigsaw or in imaginative castle building with bricks: my picture, rather, is of him smoking his pipe on the sofa, doing *The Times* crossword or occasionally drawing in his sketchbook. A sketchbook of the 1920s contains a drawing of a castle of bricks on the floor, and there exists more than one sketch of our mother reading aloud to us before it was time for us to go upstairs to bath and bed.

Tight though their financial means must have been, Compton village school was never an option. After attending a private day school, run by a Miss Taylor at the top of the hill above Shawford village, all four of us were sent in succession, at the age of nine, to a boarding preparatory school, Hordle House. It distanced me from my parents, to whom I issued rather guarded communiques in Sunday letters home. It would have been the same for

Pat sketched by his father, Charles Sylvester Nairne.

my brothers. My mother would write to each of us each week about her local activities; but, home only for the holidays, we could not share in the normal routine of my father's life, even less in his hopes and aspirations. But promotion to boarding school meant release from nursery life, meals in the dining room, and, subject to good behaviour, the freedom of the drawing room. In short, observer status, if not full participation, in Nairne family life at Plover Hill.

My mother's diary recorded, day by day, a sketchy picture of her life, though it conveys the impression of little more than a walking-on part for my father. He was rarely away; but there is only an occasional account of how he was spending his days at home.

James, Alastair (Sandy), David and Pat, Plover Hill, 1930s.

Sandy by Charles Sylvester Nairne, 1933.

Typical entries for April 1928:

19 April: The children had tea at the Sandfords. Jimmy took his bicycle and explored the I. of Wight.

25 April: Took Mother to a matinee in aid of the golf club. It was held at Twyford. They did 'The Drums of Oude' and 'The Rest Cure'. Rather bad. Jimmy lent the uniforms for the former.

A more active day on 24 May:

Empire Day. Jimmy addressed the school children down at Compton. We went to play tennis at the Godwins.

These quotations reveal little about my father. My mother never gave much away in the record of her life, but she was not apparently interested in providing a regular record of his. By 1928 he was in effect committed to a life of active retirement – a life devoted to some voluntary work outside the home, but also to an orderly routine of running his share of the house, painting water-colour landscapes and still lifes, and supporting my mother at small tea parties with neighbours. My holiday recollections are of his being busy enough in a quiet way: at his desk in what he called the studio, scrupulously careful, as he had to be, in watching over expenditure and given to answering all letters without delay; work-ing in the garden, while employing a gardener, Herbert Stratton, on one or two days a week; accompanying my mother when she went shopping in Winchester; and exhibiting his watercolour paintings whenever he could.

But he also undertook more onerous tasks: the organisation of the pageant, 'Scotland', at the Royal Tournament of 1928 (of which the poster he designed hung in the nursery for many years); the oversight, with the support of close neighbours, of the 'un-made-up' road along the Downs below Plover Hill; membership of the local committee of the Council for the Preservation of Rural England and later of the committee of the Friends of Winchester Cathedral; the setting-up and running of the Compton and Shawford Painting Circle; the honorary secretaryship of the Cuidich 'n Righ (Seaforth Highlanders) Dining Club; and, almost certainly most demanding of all, the role of honorary secretary of the Winchester Art Club, which held a large annual exhibition, including some professional work borrowed from London galleries, every autumn in the Judges' Lodgings in Winchester Cathedral Close.

These varied tasks composed, for differing periods, the bread and butter of his retirement life for some twenty-five years. But there were also two other, more substantial and important, com-mitments.

Once well established at Plover Hill, my father undertook the exacting task of preparing and publishing up-to-date genealogical tables of the descendants of the Revd John Nairne (1711–1795) of Anstruther Easter, to which he added his own sketch of family history and contributions by other members of the family, as well as by himself, about each of the five members of his grandfather's family who had lived to old age. He gave me copies of the book for my children and myself but it is a typical example of how children can take their parents for granted that I cannot remember asking him about it, even less congratulating him on the notable achievement of producing it. His foreword to the book explains its origin by saying that it was begun 'because a firm of family solicitors considered that a "Tree" would be not only useful to them, but in time almost essential'. He added that, 'older members of the family thought it their duty to pass on what they knew of their origin and kin to the rising generation'. I suspect that his elder brother, Cyril Nairne, partner in Baker & Nairne, presumably the 'firm of family solicitors' and his cousin, Canon Alexander (Sandy) Nairne, eldest son of the Revd Spencer Nairne and one-time Regius Professor of Divinity at Cambridge, had been chiefly responsible for encouraging him. The family history and tables, published under the title of *John Nairne (1711–1795) and his Descendants*, were a monument to my father's meticulous care, to his thoroughness in securing the information he needed, and to his personal modesty about what he had achieved.

His other major commitment was – at last – an appointment for which he received a salary. In September 1939 Professor Gleadowe, the art master at Winchester College, a distinguished, autocratic and eccentric man, was called back to Whitehall, where he had served in the 1914–18 war. The headmaster, Spencer Leeson, immediately offered my father the post and he readily accepted. He was confident that he knew how to teach drawing; and, at the age of fifty-nine, he was glad to have a job in the wartime period. Although it must have been an important moment in the lives of them both, my mother's diary makes no mention of it until there is an oblique reference in late October to 'Jimmy always late for lunch on Thurs'. And an entry for 23 November 1939:

> Pouring all day. Walked to Winchester. Changed from gum boots in
> car and J and I lunched with the Headmaster and Mrs Leeson. Got

home at 3 and went down to Sh. Pk. where 1st. Home Nursing
began.

The last few words provide a clue: her mind was fully engaged
in her own work. While my father joined the staff at Winchester,
my mother was 'mobilised' as a member of the local Red Cross
Voluntary Aid Detachment, which was required to undertake the
nursing at a wartime maternity unit established in Shawford Park.
Her diary entry for 2 September 1939 – the first of many about
her daily duties – on the day before the prime minister, Neville
Chamberlain, announced on the radio at 11:15 a.m. that the country was at war with Germany:

At Shawford Pk all day except for lunch. Nine mothers and four
sisters came at lunchtime. No more coming. Germany attacked
Poland yesterday. Thunderstorms.

My father worked at the college until after the war was over
– more than six years in all. Art was not then the academic subject
that it is today, and his teaching was confined to those boys
who took drawing (and presumably painting) as an 'extra'. But
it was a considerable effort on his part since the arthritis in the
knee, which eventually disabled him, must have been deteriorating year by year. Fortunately he could drive his car and manage
to climb the many steps to the room at the top of Chantry where
he did his teaching. He was apparently popular with his pupils:
I have met one or two men, only a little younger than myself,
who have asked whether I was the son of a Colonel Nairne
with whom they had enjoyed learning to draw at Winchester in
the war.

My father knew how to draw and described his own watercolours as 'watercolour drawings'. He wrote, in his 'Family Notes
1941', that he had been introduced to painting by a lifelong friend,
Mrs Day (it is characteristic of his period that he never mentions

her Christian name), wife of the Nairne family doctor in Baldock. She, and a retired doctor's daughter, Miss Milly Hicks, used to take him and his elder brother, Cyril, out sketching:

> Cyril had as a small child a natural gift for drawing, and in early days in the Chelmsford nursery he used to draw animated pictures of battles. I had little talent, but used to imitate him. Cyril was good enough to be given lessons.

My father 'took' drawing at Haileybury, but he did not, to quote his own account:

> do any drawing beyond mere scribbles until in about 1903, after the South African War, I found that Bobby Vandaleur in the Regiment painted very cleverly. He encouraged me to start again, and in 1905 when I went up to Chamba in the Himalayas to shoot I took watercolours and tried to paint in my spare time. My efforts were so distressing . . . that I determined, when I went home on leave from India, that I would take lessons. Eventually, in about 1906, I went for a few months to the life class at the London School of Art in Kensington, where the teacher was J. M. Swan RA, the animal painter. It was only then that I learned the beginnings of what drawing meant . . . I am certain that the first three months in a properly conducted life class will teach an amateur more than he will ever learn anywhere else in three years . . . Later I went, on two occasions of leave from India, for varying periods of a month or two to the Slade School, where among the teachers were the famous Henry Tonks, Sir Walter Russell RA and Derwent Lees . . . I found, on my return to India, no need to go on any more shooting trips for my leave. I used to go on painting trips instead, sometimes accompanying a friend who was shooting. But I had no more time for shooting: I only wanted to paint and draw. A painting holiday too worked out much cheaper than a shooting holiday.

Charles Sylvester Nairne's drawing of his father, Revd John D. Nairne, *c*.1905.

Painting filled his spare time for the rest of his life – until, in his late seventies, he became too disabled to go out painting any more. I enjoyed going out sketching (his word) with him whenever I could.

For some fifty years watercolour landscape painting has been my own priority on holiday and in whatever time could be spared

Boer War
cartoon by
Charles Sylvester
Nairne.

Sketch of Pat as a civil servant by Charles Sylvester Nairne from a family
storybook, *Two Girls*, 1952.

Charles Sylvester Nairne, a family dance at Plover Hill, 1956.

at home. And I must have influenced our children, as my father had influenced me [*see Chapter 29: The Perfect Pastime of Painting*]. Where does this dedication to – this enthusiasm for – the visual arts come from? Nature or nurture? My father's story explains his own development: the encouragement by chance, in South Africa, of his brother officer, Bobby Vandaleur, may have been crucial. My father similarly encouraged me, and I was exposed to his frequent practice of drawing us as children in his sketchbook and painting watercolour landscapes on our holidays.

But nurture is unlikely to have been enough without some genetically inherited skill and family talent can be traced back, not to the Nairnes in Fife, but to the Domett family. My grandfather's mother was Anne Domett, sister of John Domett, who had served under my great-grandfather, Captain Alexander Nairne, captain of a ship, the 'Alexander Kyd' (named after his great-uncle), in the East India Company sea service. John Domett was a most accomplished painter of sea pictures in watercolour. But that may be the end of the family trail; I do not know – and my father's book offers no information – whether earlier Dometts were painters.

Charles Sylvester Nairne, Pittenween, Fife, 1939.

It is likely that his time as an art student in London shaped my father's character almost as much as his childhood in the rectory at Baldock and his regimental experience in a highland regiment. He greatly enjoyed the company of artists but acquired no bohemian ways of his own. He became devoted to the quiet pastime of landscape painting but never lost a parade ground voice for occasional use. He was an excellent amateur painter with his watercolours hung more than once in the Royal Academy Summer Exhibition and frequently found on the walls of Hampshire houses.

In later years he was known to inspect a watercolour in a neighbour's home in Compton or Shawford, express admiration, and receive the response: 'One of your own, Colonel . . .'

Whenever I came back to Plover Hill, I would go to his studio beyond the drawing room and look at his latest watercolours hung on the wall at the end of the room. I would discuss painting and pictures with him and he would always be ready to look at my latest work and, with a characteristic clearance of the throat, would give advice if asked to do so.

We certainly talked of subjects other than painting but I do not recall either of my parents initiating general conversation for its own sake. There was a strict timetable for meals at Plover Hill – an important regime perhaps for those in retirement, and probably reflecting my parents' experience of their own homes in which servants necessitated fixed mealtimes. There would be conversation at the lunch and supper table, chiefly local chat between my father and mother or questions put to us about our lives at school or our activities in the holidays. My mother showed little interest in wider issues and I doubt if we were more communicative as boys than our own children were in their school years. My father would return for lunch complaining about the autocratic ways of Dean Selwyn at the Friends of the Cathedral committee meetings or groaning over a problem under discussion in the Winchester committee of the Campaign to Protect Rural England; he was not in the chair of these bodies, but he appeared to be valued as a sound man to have at any committee table. My mother was a member of Compton Church choir, of the Women's Institute, the Heathcote Players Dramatic Society, and the Red Cross Voluntary Aid Detachment: a large cast on which to draw for casual gossip about life in the villages of Compton and Shawford.

There were fairly rare occasions at the end of supper when my mother might be drawn out on, for example, her family holidays as a girl on the island of Lismore (my aunt and an uncle rowing some ten miles to Oban to find out if war had been declared on 4 August 1914) or my father might be encouraged to entertain us again with an account of some of his more remarkable or eccentric brother officers in the regiment (the impudent telegram received from one officer summoned back to duty: 'Regret many engagements in town and country'). In the 1930s there was no lack of severe national and international problems: serious unemployment, the increasing threat from Hitler in Europe, troubles in India and in the Far East (where the 1st Battalion of the Seaforths was stationed), while politics at home were dominated by economic constraints and pressures for rearmament. My father may have had

Colonel Nairne with David, Pat and James, Scotland, August 1938.

strong views on such serious important issues, but I cannot remember him initiating a discussion with us.

The deeper questions of religion, sex or the general character of society were not on the agenda at all. This may have been partly our fault, chiefly mine as the eldest surviving son. Much of my conversation would, I think, have been self-centred: about golf, which I played as often as possible, about a film I wanted to see in a Winchester cinema, about a book I was enjoying, about where my father and I might go and paint after tea, or about people we knew (though cautious about ever mentioning any girl I was interested in). The title page of G. M. Young's book, *Victorian England – Portrait of an Age* carries a quotation: 'Servants talk about People; gentlefolk discuss Things.' The Nairne family talked about people.

But, more to the point in reflecting on the past, the question which puzzles me now is: why did I never ask my father about the many aspects of his life? His upbringing in Chelmsford and in the rectory at Baldock and how that compared with our life at Plover Hill; about his army service and the frustrating post-war years; or, more deeply, about what his own ambitions had been?

I was keenly interested in history. I had an easy enough relationship with my father: why was I never interested in asking more about his experience in two wars? He once explained that his two years of the Boer War were after the main fighting was over but I recall that, on my joining the army, he mentioned the long and exhausting marches in South Africa in the context of warning me about the painful effects on soldiers of venereal disease. I did not press him for details about that – nor, as I might have done, about the Western Front in the 1914–18 war. He was abroad from 1915 and, in the years of 1917–19 he commanded successively battalions of the Black Watch and the Royal Scots Fusiliers in France, Salonika and Germany. Did that go well, and were he and my mother right to feel deeply aggrieved that he was passed over for promotion in 1925 by the much-decorated Hopkinson? My father never spoke of that to me. And yet his repeated lack of success in securing a job in the interwar years must have left him with a nagging sense of failure. Perhaps the modesty and diffidence, about which my mother had remarked in her diary, gave him a psychological skin of protection?

There was, I suppose, a practical reason why I never asked all the questions I could have asked. By the time I was of an age at which I might have raised with my father almost any question I chose about his life, I had in effect left home. From the age of nineteen my five years of war, my post-war terms at Oxford and then my marriage to Penny took me away from Plover Hill except for leave, vacations, and relatively brief visits. My parents did not stay up late; I was never offered a nightcap and the opportunity to talk by a dying fire. Routine questions would be asked about my health and that of Penny and the children and about the current pressures of my Admiralty work but the circumstances never seemed to offer easy opportunities for a relaxed and leisurely chat about the wider features of our lives.

But that was not the complete explanation. In 1950 I spent many weeks at Plover Hill recovering from my first period of mild TB: an admirable time at which to engage my father in conversations about the past. It did not occur to me to do so – partly perhaps because of the characteristic self-centredness of the young. The fact is, I believe, that in the normal way of life it does not occur to children, and especially those who have had a happy childhood, to question their parents about the whats and wherefores of their own lives. Personal experiences may readily emerge if a family is given to discussing the deeper issues of life. But, if not, not.

I never, therefore, came to know what my father felt about spiritual matters. He had been one of his father's choir boys; he would have labelled himself 'C of E' in the army but he attended church only at Christmas and Easter and for weddings and funerals. In spite of the entrenched family background of the Presbyterian and Anglican Churches he would probably have described himself as an agnostic. The son of an ordained father has to decide for himself where he stands and my father's outlook may well have primarily reflected the social environment of a Highland regiment and the Slade School of Art, and also his experience of the large-scale, and apparently random, casualties of the 1914–18 war. Neither he nor my mother were given to exposing, even less to expressing, their emotions.

They suffered together the sudden tragic death in 1937 of my elder brother, Sandy; I can scarcely bear to read my mother's few sentences in her diary. It was an acutely painful experience for us all but my father never felt able to talk about it to me. I would probably have felt embarrassed if he had.

Did or does any of this matter? Perhaps only as an insight into the character of one man and as a revelation of the undemonstrative fatherhood in families like ours more than sixty years ago. It is a truism that, while many may take the same view of the general character and personality of an individual, those views may also reflect, in different ways, a personal experience of their own.

My father was known by different names – 'Vester' in his own family from his Christian names of Charles Sylvester; Jimmy to my mother: his nickname perhaps in the army hospital where she met and nursed him, and the name adopted by my mother's relations; 'Baloo' to his regimental friend, Wiggy Thomson; 'The Bile' to more junior officers who remembered him as a fierce adjutant at the regimental depot of Fort George in 1914–15. On the other hand, his local friends, including as close a friend as the family doctor, Marsden Roberts, addressed him as 'Nairne' – unless, as many did in that period, they always kept their distance with 'Colonel Nairne'. To a succession of daily helps at Plover Hill he was simply known as 'the Colonel'.

I was told about the last nickname, 'The Bile', when I joined the Seaforths at Fort George in 1941. It had some justification in my own experience – my father suddenly jumping up from the lunch table, thrusting the window up, and yelling at a man doing some work on the house or in the garden, 'You oaf, what the hell are you doing?'; frustrated in a Southampton shop which could not provide some article of clothing, stumping out with angry words; 'How absolutely agonising!' was his response when Dundee cake could not be produced in the restaurant at the Glasgow Empire Exhibition of 1938. The nickname would have puzzled my own friends, the boys who knew him at Winchester, and the younger people whom he came to know during the years at Plover Hill. My parents were hospitable at weekends to Winchester boys they knew; they were particularly kind in the 1939–45 war to my close friend from schooldays, Peter Way, whose diary of the time provides an account of his visits to Plover Hill when under training with the King's Royal Rifle Corps at Bushfield Camp:

August/September 1941. The Sunday visit to the Nairnes at Compton. This was as usual most pleasant and I had a glorious, luxurious bath and washed my hair ... Came down feeling fresh and sat talking in the garden with Colonel Nairne. Tea – a good one, with home-made strawberry jam and decent tea for once. I could have eaten a lot more than I did.

My father may have condemned, half seriously, carnations in buttonholes, but he regarded the ways of the world with a sense of humour – and with charity as he, and also my mother, showed when my brother David's first marriage broke up. A condemnation of cads reflected his lifelong view of correct behaviour – based, in particular, on how an officer should behave in a good regiment. But he enjoyed himself in the company of artists; and he found a satisfying fulfilment as a watercolourist, and in the teaching of painting and drawing. As he moved into his eighties his arthritis increasingly disabled him, and painting was abandoned. He had a slight stroke; he found it increasingly difficult to get upstairs; he was almost entirely dependent on my mother and given to expressing concern that she might die before he did. He had one serious fall in the road outside Plover Hill and then, in May 1963, he fell in the garden. On 16 May my mother wrote:

To Win. with Mrs Dacombe. The painters Lyneham arrived to do the house. When I got back I found Jimmy had had a fall a few yards from getting in again. The painters got him into his chair. He said his bad leg was hurting. Marsden [*Marsden Roberts, the doctor*] came about 12.30 and got the Lynehams to carry him up on a chair. I gave him codeine but he wanted lunch. He slept in the afternoon ...

He never walked again. The X-ray showed a fractured thigh, and he was taken to Winchester Hospital where he stayed for nearly three months before, in default of finding a bed in a suitable nursing home, he was discharged to Plover Hill, now permanently bedridden, to be nursed there under the constant and heroic care of my mother. Three years later, in 1966, he died at the age of eighty-six.

Six years earlier we had had a family celebration for his eightieth birthday. A special birthday book was presented to him, containing paintings and drawings by my brother James, Kathy, Fiona, Sandy and myself, photographs of my parents, Plover Hill, Penny and all our family, including James and Andrew in Penny's arms, and a set of light-hearted verses which I had composed for the occasion. The verses did not attempt to convey my father's character: his integrity and self-discipline; his intelligence, skill and humour; his uncomplaining acceptance of the hand which fate had dealt him; above all, the legacy to his sons of his personal example. But, in a light-hearted way, they go some way to conveying how we viewed his long life:

THE COLONEL'S TALE

The paradox of CSN to some extent defies the pen.
  Son of a parson; in the choir; followed the pipes in
danger's hour.
  When the Boer War was ended, his service was then
extended:
  Smart and efficient he became; subalterns quaked to
hear his name.
  And in Fort George and Ardersier men heard his
voice ring loud and clear.

A regular soldier by trade, as tough as any on parade.
  And yet he had been at the Slade (so thus the
paradox was made).
  He rose in rank; he travelled far – from Havrincourt
to Srinagar.
  When in uniform he stood, he looked just as a
colonel should.
  His stern command made privates faint, but off
parade he loved to paint.

This is the point to understand: an iron glove, but velvet hand.

When a paint brush had replaced his sword, he was retired, but never bored.

A 'Local Artist' he became: College and Close respect his name.

For all who sketch he has advice; he'll sell his work at modest price.

There's nothing he does not know about arranging the Art Club Show.

From Judd's to Best's a well-known sight, painting away (despite dull light).

And now that CSN is eighty, his wisdom is both wise and weighty:

Expert on tones and forms and shape, Grand Old Man of Hampshire landscape.

While to the Seaforths he's the Colonel still, no less an expert on dress and drill.

A famous name in the Regiment's story: a painter tinged with military glory.

3

The End of the Thirties – A Radley Rite of Passage

Written in 1997 for the Radley College magazine

Over sixty years ago: a new boy of September 1935. No family car; trunk and bicycle sent by rail in advance; walked from Radley station with my father. Tea at the house of my tutor, Kenneth Boyd; my father departs; and after unpacking in my cubicle in Long Dormitory, am at a loss to know what I should be doing next.

I remained, more or less, at a loss for the next two weeks. Life since then – wartime infantry soldier, shortened Oxford honours course, the long Whitehall years, back to an Oxford college – has

The Mansion, Radley College, 1935.

included a full share of uncertainty, fears, pressures, rush; but I remember my first fortnight at Radley as the most harassed and confused period of my life. What next? What clothes next? I had moved – as so many new boys have done and probably still do – from the familiar and tight routine of a preparatory school in a single building to a strange 'village' in which I had to find my own way, and where I was not sure if the natives were friendly.

But suddenly it all fell into place; there was a moment when I became conscious that I was enjoying Radley. I was at home in the classroom in which my form master, Kenneth Boyd, would begin each day with 'Take half a sheet of paper . . .' followed by ten questions to test the memory and alertness of the form. I had become accustomed to the weekly routine: the morning cold bath and compulsory self-inspection for a skin infection called tinea; 'rest' after lunch when I could read the newspaper or one of the compulsory works of literature which members of my form had to choose for the term; a junior rugger game on a distant pitch or a run round Junior Short; lining up in a covered passage in a surplice before chapel; occasional Sunday cooking duty imposed on a fag – or was I let off that in my first term?

In spite of modest academic status as a scholar, I was bottom of the heap in Radley society. The self-confident head boy of the prep school had become the wary small boy of the public school, sitting at meals in the middle of the Social table, responding quickly to loud demands to pass up their (shop-purchased) marmalade, jam or cereal from the Social grandees at the ends of the table.* Warden Ferguson appeared an awesome figure of great age and authority, with the stature of an Old Testament prophet; Walter Smale stood out as an eccentric don, kindly by nature, but with a potential to bite, conveying an unanswerable greeting – 'Well, dear boy . . . ?' – if we met anywhere in college; there were wilder senior boys who were said to break out at night to drink

---

* At Radley College the 'houses' where students have accommodation and by which they are grouped for some games and work are called 'Socials' and therefore the student's common room is 'Social hall'.

Pat in the steeplechase, Radley College, 1938.

in the local pub. I have a visual image of my earliest years: walking exhausted off the pitch on a dark December afternoon at the end of a furiously fought Social rugger match – a somewhat heroic image resembling an illustration from a school story of the past in which the boys' code of values was little different from that of young Radleians in the mid-1930s.

Four years later, an entirely different image. I had inescapably become a different person; and, as a member of the Classical VIth, head of G Social, and a school prefect, my position in Radley society was fundamentally altered. Does my retrospective view merely reflect that I had undergone a predictable change due to age and seniority; and that Radley was unchanged? I think not. What was significant, and probably for all my generation, was the impact of a young new warden, John Wilkes. In his history, Christopher Hibbert has vividly described the character, personality and practical philosophy of Wilkes.* He aimed to shift Radley from

---

* Christopher Hibbert, *No Ordinary Place: Radley College and the Public School System*, John Murray, London, 1997.

(to use the jargon of today) the dependency culture of the school-boy to the more responsible culture expected of the university student. Study periods were introduced: a temptation to waste time, but the work set had to be done. The whole academic voltage became higher; the priority for the VIth form was an Oxbridge award, the Higher School Certificate set aside; Herodotus read round the form, the ability to translate taken for granted; Monday evening meetings of the Shakespeare Society in the warden's drawing room, the day's prep to be done as best one could. I was sixteen, by no means an academic star when John Wilkes arrived; but I felt swept into a stimulating and civilised environment by an enthusiastic warden who was to become a friend for life. The earlier visual image of a dark evening in December had changed to a brighter image of a sparkling morning in Spring.

And yet it was a time when the country was conscious of an increasing threat of conflict in Europe. Perhaps it was to the good that we were, as it seems in retrospect, surprisingly detached from the agonising political issues which engaged the university generation ahead of us. My memories are mainly of laughter among my contemporaries and celebration in college. There were two weddings at which I was a privileged guest: the marriage of Clem Morgan, the most urbane of Social tutors, to the auburn-haired Sheila Danby; the wedding of the Warden to Joan Allington amidst the grandeur of Durham Cathedral and Deanery. And, to roars from Radleians and the music of Snow White at the finish, Radley rowed to a historic victory in the Ladies' Plate at Henley in 1938.

In my last two terms we were at war. Windows were blacked out and bombers flew over at night from RAF Abingdon, but little as yet had changed for Radley. I remember a late afternoon in March 1940 – glorious sunshine, slight smell of frost – chatting happily near the Pavilion with one of my closest friends. He had recently infected me with an enthusiasm for Mozart and, killed three years later in Italy, his memory is inseparably linked with the final movement of the last piano concerto. I was being allowed to leave and start at University. For me, at that moment, the summer

The Emergency Ration, 1939, a Radley College magazine to which Pat contributed.

lay promisingly ahead: farewell to Radley and welcome to the inviting prospect of a first term at Oxford.

But it was to be the only term for six years. Exactly a year later, in March 1941, I was a new boy again – and feeling rather at a loss once more, hoping that I was convincing an infantry platoon of Seaforth Highlanders that I knew something about training for battle.

WORLD WAR TWO: 1940–1945

Introduction

We can learn little from history unless we first realise that she does not, in fact, repeat herself. Events are not affected by analogies; they are determined by the combination of circumstances. And since circumstances vary from generation to generation it is unwise to suppose that any pattern of history, however similar it may at first appear, is likely to repeat itself in the kaleidoscope of time.

Harold Nicolson, *The Congress of Vienna*
Commonplace book, entry no. 156

It is a truism to describe how my father's generation was plunged, as young men and women, into terrible experiences in the Second World War that no one anticipated or desired. As a child I was curious about his part in the war (and his Military Cross), but he never spoke much about that, and referred me to *Sans Peur*, Alastair Borthwick's 1946 history of his battalion of the Seaforth Highlanders. Only recently I discovered that Borthwick drew on those around him and that the description of the battle of the Sferro Hills is taken almost verbatim from my father's account.

A few letters home and occasional diaries survive from the wartime period. Writing in a new diary in June 1942 as he set out for North Africa, he refers to having recently been shown a nineteenth-century manuscript and comments: '. . . the fact that it was *true* made it vital and fascinating reading. So I shan't bother to argue sententiously whether I write for other eyes but my own to read. If this writing – and my patience and energy will probably soon be exhausted – should be read in 2042, it would make most interesting reading. We'll leave it at that.'

The pieces selected here follow a pattern in which my father utilised a period of recuperation for writing, as he did in Leeds Hospital in 1943 and again in 1945, while recovering from wounds. There is a boy-scoutishness to some of these narratives – with an occasional sporting metaphor ('fast balls' from the German tanks). Writing must have been one form of processing extreme wartime experiences that were not just unfamiliar but deeply shocking – as it also was for many others. Only when writing an account of fighting in Holland in 1944 does he refer to his 'experience': feeling by then, perhaps, like an old hand, even if only twenty-three.

SN

Citation for Military Cross – Lieut. Patrick Dalmahoy Nairne, The Seaforth Highlanders – On July 13th and 14th (1943) this officer displayed the greatest gallantry, initiative and devotion to duty. On July 13th he showed great courage under fire by reconnoitring forward by himself to ascertain the enemy's dispositions. By his quick action and as a result of his reliable report on the enemy a very confused situation was made clear, thereby enabling the column to continue its advance. On July 14th this officer again under heavy fire made a very close and exhaustive search of the enemy's dispositions, spotting many strong points which were holding up the advance of the Battalion. He exposed himself to snipers on several occasions by climbing trees in order to obtain a better view of the enemy's positions quite regardless of his own safety. His calm bearing under fire was an inspiration to all around him and his keen perception at the most critical moments of the battle saved many lives. His courage was of the highest order and his conduct worthy of recognition.

4

Novembers – *1940: Into the Army and 1942: El Alamein*

Written in November 1999

A dark afternoon on the last November of the second millennium. I walk down the straight and empty Oxfordshire road to the bridge over the Evenlode: a regular constitutional when I am at home for the day. My thoughts turn to past Novembers – to a few darker as well as to some lighter days.

Why has the month of November had a special significance – a month in which I seem to have often experienced some particular, even notable, event, change, or development? Battle experience in the Second World War; engagement to Penny; release from a sanatorium and from the threat of tuberculosis; the Suez Affair of 1956; arrival as the permanent secretary of the Department of Health and Social Security; the first day as the new Master of St Catherine's College, Oxford; return from Hong Kong after monitoring the consultation about the reunification agreement with China; finally home at Yew Tree, Chilson, after departure from the college, with the prospect of genuine retirement ahead.

Other months over more than half a century can claim their own share of significance but November especially so. Chalk it up to chance? Difficult to be sure about that.

NOVEMBER 1940: INTO THE ARMY

I have never kept a regular diary for long but I did so for a short time in 1940 – from mid-September until the first week of November. Not primarily, as one might think, to record my recollections of a critical autumn in English history – the imminent threat of German invasion and the RAF victory in the Battle of Britain – but because I was teaching myself to type during the months after I had abandoned Oxford and had vague aspirations of becoming a writer and time on my hands while awaiting call-up to the army.

A self-conscious, somewhat pompous, entry for 3 November:

> When I write my autobiography, I shall doubtless refer to next Thursday and Friday as the closing of a chapter of my life. I put away childish things etc. etc. . . . It appeals to my sense of the dramatic to think that within a week I shall have finished with all the sentiments, memories and pastimes that have for years been associated with existence at Plover Hill. I have never felt particularly conscious of the act of growing up – I feel as young in spirit as I did five years ago. I reckon a time will come when I shall look on Plover Hill as nothing more than the place where I spent my youth. I wonder . . .

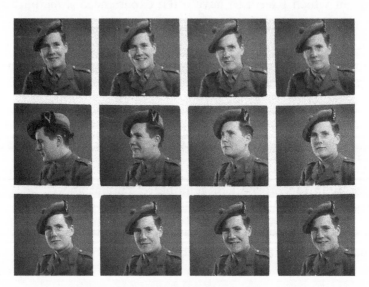

Pat as a new Seaforth Highlander, late 1940.

It was a true prediction. On Thursday 7 November I left Plover Hill to travel by train to Liverpool, spending the night with my father's youngest brother and his wife, Dr Spencer and Florence Nairne. On the following day, following War Office instructions, I boarded a ferry boat at Fleetwood and endured a rough crossing to Douglas, Isle of Man, as one of a new batch of officer cadets joining No. 166 Officers Cadet Training Unit. It was a daunting and uncomfortable start to five years of active service in the infantry.

NOVEMBER 1942: THE BATTLE OF ALAMEIN

I was in a more daunting situation almost exactly two years later: 1–2 November 1942. Active service had become serious action. I was then intelligence officer of the 5th (Caithness and Sutherland) Battalion of the Seaforth Highlanders, one of the three battalions

Second Lieutenant Patrick Nairne, seated left, Infantry Training Centre, Fort George, 1941.

of 152 Brigade (2 Seaforths, 5 Seaforths, 5 Camerons) of the 51st Highland Division. The Division, a division of the 8th Army under General Montgomery, was engaged in its first direct experience of battle – against General Rommel's Afrika Korps on the battlefield of Alamein in the Western Desert. Some months later I recorded my own experience:*

> I remember the Battalion's first attack . . . The Battle of Alamein had lasted eight days, bringing mixed impressions for us. On the warm clear morning of 23 October we had no idea what to expect. On 1 November we could not have decided what we felt – had we been given the leisure to do so. One chap might have said that the shelling wasn't as bad as he had expected; 'but I'm not liking those 88s,' he would have added. Another would have smiled philosophically with nothing to say; as long as the grub was OK and he got his spot of kip it was all right by him. Some would have just disliked it.
>
> I find that I have one fixed impression mentally docketed as The Alamein Impression. If I shut my eyes . . . one picture fills my mind. I see a cattle fence marking the front of our own minefield; from it a track comes towards me, dusty and furrowed as if generations of farm carts have been driven on it rather than forty-eight hours of tanks. On either side of the track vehicles of every kind are parked with sometimes less than five yards between them: company 15 cwts, ammunition 3-tonners, tanks, guns unlimbered and in action. As far as the eye can reach this is the scene – all overhung with a pall of fog that might be mistaken for autumn mist were it not for the smell of cordite. That is the picture of the early days of the Alamein battle – a picture of the armour of the 8th Army trying to break through.
>
> Of 1 November I have a jumbled memory of much to do and little time in which to do it. It is All Hallows Eve. Soon after midnight the Battalion must advance four thousand yards westward and dig in on a piece of ground from which the tanks can operate clear of enemy mines.

---

* A version of this text was published fifty years later as part of an article by Patrick Nairne in the *Queen's Own Highlander* magazine, Winter 1992.

I left the Battalion concentration area soon after five-thirty with a 15-cwt truck into which were crowded the intelligence section and four members of the pioneer platoon. I dropped the former at intervals along the track as guides to the Battalion forming-up place; I needed the pioneers to help with any further taping that might be required on the start line.*

As I stood in the forming-up place I remember how strongly the commanding officer has impressed on me the fact that only the company commanders have seen the start line and forming-up place by day. I understand well the importance of the Battalion getting into the correct formation without fuss and, because of the timing of the artillery barrage, crossing the start line – scarcely three hundred yards away – dead on time. I am at this moment worried that the route into the forming-up place and from there to the start-line tape will not be clear to the platoon officers and sergeants. I must walk over it myself and check that it is.

How often have I thought that anxiety is the chief horror of war! I do not find walking easy. Already I am feeling the weight of my small haversack with its additions of twenty-four hours' rations and an entrenching tool through the straps. The Battalion will not have left the concentration area yet. But I must be certain to be in time to meet the leading company on the track where my last guide is now standing.

The moon will not be up until after midnight. Occasionally a flare goes up from the German lines, green or yellow. There is suddenly a small salvo of shells to the north; it might be the Australians or it might be the Germans firing. Often odd bursts of German Spandau fire: some jittery Jerry lost his nerve?† Tanks can be heard rumbling menacingly to their forming-up place behind our attacking brigades. In the darkness I run into sappers preparing to light the axis of our advance and signallers laying cable as far forward as they dare: some brigadier will want to move his headquarters forward quickly.

The Battalion is now in the forming-up place. Blankets, under

---

* The process of 'taping' involved marking with white tape the planned route that would guide infantry soldiers into battle, often having to avoid mines.
† The German 'Spandau', the MG 42, was a 7.92×57 mm Mauser machine gun.

which men have been resting, are being collected. The companies are standing like football teams before a match, cold and longing to get started. The commanding officer has said his last word of encouragement. I snatch a tepid mug of tea from the regimental quartermaster sergeant.

The silence is broken only by the irritating noise of the Valentine tanks now close behind us. How can we hope to surprise the enemy? All at once the darkness behind the start line is lit up by countless tongues of flame – a deafening noise followed a few seconds later. The barrage has begun.

Our Brigade advanced as planned, pipers playing; a New Zealand Brigade was attacking simultaneously on our right. As dawn broke, the tanks came from behind us and parked themselves nearby, unable to risk moving farther forward in the face of constant and heavy German shelling – which we shared, dug into slit trenches so far as the hard surface of the desert allowed. At some time during the day, I somehow found my way back to where the quartermaster had temporarily established himself and arranged for food to come forward to the front-line companies.

Different units of the 8th Army were maintaining pressure along the whole front; the Italian forces, cut off by the New Zealanders

Pat, seated centre, with his platoon, North Africa, 1942.

and ourselves from the Germans farther north, were surrendering in large numbers. On 3 November the Germans suddenly ceased their resistance and rapidly withdrew their remaining forces westward. The Battle of Alamein had been won. The 5th Seaforths had lost twelve officers and one hundred and sixty-five other ranks killed or wounded. A week or two later the church bells in England – silent since in 1940 it had been decided that they should no longer be rung except to sound warning of German parachutists – were specially rung on a Sunday in celebration. As Churchill put it in his history of the Second World War, 'Before Alamein we never had a victory. After Alamein we never had a defeat.'

As November gave way to December, it was on with the war in the Western Desert. The weather had been good during the Alamein battle – though sometimes oppressively hot in the day and always sharply cold by night when we had no protection except our khaki pullovers. But, as we moved westwards, the rain came, assisting the German retreat to Benghazi and Tripoli, and ending our hopes

Sketch of the desert at Ras al A'ali, January 1943.

of a return to the warm sunny weather which had enabled us in September to strip off and bathe in the turquoise Mediterranean.

The rainstorms, nourishing the flowering desert stock while dampening our open-air lives, foreshadowed another November experience. Two more years had passed. The Highland Division had left Tripolitania, Tunisia, Algeria, Sicily and Normandy behind and, in autumn 1944, was engaged in the gradual liberation of Holland. 152 Brigade and the 5th Seaforths were somewhere north-east of the town of Eindhoven [see Chapter 7: Novembers – 1944: The Night We Crossed the Canal].

5

Christmas Day in the Desert, 1942

Written in December 1943 while in hospital in Leeds

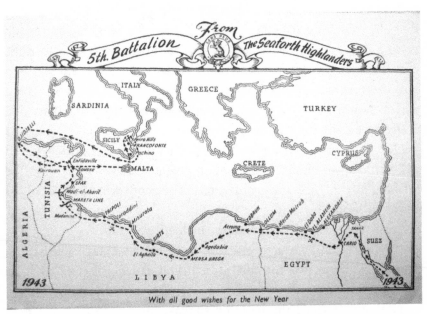

Route of the Seaforth Highlanders across North Africa, 1943.

Imagine a straight tarmac road whose monotony is only relieved by kilometre stones leaning drunkenly and by telegraph wires needing repair. Picture a brown, rocky ridge stretching for four hundred yards north of the tarmac road to a marshy flat coloured like milk chocolate. Then let your mind's eye cross the flat and pass over the undulating grassy sand dunes, reminiscent of a first class (golf) bunker, until it rests on the grey sea that is the Gulf of Sirte [*Libya*]. The Battalion lived, stretched out from east to west, in the edge of the sand dunes. We slept to the roar of the waves. The quartermaster and B Echelon [*transport for stores and work-shops*] camped under the ridge on the road side of the flat and watched the marshy two hundred yards between them and the Battalion Headquarters become impassable for vehicles as a result of the December rains. Here we stayed for nearly four days, and here we passed Christmas 1942.

On 25 December I got out on the wrong side of bed. Mentally I mean, for the size of the bivvy allowed no choice in the matter. My batman Harwood clearly thought it only right and proper that I should sleep on a camp bed on Christmas Eve. But I had not dug that slit trench deep enough and the low roof of the bivvy made getting into bed an irksome, slow and difficult operation: so difficult that as soon as my toes touched the bottom of the sleeping bag the top end of the bed collapsed with a sudden jerk. There was a minute or two of exasperated contemplation. But it needed a stronger man than I was to get out of bed and make repairs. I awoke with my head at least two inches below my feet. I heard my batman shuffling about outside. I did not feel somehow like wishing anyone a Happy Christmas. The reply would have added insult to injury.

'You orlright, sir? Yer water's outside.'

'Right.' Pause of five seconds for an effort. 'A Happy Christmas, Harwood. I'll put on another shirt if you can dig it out.'

'Same to you, sir.'

Harwood opened the battered suitcase, protected from the dew by a gas cape, and left the shirt on the bed. I started to dress and stumbled out of the bivvy pulling on my battle-dress trousers. The Signal Platoon was marching by on their way to breakfast at Headquarter Company cookhouse. I celebrated the day with a new razor blade and shaved in the icy, salty water. There was sand in the toothpaste again. I wound up my watch and climbed the hil-lock that stood between me and the Mess tent sixty yards away.

I picked up a September *Spectator* and sat down at the trestle table. The custom of reading a paper at breakfast seems to be an essential tradition of the British Empire. There was not much conversation this morning anyway. A conventional Happy Christmas from everyone as they came in, grumbling that there was no porridge for the fourth day in succession, shouts for more tea . . .

'And I hope someone is doing something about it, George. The only thing to do is go and kick up the hell of a stink at the F.M.C. It's bad for the morale of the Highland Division.'

The P.M.C. smiled as placidly as the Cheshire Cat.

'Good morning, sir. A Happy Christmas.'

The Commanding Officer entered followed by the quartermaster.

'News this morning, Intelligence Officer? [*i.e. Patrick Nairne*] My staff at B Echelon haven't seen a paper for weeks now . . .'

It might have been any day in any Mess of any battalion on active service.

'Is there any tea in that pot, Nigel?'

A look of disapproval puckers O.C. [*Officer in Command*] C company's face.

'You're a menace. That must be your third mug.'

When I came back from breakfast to my bivvy I found the I Section making porridge. They always had a little oatmeal up their sleeves reserved for special occasions. 31 October had been one when we rested before our attack, and 5 November had been another when the Afrika Korps was on the run. Sgt McKirdy was expert at making it. I lay on my bed and reread some old airgraphs, loitering with intent. A courteous hesitating invitation was offered within a few minutes.

'Well, thank you very much, sergeant. I must say I wouldn't say no to a mess tin of porridge.'

I ate it slowly and luxuriously and read another chapter of Mottram's *Our Mr. Dormer* which had arrived as a Christmas present. At 0945 I put on my belt and pistol and went over to the Battalion Headquarters for Church Parade.

We stood at the foot of the sand hills between the Mess tent and the Adjutant's 15-cwt truck. There were not enough paper carol books to go round. 'While shepherds watched their flocks by night', 'Hark the herald angels sing', 'Noel', a short seasonable sermon. The padre paused and asked the Commanding Officer if he would choose the last carol of the service. The Commanding Officer, taken by surprise, swayed characteristically on his heels – obviously fighting against complete mental vacancy. Half a minute elapsed before he chose 'Noel'. Amidst the suppressed amusement of the congregation his choice was tactfully altered by the padre to 'O Come all ye faithful'. The rest of the day was a holiday. That was official throughout the 8th Army. Andrew, abetted by Quinton, sent a phonograph of greeting in Gaelic to the Brigade Commander.

It has always been a regimental custom for the companies to enjoy a special dinner on New Year's Day. Turkey, plum pudding, a beer ration and the Commanding Officer's speech made up an unchanging programme. This year the occasion was on Christmas Day; for operational reasons, some said, but chiefly, we thought, because the pork would have been bad by 1 January. The NAAFI had supplied pork, a few turkeys, plum duff and half a bottle of beer for each man. George Willock had collected it all from Marble Arch on Christmas Eve.* (The supplies had been flown up from the Delta, he said.) Some companies had made elaborate dining halls by digging a broad rectangular slit trench and using the sand left inside the trench as a table. Petrol tins were cut and used as platters. The Commanding Officer, accompanied by the Adjutant and R.S.M., was piped into each company area, where with a glass of whisky he proposed the company's health. His speech became inevitably longer with each company he visited. I stood with Angus at Headquarter Company cookhouse which he attended one from last. The Commanding Officer arrived to the tune of the Company March on the shoulders of two strong men. He spoke cheerfully with a tendency to repetition:

'Headquarter Company produces the trained specialists . . . the cream of the Battalion . . . It is only by pulling together . . .'

---

* Marble Arch was the name given to the 31-metre high Arch of the Philaeni constructed by the Italians in Libya in 1937.

A pause as he leaned forward on his cromach.

'I remember I said last year at Stonehaven that . . . well, let us in 1943 . . .'

George replied suitably. The Commanding Officer departed amidst cheers. Dinners were served. Angus and I joined George and insisted on drinking his health. It made an excuse for finishing the whisky.

The afternoon slipped idly away. The Jocks were sleeping off their Christmas dinner, the Commanding Officer was smoking a cigar in his tent, Andrew was writing letters in his truck. I lay on my bed – (Harwood had comfortably deepened the slit trench) and read *The Moon is Down* by Steinbeck, borrowed from one of the Intelligence Section. At four o'clock the pipe-band beat retreat on the edge of the marshy flat. The sky was the colour of lead; it was to pour with rain in two hours. The pipes and drums were the only sound in that wasteland. It was a dreary and yet distinguished spectacle. We were fascinated as we stood there, charmed like snakes by the pipe-band and by the desert landscape. No cloud moved in the sky; not a blade of grass rustled in the dunes; no bird flew past. Only the band playing and marching on the un-echoing sands. And then I saw a convoy of 3-tonners in the distance moving westwards on the main road.

'The Brigade I Summary says we're into Sirte today,' said Andrew.

'I simply refuse to believe it's Christmas,' remarked David emphatically, moving towards tea in the Mess.

We dined well that night. The Mess tent had been garnished with greenery from the edge of the dunes and cotton-wool 'snow' from the RAF. Hurricane lamps hung above the tables. Someone had produced some decorated menu-cards. The pouring rain made service from the cooks' truck difficult for the waiters. But there was onion soup and turkey, plum pudding, tinned peaches and a mug of Canadian beer. Quinton was in irrepressible form – apparently he had shared a bottle of whisky with his brother-in-law earlier in the evening – and told a genial Commanding Officer loud stories of his days in the Pioneer Corps. Andrew arrived late and bustling from the orderly room truck. Incipient jaundice had been too much for Bill Gray and his place was empty. The Army Commander's Christmas message was passed around. Quinton gave a recital and translation of the Battalion message to Brigade. Someone was collecting signatures on the back of a menu-card.

The party broke up at half past ten. I climbed the hillock on my way to bed. Rain had stopped and the moon was up. The sand was glistening white like icing on a cake. I tried to pretend it was snow. I thought of Britain. Was there snow on the ground at home? Had the village bells been rung in the morning? Was it a good year for the holly berries? Home thoughts from abroad are usually sentimental nonsense. No doubt it had been a mild rainy day in Scotland. I pictured Stonehaven in 1941 and wondered where we should be in 1943. I could see the tracer of ack-ack farther up the Libyan coast, followed a few seconds later by the noise of the guns. Andrew's voice could be heard outside Battalion's Headquarters. I saw that there was a lamp alight in the Intelligence Sergeant's bivvy.

'Some work on, Sergeant?' I asked as I walked past.

'Only a cipher message from Brigade, sir.'

'If it's important, bring it to me when it's finished, will you?'

I went to bed. The camp bed had been mended with string and stood firm. There was a wind flapping the sides of the bivvy. I reckoned it would be raining on the morrow.

6

Sferro Hills, July 1943

Written in May 1945, as a contribution to Sans Peur
by Alastair Borthwick

As intelligence officer I had sent the two intelligence men away from the Battalion Observation Point to their tiffin and now lay uncomfortably in the shallow stony trench camouflaged by wheat-sheaves. I slowly searched the Sicilian landscape through my field glasses. It was a magnificent scene whose sweeping grandeur and delicate detail a middle-aged great-aunt (on one of her daring Victorian tours) would not have hesitated to express on cheap cartridge paper with misguided watercolours. In the foreground a colony of small farms lay irregularly on either side of the Dittaino wadi; in front one of our companies occupied the area where the 2nd Battalion had spent several unhappy isolated days; on the left it was possible to distinguish the bridge, code named Jaguar, into Sferro, where shells fell persistently on 153 Brigade.

On the right of the middle distance, wrecked Messerschmitts glinted in the sun on Gerbini Airfield. Near them I counted four burnt-out Shermans of 50 Royal Tank Regiment. From Gerbini a railway line drew a straight black shadow beneath its telegraph poles north-west to the base of the Sferro Hills. In the background the foothills of Mount Etna rose from the plain like cumulus clouds from the sea. In the centre of the distant green terraced slopes the town of Paterno shone white like a water lily amidst its cluster of leaves.

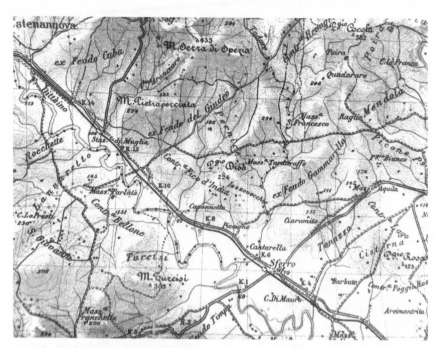

Pat's 1943 map, showing Sferro above the Dittaino River, Sicily.

I concentrated my glasses on Paterno. Its stillness and whiteness both flattered to deceive. All towns of Sicily gleamed like ivory in the distance only to reveal on closer view walls as grey as a Durham mining village. And no doubt its narrow streets were as filled with the dust and roar of German traffic as the streets of Ramacca with the transport of the Highland Division. For it was clear from the map that Paterno was an important communication centre for the enemy guarding the approaches to Etna and the right flank of their Catania position. If Paterno was taken, 13 British Corps could capture Catania. So for nearly eight days now that white town on the green terraced slopes had been the objective of the 51st Division.

On 18 July we had risen hastily from a few hours' sleep in the dewy grass among the rocks above Ramacca and descended from the hills into the Catania plain. We had lazily breakfasted in a cornfield while the Commanding Officer was on a recce. Somehow we had felt more optimistic than a breakfast of compo rations – sausage, the inevitable biscuit and a slab of chocolate (uneatable by midday) – could have justified. Behind us we still had the taste in our mouths of the unripe oranges at Francofonte and the tomato fields at Scordia. There had been a sense of satisfaction that we were free of those narrow, steep, winding roads and clustered fortress villages and into country which the nostalgic might mistake for a bit of Salisbury Plain baked hard by the summer. Here tanks could operate in undeniable tank country; indeed a day or two earlier the Camerons had mistaken a field of corn-stooks for a squadron of camouflaged [*Panzer*] Mark 4s. Ahead of us the outlying slopes of Etna had smiled encouragingly with their shaded terraces. Already two bridges over the River Dittaino had been captured intact. We had been told that Catania would fall any day. We had marked the code name 'Anglesey' beside Paterno on our maps. No wonder confidence had blossomed brightly that the battle groups of the Hermann Goering Division would not long delay us.

Two axes had been tried: through Gerbini and through Sferro. But the Germans had been determined. The Gordons and Black Watch in Sferro village had found the Boche Forward Observation Officers in the hills above them a gross inconvenience during daylight. The 2nd Battalion had done a night excursion up the line of the Dittaino wadi and had lost their commanding officer, second in command, two company commanders and intelligence officer as prisoners in the process. A battalion of Royal Marines had been brought up from the beaches to be 'additional bodies on the ground'. They had done a successful advance by darkness on the left of the 153 Brigade but had found their new positions untenable under daylight mortaring. 50 RTR [*Royal Tank Regiment*] had launched a squadron one morning across Gerbini Airfield and had met dug-in 88s [*German anti-aircraft guns now used against tanks*] behind the Gerbini railway line. 154 Brigade had done a full-bloodied night assault on Gerbini itself and had got a deal more than a bloody nose so that a reluctant GOC [*General Officer Commanding*] was forced to withdraw them. Even Rear Div. had not been without its alarms, for Jack Angus had been dispatched one day with his platoon to hunt German paratroopers who had been reported sniping their area. We alone had been the divisional reserve, condemned to an hourly existence of harassed uncertainty.

But now it was 25 July (it may have been the 26th). All three Brigades of the Division were in the Line while the Americans drove eastwards from Palermo and 78th Division came north from Syracuse to reinforce the 8th Army between ourselves and the Canadians.

I crawled cautiously out of the Observation Point, exchanged a few words with the Royals armoured car parked in the wadi and walked the sixty yards to the Battalion HQ. My legs were stiff and I felt a bout of gippy tummy coming on. I found the Adjutant dealing with a strength return on the edge of his slit trench.*

'Any news?'

Douglas said that the General had paid a visit.

'We're being relieved by a battalion of 13 Brigade. You know, Lorne Campbell's Brigade in 5 Div. Probably tomorrow.'

The divisional axis, he casually explained, was apparently being changed from north-east to north.

I looked at his mapboard. His eyes moved from Paterno westwards and paused at the neat brown lines that marked the hills above Sferro.

Next morning found us encamped round a dirty black-stone farm called Massa Ogliastro. Here we heard of the plan to attack the hills north-west of Sferro. The Highland Division had to do two things: first to open the road, at present in no man's land, joining Sferro and Catenanuova, secondly to attract the few remaining German tanks towards its front. When these jobs had been done the 78th Division would make the main 8th Army thrust towards Centuripe farther north.

Patrol areas were allotted to each battalion of the Brigade. New maps were issued. The GOC held a conference down to company commanders. Recces were made. The contours on the Commanding

* The Adjutant was reporting on the number of men fit for the next battle.

Officer's map were painted distinctive colours. The Bofors fired a demonstration of tracer at night. First reinforcements joined us from Sousse. Conscientiously, but with little realism, a rehearsal was carried out. I took an afternoon off to draw a panorama of the Sferro Hills.

I lay next to a Middlesex machine-gun post in the thick, dry couch-grass on the north-east slope of Monte Turcisi. The landscape in front was at peace – deliberately, for jeeps were stopped by a notice well back, while two miles south on the Gerbini front, 5 Division were at pains to patrol aggressively and raise dust on their skyline. Below on the right I could see the roof of Massa Turcisi, a huge and squalid farm. A track for vehicles had been found round the south side of Monte Turcisi leading to the farm and down to the dry, stony bed of the River Dittaino where Russell's patrol reckoned Motorised Transport could cross. On the far side of the curling Dittaino wadi a white path twisted past a cottage and ran between gorse bushes and a cornfield to the line of the road and railway stretching together across no man's land to the huddle of rooves glistening in the sun away to the left which I identified as Catenanuova. Across the road the Sferro Hills rose steeply; the grassy slopes mounted deceptively smoothly to Pt.224 at the northern end of the ridge.

I turned my glasses on to a farm which stood halfway down the hill from Pt.224. It was called Iazzovecchio and a patrol had reported that the dogs still barked there. Not a sign of life now. I shifted my elbows and moved the glasses right-handed up the crest to where a stick grenade had forced Jack Angus back and along the ridge till they reached a light green copse. This end of the ridge with the green copse and a farm named Angelico, a hundred and fifty yards below it, was the Battalion objective. I could see no Germans now. Yet no doubt the reverse slope of the ridge was pitted with crowded dugouts. At this moment enemy observers were probably concentrating their glasses on Monte Turcisi.

It was to be a divisional battle. 152 Brigade were to take the Pt.224 feature and 154 the hill to the west of it. The Brigadier's plan was for 5 Cameron to lead and capture Pt.224 itself; 5th

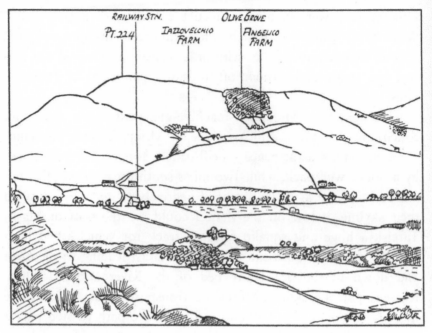

RAILWAY STN.   OLIVE GROVE

PT.224   IAZZOVECCHIO   ANGELICO
          FARM   FARM

A sketch of the Sferro Hills as seen from our Observation Post.

Drawing by Pat, as intelligence officer, of the battle objective, Sferro Hills, as
reproduced in Alastair Borthwick, *Sans Peur,* 1946.

Seaforth would follow the Cameron axis as far as Iazzovecchio
farm and then attack north-eastwards to take Angelico farm, the
green copse and the right-hand side of the hill. 2nd Seaforth would
be in reserve and six gunner regiments and two machine-gun companies would support the attack. The C.O. had chosen two routes:
he did not want all his eggs in the Cameron basket. A, C, D Companies, Bn. Hq and a few Bn. HQ vehicles would follow the Camerons up the direct track to Iazzovecchio farm. B Company and
the supporting weapons would cut across the cornfield from the
Dittaino wadi and climb another track farther east from the main
road to the same farm. At Iazzovecchio the Battalion would deploy
for the assault and would exploit, if possible, the line of a wadi
on the far side of the hill. It seemed a simple enough plan. But as
I put the finishing touches to my panorama I thought of the vehicles and supporting weapons. Not so easy for the chaps on their
feet carrying picks and shovels, ammunition and rations; but to

move the carriers, mortars, machine guns, anti-tank guns of two battalions, one behind the other, down a rocky mountain, across a shingle river bed and up a steep hill against an enemy whose positions we could only guess and whose strength we did not know appeared a most hazardous business.

On the night of 30 July the Battalion moved from Massa Ogliastro to a concentration area in the narrow grassy gullies on the west side of Monte Turcisi. For several days thunderclouds had threatened and there had been anxiety for the Dittaino wadi. But on this evening the stars shone from a clear, sultry sky. When the Battalion was settled to sleep Ian and I, with a clodhopping escort from the defence platoon – (they always called themselves the O Group) – strolled to the Dittaino to have a look at the crossing place. On our way back we paused for a gulp of whisky with Jimmy who had been sent with a 15 cwt to evacuate the vast Sicilian family from Massa Turcisi. It was nearly 0300 when we reached the Battalion area. Our weariness made us glad that the minimum movement was allowed on the following day.

31 July was a day of waiting. Perhaps the subtlest thing in army training is the fact that it teaches a soldier how to wait, although on active service most soldiers don't wait – they sleep. Yet one cannot sleep all the time. Soldiers, like boxers before the fight in the evening, cannot help thinking . . . On All Hallow's Eve at Alamein there had been no time; we had had one day only out of the Line and that had been a whirl of recces, O Groups, and weapon cleaning. Besides we had little idea what was coming to us. Corradini had been a scramble; not a moment for anything but the most practical thoughts. The day before Akarit has been fully filled with route recces, kit packing, conferences and a long march to the start line. At Francofonte we had found ourselves in the fight almost before we knew it. But on this occasion all preparations had been completed in good time and we sprawled all day in the sun like picnickers on bank holiday. The I section marked code names on maps; I chatted to Brigade on the field telephone about Henderson's patrol which had reported contact with the enemy; the Adjutant made a circumspect trip to the vehicle

concentration area. The General and Brigadier paid visits, exuding hearty optimism. The C.O. held a final conference. Apparently Corps were referring airily to the operation as 'the Highland Division's skirmish'. Our natural scepticism was reinforced.

The Battalion was not moving from its concentration area until ten o'clock but – with a party of company guides and I Section – I left over an hour earlier. There were three tasks to be done: to see how the Brigade sappers had taped the wadi crossing, to place the company guides in the wadi where the Battalion was to wait until the Camerons were clear and to tape a route for B Company and the supporting weapons across the cornfield to the road. We hurried down the rocky mule-track to Massa Turcisi with shovels clanking in our hands and haversacks rattling on our backs.

Massa Turcisi had been made a Brigade report centre. I found it very different from the silent ghostly farm I had visited in the early hours of the morning – as different as a pub on a Saturday night is from a pub on a Sunday morning. Here each battalion was to 'marry-up' with its supporting arms, and already a Liaison Officer was acting 'mine host' to a gathering of gunners, sappers, guides, recce parties and vehicles. My party was joined by the Intelligence Sergeant, beaming efficiency, with a drum of tape tied to the carrier of his motorcycle. We continued down the white track to the Dittaino. There was no moon but we could see ahead of us a clump of tall cypresses as artificial as a Shakespeare stage set. Not a word was spoken. The Intelligence Sergeant's bike chugged steadily behind their single file, and in the distance to the south occasional mortars growled, perhaps at the lurid glow in the darkness provided by a clump of burning haystacks.

When we reached the bushy banks of the wadi some sappers were just clambering from a truck. I took a look round. Not a strand of tape in the bed of the wadi. I quickened my pace to the far bank. Not a shred of tape anywhere. Perhaps I was looking in the wrong place? But now the sappers from the truck had arrived noisily on the scene. Were *they* here to mark the crossing? And just starting now? I had a word with their officer.

'My God!' He looked at his watch as he rejoined the Intelligence Sergeant, 'The Camerons will be here any minute.'

A wave of exasperation flooded my mind. It really was too bad. Sudden memories of Alamein and Akarit pointed accusing fingers from my brain. The taped start line which had materialised so late on operation 'Supercharge', the precise plans for lighting that had never been carried out before Roumana. And now the wadi crossing at Sferro. It seemed more doubtful whether the sappers could finish their work in time. I saw them begin reeling out tape and digging away the banks of the wadi while I showed the guides where to lead their companies on arrival.

I left my haversack with the motorbike, collected the tape and led three Intelligence men across the wadi and into the cornfield. It would appear a simple enough job laying some four hundred yards of tape across a field with corn-stooks and a stretch of plough; it shouldn't take longer than twenty minutes. Or so I reckoned confidently. The artillery barrage would be opening in half an hour along the line of the road. I had to be well on my way back by that time.

But it wasn't that easy. The drum of tape had no bar through its centre so two men clasped it between them in their arms while the third awkwardly unreeled the twisted tape from behind. They stumbled ponderously over the stubble following as straight a course as possible through the stooks.

'Come on, come on. We haven't got all night. Get a move on with that tape . . . And try and make a little less noise.'

I had felt the same irritation at the roaring Crusaders moving to their forming-up point behind the start line at Alamein and at the 154 Brigade Scorpions proclaiming our purpose to the desert air before Akarit. We could not be far from where Henderson had reported the German patrol on the night before. We reached the plough and our pace became more laboured. But a few minutes later we were cheered by relief on seeing telegraph poles and a small hut appear dimly in front. This would be the level crossing where B Company and the supporting weapons must cross the railway and road before ascending up the hill to Iazzovecchio. The tape was quickly tied to a fence pole.

We retraced our steps and went two hundred yards when the barrage began. Monte Turcisi and the ridges right and left suddenly flickered with a hundred dancing flames. Immediately the air above us began to hum as rhythmically, but more harmoniously, as the symphony of seagulls on a seashore. We sniffed cordite and, looking back, saw the line of telegraph poles already obscured by a fog of dust punctured every second by the red flash of a shell burst. We broke into a dog-trot. It was mentally disturbing to move away from the barrage: like turning one's back on a house on fire. By now, I thought, the Camerons will have started. Yet there did not seem to be any German Defensive Fire. We were out of breath when we reached the Dittaino wadi.

The Cameron guns and vehicles were slow getting clear and the Battalion was delayed by nearly half an hour. The companies, wearing pullovers, khaki drill slacks and anklets, were huddled under the wadi bank. It was like a last war picture of men waiting to go over the top. The C.O. repeated last-minute instructions to company commanders and grumbled that our own transport would be late. Douglas was shouting orders not to bunch. But no German shells were coming our way; there was only the relentless musical hum of our barrage – with one of our guns firing persistently short.

At last A Company could start. Plodding in single file, they followed the sappers' white tape out of the wadi and along a sandy track through thick gorse bushes typical of a seaside golf course. C and D Companies came behind with Battalion HQ at the back. The Adjutant and I were walking together and had scarcely gone a hundred yards when the column halted. We waited resignedly; it was the hopeful resignation of those who sit for a few moments trusting that a BBC technical hitch rather than spent accumulator has suddenly silenced their wireless set. The column moved once more. Within two hundred yards it stopped again. Our advance was revealing characteristics similar to a Bren gun with an ill-adjusted gas regulator. After three minutes of patience the Adjutant sent me up the column. There should be no cause for delay; and at this rate the Battalion would never reach the ridge. While pushing past C Company I guessed what had happened. The tape had finished, the track forked right and A Company had chosen to continue left. At the front the officer commanding A Company spoke with resentment.

'Paddy, your Intelligence man has led me wrong.'

There was no time to argue.

'You ought to have forked right just back round the corner, James,' I said vigorously. 'Come on, I'll lead you myself.'

The column wheeled round, got clear of the gorse bushes along the correct path and crossed the railway and the road. The C.O. stood on the track to Iazzovecchio shooing the companies past him. A section of C Company was told off for breaking into the double.

We were now out of contact with the Camerons in front. The smoke from the barrage hung about us as thick and yellow as a London fog. From the Observation Point on Monte Turcisi the track up the slopes to Pt.224 had shone white in the sunshine. It had never occurred to us that it would be difficult to follow. Under the July starlight our patrols had had no difficulty in using it. But now visibility was down to ten yards. It was even hard to see the red tracer fired for direction by the Bofors. Suddenly A Company was again confronted with a choice of two tracks. One forked right, one left: nobody remembered this track junction. It was then a toss-up and I favoured the left. But we had been bitten once . . . The column stopped while investigation was made. We could not afford any error in the matter. To follow the Cameron axis to Iazzovecchio was an essential part of the plan.

Our three companies were struggling up the hill, as ill-disposed as the Highland Brigade column led personally by Wauchope (with his brigade major holding the compass) into the disorganised disaster of Magersfontein.* Finally the right-hand track was chosen

---

* A reference to the Boer War campaign, and the battle of Magersfontein in 1899, when the Highland Brigade suffered very heavy casualties.

and in a few hundred yards we came upon the Cameron RAP [*Regimental Aid Post*] digging in.

We began to hear the *beripp . . . beripp* of Spandaus ahead of us. As A Company with difficulty located Iazzovecchio – (someone kept referring on the wireless to the farm with the Jewish name) – and found it deserted we sat on the ground under a constant whine of bullets. But the enemy was firing high and we were having no casualties. Yet we were over an hour behind the artillery programme and the barrage had stopped some time ago. Concentrations only were going on down on the far side of the hill. It was bluntly obvious that the enemy was still on the crest in front of us. A and C Companies deployed and advanced on Angelico farm and the green copse respectively. The second in command was bustling about in order to hasten them on their way. D Company and the Battalion HQ followed A Company's axis, while B Company arrived at the top of the easterly track to report two 17-pounders overturned on the steepest part of the slope.

The night passed too quickly. D Company made itself firm at Angelico and Jack made a decision on the spot against exploitation beyond the ridge; A Company spread eastwards and sent its left-hand platoon to the assistance of C Company in the copse; B Company pushed resolutely towards the line of the ridge between the Camerons and ourselves; over a hundred prisoners trooped back to the shallow stony ditch where Battalion HQ was attempting to dig in. Some planes loosed orange flares and with an accuracy attributable only to the RAF set two of our mortar trucks ablaze with three bombs. There was a tireless traffic of officers and NCOs guiding carriers, anti-tank guns and mortars into position.

A misty dawn revealed our job unfinished. The green copse had been a German strong point and the going had not been easy. We could not yet stand among the bushes on the crest and survey the country on the other side of the hill. Scattered snipers prevented us. Nor had the Camerons yet cleared Pt.224 that overlooked us from the left. As the sun rose men were digging all over the hill. The C.O. moved Battalion HQ farther down its ditch, the second in command was seen gallantly crouching in the open with a rifle beyond A Company, Henderson the Forward Observation Officer manoeuvred his Honey [*US built M3 Stuart tank*] as far forward as he could and someone urged three Shermans round the right flank of the copse. Heavy German shells had started to whirr majestically overhead to burst near the road and the railway, clothed in dewy mists below us, and the inevitable mortars had opened their fast bowling. We were glad of a piece of chocolate for breakfast.

By ten o'clock the scene was quieter. The forward platoons had not spared their Bren magazines, the Middlesex guns had fired aggressively, if blindly, from east of Angelico, the mortars had practised tireless indirect fire on to the far side of the hill, the Shermans had made a show of strength and were now parked, with turrets open under looted orange sunshades, on the slope behind C Company. The Germans – for reasons they could best explain – had left the ridge and the copse to us. Although the shelling had not slackened – a direct hit on Angelico had wounded Jack – the whole objective was firmly ours. The Brigade Major said on the blower that there was reason to think the enemy were pulling out. I limped wearily from Battalion HQ up to the copse to see for myself.

Under the delicate green trees lay dirt and disorder. The entrances to dark dugouts were strewn with carbines, egg grenades, belts, respirators, lemons, aluminium mess tins, bread, bottles, note-books, clothing: all overlaid with the well-known bittersweet odour of German occupation. A few German corpses were gathering flies and from the bottom of the copse dead mules stank in our nostrils. Platoons of A and C Companies were relaxing or sniffing about the abandoned trenches with a bit more than mere curiosity. I walked to the left edge of the copse and wondered why the Germans did not shell such an obvious landmark. Perhaps they thought their infantry were still in possession. Beyond Lorie's HQ I came on a Scottish horse major crawling with a tommy gun.

'Isn't it safe to walk over here?' I smiled in greeting.

'I don't know.' The gunner major smiled back and stood up. 'This is my first day's shooting and I wondered if there was a chance of bagging a jerry myself.'

We walked together, as warily as stage villains, down the German side of the hill and sat down on the edge of an empty dugout. The major called up a signaller who had been following as discreetly as a private detective and began testing his wireless. I studiously compared my map with the glorious panorama in front of us. Immediately below was a parched valley planted with a handful of squalid farms. On the right rose brown hills stretching back left-handed like a succession of sandcastles towards Mount Etna. On the left a sun-baked track, leading from the middle of these hills, disappeared below Pt.224. On the far side of this track farms were scattered; I spotted some German vehicles parked round one farm. (The major licked his lips.) In the distance the terraced slopes of Etna shimmered in the heat.

'Brigade reckoned the Boche were skinning out,' I remarked casually as I gazed steadily through my field glasses. (But the Major was now having trouble with his wireless.)

'Hi! Look! Look!' I shouted to interrupt the Major's bickering to the signaller. 'Are those tanks ours?'

A dozen tanks with a picquet of motorcyclists were serenely driving along that sun-baked track towards the northern end of the Sferro Hills.

'They might be Shermans.' He paused doubtfully, glaring again through his glasses. 'They can't be, *can't* be . . . I can see now.' His voice was triumphant. 'They're Mark 4s. This'll mean the start of a counterattack.'

(Slowly and happily the Scottish horse major was issuing a fire order on his wireless.)

The next three hours were the wearisome climax to the battle. The German tanks were dropping 'fast balls' all over the hill. Heavier calibre stuff droned overhead to the Sferro road behind us. Panzer Grenadiers assaulted Pt.224, and one German tank forced its way gallantly to the peak. But six gunner regiments, backed by every anti-aircraft gun on the slopes, put down all they had in support of the Camerons. By two o'clock the Hermann Goering battle group had had enough. The surviving tanks were seen driving away. The shelling slackened. By six o'clock it was just another still sunny Sicilian evening. The battle was over.

On the next day vehicles drove from Sferro and met the Canadians in Catenanuova. A day or two later 78th Division attacked with success at Centuripe. So the Division had done its job again. A radiant Corps Commander stopped Jack Latta on the road and told him Catania had fallen. Paterno was reported taken. With their Etna position outflanked the Germans were scuttling for Messina.

With about thirty-five casualties in the Battalion it had been a 'cheap' victory for us. Perhaps this fact made the loss of Jack [*Davidson*] seem all the sadder. For he died of his wounds in a dressing station below Monte Turcisi. No finer man ever fought and gave his life with 5th Seaforth.

On 7 or 8 August, 152 cautiously followed 154 Brigade in glaring daylight down the cliffs below Monte Cocola and across the shallow Simeto river. By evening the Battalion was astride the road below Biancavilla. We found ourselves among shady groves of orange trees, cactus bushes with their prickly yellow fruits, orchards hung with figs and warm stone walls luscious with ripe grapes. Etna towered above us and Douglas was reminded of the Argyllshire mountains. I compared the early mornings to a classical landscape by Turner. The C.O. looked round for a horse to ride. The second in command was sent to scrounge vino. After arid fields, the dried wells, the sordid farms and the dusty tracks of the Catania Plain below Ramacca, our new surroundings seemed like the Promised Land. We too had come out of Egypt; almost a year to the day we had disembarked at Suez. Now our last battle in the Mediterranean had been fought and won.

7

Novembers – 1944: *The Night We Crossed the Canal*

Introduced and edited in 1999

In mid-October 1944 I had returned to the Battalion as adjutant – after more than a year away, evacuated with lung trouble at the end of the Sicily campaign and, while graded unfit, promoted to captain and – unexpectedly at the age of twenty-two – appointed adjutant of the Seaforth and Cameron Training Centre at Elgin. I was in time for the winter campaign in Holland, and in Spring 1945 I wrote an account of a memorable night in November: 17 November 1944.

We sat in the small front room of the red-roofed cottage while the rain beat mercilessly on the tarmac road outside. On the table three hurricane lamps – why were they never well cleaned? – jostled for space with the crockery set for dinner and scarcely succeeded in lighting the room with its drab curtains and two coloured photographs of Tyrolean snow scenes. In the kitchen next door the mess staff and batmen were chattering and laughing with the large Dutch family whose friendly spirit was undiminished by their relegation to two rooms on our arrival the day before.

As we began to eat a sudden dull thud in the distance was followed by three more irregular thuds. No experienced ear could miss their meaning, but undisturbed security during the day and the homely atmosphere of the room led us to be caught unawares. An unmistakable whistling screech forced us instinctively to duck and three more shells in rapid succession found us sitting on the floor. The civilians began hustling down to the cellar; upstairs the commanding officer lay unmoved in bed with a bad cold. Two more shells – within a hundred yards of the house – while we listened with respectful patience: three minutes silence and we slowly resumed our places at the table.

The commanding officer's batman put his head round the door and the second in command went out to speak to Brigade HQ on the wireless. Nothing was said while he was out of the room; we were all guessing in our minds what Brigade had to say.

'We've got to go over the canal tonight.' The second in command broke the news quietly as he sat down again to his soup. 'Probably not before midnight. The 2nd Battalion is going first and Brigade wants to wait and see how it gets on before committing us.' He broke off a piece of bread. 'We've now got to go over by the Cameron crossing. Brigade is sending along a liaison officer later.'

No one spoke. This was not what we had hoped to hear. Outside the wet blustery weather damped the spirits on a moonless night, and on the far side of a narrow, muddy canal a mile or two away were the Germans.

It is impossible now to remember the name of the canal or the names of the villages which the Brigade had occupied in Holland. But somebody in the Battalion has only to refer to the Night We Crossed the Canal and we know at once what occasion he means. The commanding officer probably thinks of a cold that forced him to bed in the evening; George, as O.C. HQ company, remembers an exacting night on the Brigade rear link wireless set; Leslie, O.C. D company, a day of soaking rain in the woods by the canal bank followed by a malicious mortar 'stonk' on the bedraggled company when resting on its return; and myself returning from a recce with the intelligence officer, wet and muddy from boots to Balmoral. But all have vivid recollections of the relentless weather, of squelching mud, and of setting off late at night to advance over unknown ground against an enemy of unknown strength in unknown positions.

The more experienced a battalion becomes, the more it dislikes the prospect of fighting an impromptu battle. Such battles often cost the most in casualties if the enemy is determined (as the 5th Battalion had found at short notice at night, at Homs, a few miles short of Tripoli). A battalion in reserve busies itself in constantly trying to find out what neighbouring battalions are doing and how other brigades are faring in order to guess what its own next task may be. Tonight the commanding officer chats to the brigade major on the wireless; as adjutant, I cross-question liaison officers who do not escape quickly enough; the intelligence officer is dispatched to brigade HQ to *Find Out the Form*; O.C. C company telephones to ask for any 'griff'; O.C. A company drives himself down to enquire, bubbling with his latest shelling or Spandau story; O.C. HQ company arrives with a pipe in his mouth and a puzzled look; the quartermaster sends a note from B Echelon to the effect that *No One Ever Tells Him Anything*. Intelligent anticipation is the constant aim. But now we know that within five hours the canal must be crossed and the Cameron bridgehead enlarged

It was nearly an hour after midnight before the Battalion was on the move. The signals officer had eavesdropped on the Brigade rear link wireless set and reported no opposition to the 2nd Battalion's progress. A slightly dazed commanding officer had been roused from bed at his own insistence. A liaison officer visited and fixed some code names. The commanding officer's Orders Group of company commanders had clustered round an air photograph while the intelligence officer traced with a chinagraph pencil the route he proposed to the scattered village which had been made the Battalion's final objective. Our rum ration had been finished in some coffee and we were glad to be moving.

The start of an operation sets the mind at ease with the thought that there is no longer any point in worrying over preparations unmade. It was now scarcely raining and the searchlights, throwing up their broad rays of artificial moonlight, outlined the hedges and houses beside the road in a lurid purple glare. The night was quieter and there was no shelling near us. The companies tramping in single file, platoon following platoon, were reminiscent of a WWI painting – perhaps by C. R. W. Nevinson.

The Cameron crossing place had been given the code name

Pat's copy of an aerial reconnaissance photograph, Holland 1944.

'Partridge' (with Brigade's usual preference for a sporting touch); and within two hours the Battalion was across and on its first report line. The most trying part of the operation had been completed. It was to the credit of the intelligence officer who had led with A company, and to the Jocks who accepted the whole operation with their usual blasphemous serenity.

Now we were halted on a watery track while O.C. A company, ever cautious, cleared the dripping fir trees and the ghost-like farm buildings ahead. The commanding officer, O.C. B Company, and the intelligence officer were waiting in a convenient German slit trench. Behind them the long single line of men lay motionless beside the track like so many dead bodies. It was cold and wearisome. Our impatience was increased by the guns of the 15th Scottish Division which, no doubt with the excellent intention of putting down harassing fire on the Brigade left flank, began dropping their shells within a hundred and fifty yards of us. At last three bewildered German prisoners were escorted to Battalion HQ, and the whole Battalion started to move again. Some hours later a chilly November sun rose to reveal the Battalion on all its objectives with platoons spread among trees, across fields and in farm buildings. An operation which had all the makings of a Boer War Magersfontein turned out to be almost as innocuous as a school OTC field day. The Brigadier drove his jeep to our new Battalion HQ, smiling with enthusiastic delight at our night's work. Suddenly we realised that we were tired. Our battle dress was wet and mud-stained, our boots sodden and weighed down with wet earth, ourselves unwashed and our eyes aching for sleep.

It had turned out to be a very small affair. But, in J. B. Salmond's *The History of the 51st Highland Division*, he wrote of the occasion: 'It was really a very remarkable accomplishment that under dreadful conditions those two battalions (2nd and 5th Seaforths) should have arrived and dug in (still in the darkness) on the exact positions they had set out to reach.'

But the Germans had no intention of giving up. There were to be six more months of often severe fighting before the German

The bridge at Arnhem, Holland, 1944. Photograph belonging to Pat.

Pat by William Dring, pastel, 1940

South Lodge yard, 1956

River Mole, Surrey, c.1965

River Thames
from Hammersmith
Terrace, drawing
for Christmas card,
1949

Foston Church,
Christmas card,
1984

Loch Fyne,
Argyllshire,
Christmas card,
2002

Salute church from Riva degli Schiavoni, Venice, 1989

Tuscany sunset, 1999

Pat and Penny Nairne at the wedding of George and Fiona Greenwood, January 1980

Culver Down, Bembridge, Isle of Wight, 1969

Bembridge Harbour, c.1985

Italian village roofs, 2002

Port de la Selva, Catalonia, 1974

Dinas Head, Pembrokeshire, *c.*1973

Towards Snowdonia, 2004

surrender in the following year. In December came the sudden and successful German onslaught on the weak American front in the Ardennes, and the Highland Division was rapidly moved south of Liège, to the north of the German salient.

Here, in early January 1945, during an awkward afternoon attack on a snowy battlefield with the objective of capturing the defended village of Mierchamps, I was wounded by a shell in the neck and hand, while reporting progress on the wireless set to Brigade HQ. It proved to be, in soldiers' jargon, 'a Blighty one': a month or so later I was evacuated to a hospital on the edge of Leeds while the Battalion fought in the Reichwald battle in February, crossed the Rhine in March, and suffered further casualties in continuous fighting until the war in Western Europe ended on 5 May 1945.

In the autumn of 1945, fit once again, I was summoned back to the post of adjutant at Altenbruch in Northern Germany, east of Cuxhaven, where the Battalion had the task of supervising the effective demobilisation of a German division.

One evening, in early December, the daily battalion post included a brief letter from the War Office informing my commanding officer, Lieut. Colonel John Sym DSO, that T/Captain P. D. Nairne

Pat, left, with Seaforth officers, Cuxhaven, Germany, 1945.

MC should be released straight away, under Class B demobilisation, in order to return to Oxford University. I placed the letter at
the bottom of the file of papers to take John Sym by surprise later
that evening. Three days later I left the Battalion forever.

AFTER THE WAR: 1945–1967

Introduction

Personal relationships. Here is something comparatively solid in a world full of violence and cruelty . . . We don't know what we are like. We can't know what other people are like. How then can we put any trust in personal relationships, or cling to them in the gathering political storm? In theory we cannot. But in practice we can and do . . . I certainly can proclaim that I believe in personal relationships. Starting from them I get a little order into the contemporary chaos.

E. M. Forster, 'What I Believe', 1939
Commonplace book, entry no. 204

My father's description of Oxford counters any expectation that post-war university life would be idyllic after the privations and dangers of the battlefield. It was unnerving to be a student again, even on a shortened degree course. However, he started a commonplace book in January 1946 with an eagerness for knowledge – headings under which he copied out chosen quotations ranging from 'Diplomacy', 'Laughter' and 'Art' to 'Conscience', 'Moral Evolution' and 'Convictions' – and ended his time at Oxford by meeting and falling for Penny Bridges. Being selected for the Civil Service was another surprise. His idea of the significance of Novembers was established through wartime events, but the occasion of asking Penny to marry him in Cornbury Park on 23 November 1947 was life changing.

The effects of my father's work on home life are conveyed by a note written later which admitted that '. . . only a few months after I joined the Admiralty it looked as if I might have to postpone my wedding leave because of the Soviet blockade of Berlin in the summer of 1948'. The severe impact of work never went away even if it was modified over the next four decades; and family life, friends and holidays were creatively woven together.

From Sunday 19 September 1948 – the day after their wedding – my parents started a joint journal and set aside their previous individual diaries. It charts the life of the newly-weds: how much they were in love; how my father gradually shared his experiences in the war; their determination to start a family; and their desire to contribute even in a small way to making a better world (my father helping run a youth club in Hammersmith and my mother involved with a young mothers' group). But equally it reveals the strains on my mother as first Kathy and then a second daughter Fiona had to be cared for in the rented flat in Hammersmith Terrace. A garden overlooking the Thames was delightful but also liable to the alarming threat of floods. And for a period in 1950 my father was confined to one room, recovering from TB and kept in quarantine from the baby.

The young couple had supportive siblings, mostly helpful parents and new friends (such as James and Elizabeth Morris, encountered in the baby clinic). The year 1953 was particularly complicated with a second bout of TB and long recuperation at the Benenden Sanatorium in Kent. My mother organised the move to South Lodge in Cobham, Surrey, and also coped with my arrival in June. More indoor and outdoor space helped the family as it expanded with my twin brothers, James and Andrew, arriving in 1960 and my youngest sister Margaret in 1961. South Lodge became the established focus of our childhood, with schools, shops, library and church (and a suburban train station) all within easy bicycling distance.

My father often joked that after wartime service in the army the Civil Service deliberately pitched him into the navy section. But reorganisation in 1963–64 united the different service departments into the new Ministry of Defence. Much hard work and several promotions later took him in 1965 to the crucial appointment of private secretary to Denis Healey, Secretary of State for Defence.

SN

8

Post-War Diaries: 1945 and 1946

Edited in 2002

Demobbed! The 5th (Caithness and Sutherland) Battalion of the Seaforth Highlanders left behind in Germany. Back home at Plover Hill, Compton. Two letters bear witness – both from the Compton and Shawford Welcome Home Committee. One formally welcomed me home, adding: 'We offer you our grateful thanks for your services to King and Country and our best wishes for your health and happiness in the years to come.'

The other sent me 'from subscribers and well-wishers' a leather wallet and a token for three National Savings certificates, adding: 'We have had some difficulty in making the selection, for some presents we have considered are either unprocurable or in very short supply.'

Fair enough: I had not expected anything at all. And I did not intend to remain at home. As an Exhibitioner at University College, I had received early release from the army in order to return to Oxford, where I had spent one term in the early summer of 1940, more than five years earlier.

I began [*another*] diary on Tuesday, 1 January 1946. The first entry sets the tone:

Cold and frosty. Uncle Dick departs to London by 1030 train from Winchester. Chat with Michael R. at rly. stn.; he returning to Park Prewett (hospital where he was undergoing medical training). Meet

Ellises and G. H. in the town. (Listen to 'Dream of Gerontius' Prelude
in Whitwams Music Shop.) Put car in for overhaul at Reliance Garage.
To tea with Ellises; have to hear story of proposed farm in Cotswolds.
Caught for drinks after tea when Winlaws came in. Old man Winlaw
father of my Pl. Instructor for two months at 166 Officer Cadet
Training Unit, Isle of Man, Nov–Jan 1940. Listen to poor session of
'Brains Trust' with the arrogant Joad and the ass Campbell. Reading
vol.1, Clarendon's *History*, vol.1, Churchill's *Marlborough*, Pepys'
Diary, *Shining Scabbard* by R. C. Hutchinson, James Thurber's
Carnival.

Social life near Plover Hill in the late 1940s at its liveliest. But
who were all these people? Fifty-six years later I can still see them
all clearly in my mind's eye. Michael Roberts on his way to continue his medical training at Park Prewett Hospital near Basingstoke,
where I had been an orthopaedic patient in 1945 after being
wounded in the Ardennes. Michael was the son and grandson of
local doctors – an only child and given to hanging around with
nothing to do as a small boy in the 1930s. His father [*Marsden
Roberts*] was our doctor, a good amateur painter, and a close friend
of my parents.

The Ellises gave good children's parties in their large house in
Shawford on the edge of the River Itchen, in which we were
allowed to bathe. My father regarded father Ellis as a bore; there
were a son, Leslie, and two sisters, whom we had known at Miss
Taylor's, the small private primary school at the top of Shawford
hill, judging Leslie to be wet and dismissing the sisters as members
of the, for us, unknown species of girls. I think that, after his years
at Winchester, the farm was for Leslie, who had been unfit in the
war. I lost touch with the Ellises.

The initials G. H., on the other hand, were significant. This was
Gill Horrocks and there was no need to spell out the name. She
was the young daughter (and another only child) of Lieut. General
Sir Brian and Lady (Nancy) Horrocks, who had a thatched cottage
in Compton Lane, close to the house of Nancy's uncle, the architect
Herbert Kitchen, a good friend of my father's. Gill was bright and

pretty, in her last year at school and hoping to secure a place at Oxford in the year ahead. Although some seven years older, I was attracted – and in those innocent years it became evident that the attraction was mutual.

Her mother was a watercolour painter and an uncharacteristic army wife; she was much on her own in Compton and my parents were kind to her. Brian emerged as one of the most courageous and successful generals of the 1939–45 war. He was the Highland Division's Corps Commander in Germany and had visited our battalion in Cuxhaven where I was adjutant. He knew me then and he was very kind to me in later years when, on retirement from the army, he became Black Rod in the House of Lords and began to develop another successful career as an early TV broadcaster about the army in battle.

9

Novembers – *1946 and 1947: Oxford*

Introduced and edited in 1999–2000

By November 1946 I had been ten months back at University College, Oxford; once again I was writing a daily diary. My neck was healed, and the doctors had done all they could to repair my left hand; I was safe and among friends; I had a new and compelling purpose in life. But my diary struck a note of depression. For 17 November (the same date as 'The Night We Crossed the Canal' but two years later) the diary records a 'day of dreary rain'. The following day was a Monday and I wrote at the top of the entry: '10½ hours work' and then added:

> I write at 2330, despairing about my essay on J. S. Mill; sometimes my brain will not work – I can think of NOTHING.

> 1000: Mackenzie on the Civil Service – good. Rest of the day on Mill. His 'On Liberty' very stimulating and good reading, but God knows what the answer is between state control and individual human rights. I am muddled-headed. p.m. – work in Library and visit Blackwell's shop where there is an essay in McCallum's new edition of Mill. Victor Watts to tea – a good chap but as young as his age. Letter from Harwood (Seaforth batman). Cold weather.

In January 1947 I took a preliminary written examination for the Administrative Class of the Civil Service. I did not think that

I had done well but I heard nothing from the Civil Service Commission for five months. Meanwhile I was offered by John Wilkes, the warden of Radley College, a teaching post, coupled with the secretaryship of the Radleian Society and also a teaching post at Eastbourne College after an interview at the Randolph Hotel with the headmaster, John Nugee, formerly sub-warden of Radley. Both good offers to a young man unsure of his future who had not yet obtained a university degree: could I risk refusing them both when the prospect of a Civil Service place looked bleak? My diary entry for 16 June 1947:

> A letter from the Civil Service Commission. I have failed to pass my language oral test and so the Foreign Service is 'off'; my marks qualify me for a preliminary interview as a result of which I may, or may not, be called to a 'house party' selection board. Well, well . . . Might be worse is the best comment.

In May I said 'no' to John Wilkes, though he was by then an old friend and my father was inclined to urge me to accept. But in mid-July I visited Eastbourne. I walked with John Nugee on the sea front and before dinner in his house he declared, 'What I look for in my staff, Nairne, are Christian gentlemen.' I could only hope that I would not disappoint. Nugee wanted me to teach virtually every subject to the lower forms: I thought that I might well disappoint them.

But I was not to be put to the test. Although the question of a job was always in my mind, my main concern during the first six months of 1947 was history Finals – the university examination for the shortened Honours course in modern history, to which the college had allowed me to switch from Classical Moderations on my return from the war. The diary for 11 June records with some exaggeration:

> This has been one of the HISTORIC days in the Nairne career!
> This morning I finished my last Schools [*Finals*] paper: 'The principles of modern English government 2' – not an easy paper; I felt

ill-ish in the middle of it and did not do as well as I should have liked. But the exam is now over. And that is that. Relax – for a time anyway.

. . . Giles Alington and David Cox hold a history schools dinner in the Senior Common Room; and very good it is – the best dinner I've eaten this year . . . Now I feel well-fed and well-drunk; the night is warm. To bed.

Some five weeks later, on 23 July, I wrote:

A GREAT DAY – Am desperately nervous before my 'viva' – and at ten o'clock I get a horrible 'doing' from the examiners – all about Ireland and the S.A. War, about which I know precious little. I do shockingly and feel like a small boy who is caught when he hasn't done his prep. I am distraught with nerves: must be a borderline case . . . After lunch John Hennings and I feel absurdly overcome with nerves. At 3 p.m. the history lists are posted in 'Schools': we are there at five past. I have a FIRST. *Laus Deo* – what else can be said? Catch 3:35 train home and feel tired out. Finish Flora Thompson's *Lark Rise*: charming.

The clouds of uncertainty were beginning to clear and the sun was coming out in my sky. At the end of July, having heard that I had passed my preliminary interview and that the Civil Service Selection Board lay ahead in September, I wrote on 30 July to decline the offer from Eastbourne (with, if anything, a feeling of relief rather than of grief).

All hope of employment in 1947 now rested with the Civil Service.

10

Oxford Interlude

Written in 1947–48

This is not another article on contemporary Oxford; I offer no neat analysis of post-war psychology at the university, explaining the causes of the Tory reaction or why so many bicycles are parked late outside the Radcliffe Camera. I have something more personal and, at the same time, more general to say.

Here is my reason why. I have just left Oxford for ever, one of hundreds. There would be nothing interesting in that but for one fact: most of us were ex-service men. We have spent nearly two years at the university – subsidised by grants from the Ministry of Education. So it had been an academic interlude largely at the expense of the taxpayer. Has it been worth his while – and ours?

The answer must of course depend on what someone extracts from Oxford. I have had five terms and my own paramount feeling during them has been one of disappointment. I had expected something different; for I had known Oxford before the army and, during the years of war, memories of it became idealised like childhood summers whose days were always cloudless. A room of one's own and a come-as-you-please existence epitomised the personal delights, which a military barrack-room and regular parade hours denied. Standing in a queue with mug and mess tin, one remembered picnic suppers on the river; marching twenty miles beneath the sun, one recalled lying with a book on a shady college lawn. So with time Oxford came to provide a flawless mental image of carefree calm, while army life, no less superficially, represented the exact opposite. But more than that, war was a racket: sometimes a mental and physical strain, often a stimulating scramble, of sudden moves, dangerous moments, constant discomfort and ceaseless responsibility. Oxford has proved to be a racket too.

Nonsense? Only for those who do not lead the full life which the university offers. In the 1760s Charles James Fox wrote from Oxford: 'I really think, to a man who reads a great deal, there cannot be a more agreeable place.'

He is right, if a person does nothing else but read. But Oxford permits few such an austere existence. Sport, drama, music, painting, politics – the whole gamut of cultural and social life – exist to stimulate, recreate, educate. Ignore them, and it is absurd to talk about the 'carefree calm' of university life. In short, an Oxford term is, as Bagehot described the office of prime minister in Peel's time, 'a distracting routine'. There must be some routine, or the week's reading will be skimped and the tutorial essays insufficient. Yet there must be room for distractions. Nobody interested in politics, for instance, should neglect a political club; those who have acted before want to act again; there are today more clubs of one cultural sort or another than ever, while sport and social life, most of all, consume the time of their addicts. The majority therefore divide their spare time as best they can between games, recreation, social and club life. What is the result? The days are as crowded as trams in Cairo and the nights are as late as trains in the Balkans. A term of eight weeks is a relentless process of trying to have one's cake of conscientious study and yet eat it with hours spent away from one's books.

This must have always been so. Only a fool perhaps would find disappointment in so lively an existence. But the circumstances of the ex-serviceman are exceptional. While he recognises the value of university activities, he must try and subordinate them to the necessity of doing well in 'Schools' in the shortest possible time. It is moreover in their attitude towards these activities that the difference is most apparent between an undergraduate from school and from the services. The former gains most in the university life apart from his academic work; it is there, more than in the examination schools, that the sixth-form boy becomes an educated man. But it cannot be the same for the latter. After several years of war service, he cannot attach the same importance to these activities and so can never enjoy Oxford as the end in itself which it is to the schoolboy. Let me be personal about this: I have enjoyed playing games, being an active member of two clubs, and missing as little as possible of what the theatre, music, art and social life of Oxford had to offer; but all the time, as psychological flies in the ointment, there have been both anxiety about imminent examinations and impatience to get started on a career.

But these disappointments were by the way and obviously some felt them more than others. I would offset them with two especial benefits which Oxford has to bestow on the ex-serviceman.

First, one has been able to acquire enlargement of mind. What do I mean by that? Surely years of responsibility must have given one this? I think not, because I am convinced that no amount of practical experience alone can produce it. It is the quality of which Newman wrote in *The Idea of a University*.

> That only is true enlargement of mind which is the power of viewing many things at once as one whole, of referring them severally to their true place in a universal system, of understanding their respective values and determining their mutual dependence.

This 'power of viewing many things at once as one whole', the very essence of good judgement, could not be acquired on war service. There was the urgent necessity of learning and attending to the job in hand; there was the impossibility for the majority of spending leisure in intellectual or academic pursuits; there were the limitations which 'the exigencies of the service' imposed on the liberal influence of travel abroad. But the constant study of the arts or sciences and continual association with contemporaries, whose experiences have been different, have not failed to destroy personal prejudices, broaden the intellect and widen the vision. A significant effect of this has been a more balanced view towards oneself. In wartime people always exaggerate their personal prospects for the future; all war aims must tend to be idealistic. The rapid development moreover of character and personality in the forcing-house of danger naturally bred both confidence and conceit. Besides, it was 'something' to have survived. Oxford has been wholesomely disillusioning. It was chastening for the successful junior officer to be back in the invigorating and competitive society of intellectual betters and equals. Mental readjustments had to be quickly made. It did one the world of good.

Secondly, the ex-serviceman has regained the capacity for academic and concentrated study. War days had involved energetic physical activity and rapid mental decisions. It had been a service convention for the officer on operations to resent paperwork, to despise what Wellington had called 'the futile drivelling of the mere quill-driving'. There had been countless days spent on the move or in hospital, whose one redeeming feature has been their small demand on mental concentration. And there had been numerous leaves of glorious indolence. In short most of those who had not spent the war at a staff desk had inevitably lost the faculty of concentrated bookwork. Oxford has recovered it for them. Intellectual curiosity has received a fresh stimulus; what is more, the discipline of applied study and pure thought has become a reality again.

There are perhaps too many people telling us in print 'what is needed in the country today'; but enlargement of mind and the power of concentrated study are surely among the foremost necessities. There cannot be too much of the former amidst racial hatreds and class warfare; and, without the latter, the critical problems of our national economy and administration cannot be solved. University life may therefore be as packed as the Cornmarket on Saturday afternoons, its joys may be dampened by a ceaseless drip of anxiety about the future; yet, if a man can crown his war experience with as much as he can acquire of these two faculties, he will indeed be well-armed for the future – and Oxford will have justified itself in him.

11

Novembers – *1947, 1949, 1953, 1956*

Written and edited in 1999–2000

NOVEMBER 1947: IN CORNBURY PARK AND TO THE CIVIL SERVICE

By November 1947, after many anxious months, my life was entirely different and remarkably better. In early September there had been two days at the Civil Service Selection Board at the Manor House, Stoke D'Abernon – within about two miles of the Cobham house which, six years later, was to become our family home – summed up in the well-tried diary phrase, 'It might have been worse.' On 24 September the Civil Service Final Interview Board, chaired by Sir Percival Waterfield, at Burlington Gardens, and recorded in the diary:

> My main impression was that the Board did not take much interest in me – either because they mean to fail me or have already decided to pass me. I cannot be sure – and am sick of this waiting.

I heard nothing from the Civil Service Commission until mid-October:

> Thursday, 16 October: BIG DAY. The post did not come until ten o'clock; by then all were in Winchester except me. Two bulky letters from the Civil Service: one – instructions, the other – announcing that

I was successful. Second with 266 (out of 300) marks in a list of seventy-four, of whom sixty-seven failed. I jump about the nursery with excitement. Relief with a capital R. It really is TREMENDOUS news, on which I could never dare count and for which I have waited very long.

But there followed another wait of over a month. On 25 November my father telephoned me in Oxford, where I had been staying for the weekend, to say that instructions had arrived for me to start at the Admiralty at the end of the same week. A characteristic Civil Service welcome. I had heard, to my surprise, that I was being appointed to the Admiralty (where else for a man who had served for five years in the army?) only through calling and enquiring personally at the Civil Service Commission. I did not know where I was going to live in London, so I had the sense to visit the Admiralty on 26 November and secure agreement that I should not start until Tuesday, 2 December.

But why had I been staying in Oxford when my father had telephoned me? For an even more important reason than my appointment to, and arrival at, the Admiralty to begin my Civil Service career of thirty-four years. I was visiting Penny Bridges, and on Sunday 23 November we became engaged to be married. As I write this, we have been together for fifty-two years with a golden wedding behind us – living within two miles of Cornbury Park in which I had proposed marriage.

It is impossible to say whether Penny Bridges – in her second year at Lady Margaret Hall and only recently met in the previous May – had been more in my mind than my concern for a respectable degree and a good job. She certainly featured prominently in my diary – in effect, another factor of uncertainty as I contemplated the future. Diary extracts tell the story – an account of an inexperienced and rather inept young man with no sisters to advise him, no elder brother to have shown the way, a father approaching his seventies, and a mother with whom nothing of an intimate character could be easily discussed.

Penny Bridges at Lady Margaret Hall, seated second from left.

Thursday 6 November, 1947 ... p.m. play third-rate golf with Bull.
My mind is not on the game. Indeed my mind is not on anything
but Penny. I am, frankly, frightened by the unsure step of proposing marriage. But that's what I want to do. So why let cowardice
prevent me?

The doubts are understandable. I knew that, subject to a two-
year period of probation, I had an appointment as a modestly paid
assistant principal in the Civil Service with a pensionable career
ahead. I had learned, in the most casual way, that I was to be
appointed to the Admiralty. But that had not yet been officially
confirmed and I did not know where the Admiralty might send
me, divided as it was between London and Bath. An earlier November entry had briefly described a walk with Penny in Blenheim Park,
'lovely with an azure sky and amber leaves'. Its words reflect the
old-fashioned outlook of the times half a century ago: 'Convention
(and instinct) tells me that, if I say "love", I must at once say
"marry": therefore I dare not say love . . .'

Sunday 16 November ... After M has gone to bed, I tell D that I may ask P to marry me next weekend. He is not discouraging, beyond saying that one can't marry quickly. Now, anyway, the ice is broken. How absurdly hard to talk to one's father about these things!

I imagine that my father must have passed on what I had said to my mother, but the diary does not record her mentioning the matter and I do not recall her doing so. No words of encouragement nor of the opposite before the next weekend. I stayed with the Bridges family. On the Sunday the weather was good and Penny and I decided to visit Charlbury, slightly known to me because I had once lunched with a distant cousin at Cornbury Park.

Sunday 23 November: What CAN I write? At three o'clock in the afternoon in Cornbury Park I asked Penny to marry me. She said 'Yes' ... I can only slowly appreciate how my life is enriched.

Penelope Chauncy Bridges, 1948.

No. 2, Hammersmith Terrace,
drawn from the river, Christmas
card, 1949.

... We catch 12:10 train to Charlbury – lunch very well at The Bell
Inn; climb the tower of the church; walk in the Park; hitch-hike home
– New College Chapel: lovely reading of Ecclesiastes 11 and 12 –
sherry chez Hanning – 'Town and Gown' supper – home – Colonel
and Mrs Bridges very kind and pleased.

NOVEMBER 1949: WORKING LIFE – HAMMERSMITH TERRACE

Another two years later – November 1949 – living in a flat at
No. 2, Hammersmith Terrace, with a small garden overlooking the
Thames; married, a father, and to the Admiralty every day. Far
from a life of leisure, but we were very happy, and Katharine, two
months old, was the loveliest and liveliest firstborn.

But characteristic extracts from the joint journal we kept in the early years of our marriage include these words of mine on Thursday, 24 November, 1949:

> Extremely harassed with work. I realise that the drafting of the final report of the Finance Committee is an ENORMOUS job – and, if Pughe (head of General Finance Branch 1) is to tinker as much as he likes with the wording, I must let him have the draft by Tuesday.

Words of Penny's on Saturday, 26 November, 1949:

> I suppose I must be feeling very tired today: at any rate I felt upset and harassed almost from the moment that Pat arrived home at 5.00, not 1.30, as pressing work kept him at the office all afternoon . . .

These entries foreshadowed serious problems of health ahead – problems that were to beset me until 1953 and the end, coincidentally, of another November.

NOVEMBER 1953: THE END OF THREE YEARS WITH TB – BENENDEN AND SOUTH LODGE

I did not care for General Finance Branch 1 and its fussy head, though the branch was what it was intended to be – good training for a young Admiralty civil servant. But in January 1950 I escaped to a new appointment: secretary to the Re-engagement Committee, chaired by Admiral Sir Geoffrey Hawkins, required by the Board of Admiralty to review all aspects of the conditions of service for ratings in the Royal Navy in the changed circumstances of the post-war years. It was a job which quickly taught me a great deal about the navy but I could not see it through to its successful conclusion. In the middle of March my chest and lungs were causing anxiety, and I was required to see a TB specialist. But, before the date of my appointment with the specialist, I was told that I had been given another, very different, appointment – the post of private secretary to James Callaghan, Parliamentary and financial secretary to the Admiralty (and the future prime minister of twenty-five years later).

It was a most promising assignment for a young civil servant.

On 26 May 1950, however, before the end of my first week in the Minister's office, my immediate prospects were destroyed. The Hammersmith Hospital clinic told me that one of my throat swabs was positive, and that I must submit to several months of bed rest as treatment for TB.

We arranged a bed for me in the living room, overlooking the small garden of 2 Hammersmith Terrace; then moved to Plover Hill towards the end of June 1950; established in the small front bedroom, with a fine view across Compton village in the valley below, to Winchester Cathedral in the distance; back to Hammersmith Terrace in late August, returning to Plover Hill in November; and to Penny's parents at Appleford for Christmas. I never had a cough nor felt particularly ill and in the Spring of 1951 my latest X-rays satisfied the Hammersmith clinic that I had recovered. Encouraged by a gift of £100 from my aunt, Dolly Cadell, we went to Italy – Lerici and Florence – for a fortnight. It was an enchanting holiday, though darkened at the end by news of the sudden

Castello di Lerici, sketched on a later visit in 1988.

death of Penny's father; but I felt fit again and ready for work as we returned to our daily life, with Katharine, at Hammersmith Terrace. On 17 April 1951 I was back at the Admiralty as a principal in the less demanding branch of Organisation and Methods.

But, as always in Whitehall, there were some exacting tasks – for me the role of secretary of an ad hoc body, the reorganisation of the Admiralty Committee, chaired by the secretary of the Admiralty himself, Sir John Lang. This was another valuable learning experience but it almost certainly aggravated what had become a life of increasing strain. Fiona had been born in December 1951, a third child was expected in June 1953, and we needed to resolve successfully the urgent problem of finding and financing a house outside London. It was not perhaps surprising – though a serious shock at the time – that in March 1953 a routine X-ray showed that the TB had returned. The Hammersmith clinic prescribed much more drastic clinical treatment – admission to a sanatorium, leading to another absence from the Admiralty of nearly a year.

In the first week of April 1953 Penny drove me to the Civil Service Sanatorium at Benenden in Kent. There I had to stay as a patient for seven months in what was, in effect, an open prison, wholly

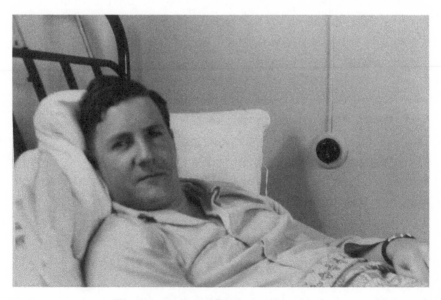

Treatment at Benenden Sanatorium, 1953.

dependent for my future on the word of the doctors. Meanwhile, Penny – seven months pregnant, with Kathy and Fiona and a live-in mother's help – moved from Hammersmith Terrace, went to stay at Plover Hill and handled, almost entirely on her own, the move in the early autumn to our new home of South Lodge in Surrey. It was a tremendous achievement, crowned in the middle by the birth of Sandy, in a Shawford nursing home, in the first week of June.

As winter approached, we welcomed another important November event: my release from the sanatorium on 10 November. Pen, with characteristic determination and cheerfulness, arrived early with the car; I was seen off in traditional Benenden fashion by the sanatorium band; we breakfasted at Goudhurst and reached South Lodge before the end of the morning.

Our journal recorded what my treatment had been – probably typical at that time for milder cases of TB: sixty-five days of strepto-mycin injections, 119 days of PAS medicine, forty-two days of some other drug of which I never grasped the name, and for the whole period one lung artificially collapsed. Benenden turned all its patients into hypochondriacs, ever checking their weight and worried by any sign of a cough. I was so anxious to reduce the risk of any return of TB infection that I pressed the doctors about the possibility of the major surgery which many fellow patients were required to undergo. I was eventually introduced to the senior consultant of the London Chest Hospital, Mr Holmes Sellors, an impressive man who was treated as a 'god from on high' by the Benenden clinical team: 'Look here, lad,' said The Great Man, 'I have been looking at your X-rays and, though there can be no guarantee, I don't think that you ought to be troubled again. There is really nothing to operate on.'

The Great Man proved to be right. His words foreshadowed the end of as uncertain a period of my life as my wartime service and my last year at Oxford. I wrote many letters from Benenden (and had many replies from Penny), but I wrote nothing in our journal about my time there until I had been two months back at South Lodge.

I could not criticise the clinical judgement of the medical staff; there was, in any case, no alternative to my accepting it. My rela-tively mild TB was almost certainly derived from serious lung trouble, a pleural effusion, at the end of the Sicily campaign. My lungs may also have been affected by the severe London smog of 1949. I was fortunate, however, to be among the first patients to receive the clinical treatment of streptomycin combined with an artificially collapsed (and thus rested) lung. I was a subscriber to the Civil Service Sanatorium Society, and it made practical as well as clinical sense to accept free treatment at Benenden; but I was an 'odd man out' among most of the patients, though I quickly came to admire those whom I soon knew well.

I described some of them in our journal in January 1954:

> My fellow patients. The friendliest lot you could imagine. On return
> from weekend leave – and the return from my first leave was especially

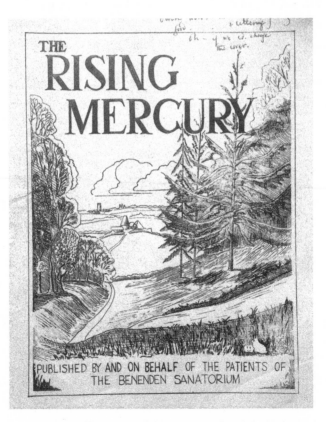

Cover of *The Rising Mercury*, Benenden magazine.

grim – the cheerful friendship of m'comrades was a real comfort. There was R. B., the only other 'gent' in the strictly social sense, recently married ... tall, good-looking, in some ways tiresome and spoilt, by no means an intellectual but quite 'a vulture for culture' ... then G. L., the famous 'oldest inhabitant'; he had been some five years in the place and was a marvel of determination and cheerful wit; H. K., who followed T. W. (a Labour councillor from Rochester) as chairman of the Social Circle, an ex-regular CSM in the Sappers and now in the telephone exchange in Reading, a man of impressive resignation and patience with a weakness for drink, a fund of good stories (telling without a sign of emotion, for example, how he tried to drown his wife at Malta), and a capacity for sitting quietly in bed sewing floral patterns for cameo brooches; O. W., clandestinely engaged to staff nurse, Penny Howell, a most capable young artist and dressed like one; ... F. B., a cocksparrow of a higher executive officer from the Air Ministry; ... J. W., a young postman from Penzance, reading nothing but the Bible and interested in little except the teaching of his Apostolic Church ... I could name a score of others ... It sounds pompous to say it, but the comradeship of Benenden was a shining feature of it. But I must be honest: I constantly missed what may be loosely called 'my own sort'.

NOVEMBER 1956: THE SUEZ AFFAIR

I returned to the Admiralty on 1 February 1954. For two busy years November kept a low profile. Then suddenly in 1956 it became for the country, and for myself, the most important month of that year. Some months after I had become head of the Middle Eastern and international law section of what was, rather quaintly, known as Military Branch of the Admiralty secretariat, I found myself, though relatively junior, in a front-line administrative post during the Suez Affair.

In July 1956 President Nasser of Egypt had suddenly declared that he was nationalising the Suez Canal – in effect, assuming political control of the normal, and fastest, waterway to India and the East. On the morning after the announcement I was one of those present at a crisis meeting in the room of the First Lord, Jim Thomas (Lord Cilcennin), while the First Sea Lord, Admiral Lord Mountbatten, wearing his small half-moon spectacles, outlined the current dispositions of the Fleet, indicating that an immediate and speedy assault to secure military control of the Canal might well be practicable. But such bold action was not a realistic option in the contemporary world of international diplomacy and the United Nations. The summer passed with secret British preparations for invasion – Operation Musketeer. In mid-August we got away for a family holiday in the Isle of Wight and from Bembridge we could see invasion support ships at anchor in the Solent. But, by the end of October, Nasser had still been challenged by nothing stronger than political speeches, UN resolutions, and visiting missions.

At least at my level in Whitehall we were left wondering what the next step would be. As emerged later, only the smallest inner ring of the Cabinet knew how the prime minister, Anthony Eden, was planning to act in secret complicity with the French and Israelis – with the objective of securing acceptable justification for British and French intervention to recover the Canal. My first intimation that Operation Musketeer might at last be launched was a meeting called at the shortest notice by the War Office and chaired by the permanent secretary, Sir Edward Playfair: its purpose, not fully explained at the time, was to formulate contingency plans for the urgent evacuation of the military and civilian staffs working in the British base in the Canal area of Egypt. Within a day or two, in the first week of November, the Israelis had launched a major attack towards the Suez Canal and an invasion force of ships was on the move from Malta and Cyprus. Armed with the little I knew about maritime international law, I was required one afternoon to walk across the Horse Guards Parade to the Foreign Office and seek the personal advice of Sir Gerald Fitzmaurice, chief adviser to the Government on international law. An unknown submarine, suspected to be Russian, was operating menacingly in the area of our invasion ships: would we be justified in sinking it? Sir Gerald thought not: we were not at war and we had not been attacked. The Government never formally declared war, but on 5 November Egypt's airfields were bombed, British and French parachutists were successfully dropped at Port Said, and our troops were landed.

Port Said surrendered within hours but all hell broke loose in the United Nations in condemnation of the British and French action. Subsequent biographies and historical accounts have told the full story, including the reaction of outrage on the part of those government ministers and Foreign Office officials who were never – and could never have been – told at the time of the Prime Minister's and Foreign Secretary's secret collusion plan with the French and Israelis. In the upshot Nasser was left in control of the Canal; Anthony Eden, by then a sick man, resigned; Harold Macmillan became prime minister and then sought with some success to restore Britain's position in the world and its economy at home. In late October 1959 he called and won a general election.

Penny and Patrick at a dance, late 1950s.

12

Admiralty Work in the Late 1950s – Diary Extracts

Friday, 1 March 1957

I am in HMS Tyne destroyer depot ship . . . Damned lucky to be here at all. The C.O., Captain 'Tich' Bennett, got on to Abercrombie in Naval Personnel and urged that somebody from the secretariat should come with Tyne on her NATO communications exercise, her visit to Oslo at the end of it, and, in particular, the informal visit to Rotterdam. Abercrombie tackled the secretary: why shouldn't Moore or Nairne of Military Branch go? They had had a good deal of extra work because of the Suez 'War'. Philip Moore was not keen, so Jim Mackay, head of Military Branch agreed that I should go . . .

After lunch. I've been reading another chapter of Bryant's book based on the Alanbrooke war diaries.* The diaries are most stimulating stuff, though Bryant is rather heavy-handed. Brooke emerges as hardheaded: tough shrewdness incarnate. It is good to be reminded of the deficiencies and self-deception of 1939–40. Are we going the same way again? Sandys [*Duncan Sandys MP*] has now been a month or so at the Ministry of Defence: the political thug who is going to stand no nonsense from the service departments, especially the Admiralty. The political objective is to put our economic affairs on sound footing; the chief remedy – to cut the

---

* The first volume of the wartime diaries of Alan Brooke, 1st Viscount Alanbrooke, edited and introduced by Sir Arthur Bryant, was published in 1957. The diaries contain notable critical commentaries on Winston Churchill as prime minister.

service votes, since you cannot cut the welfare votes. But strategic arguments have to be found to justify economies. You cannot get up in the House and explain that cuts have to be made, that these will create the most serious risks but that, nonetheless, the risks must be accepted. Of course, we are more or less taking risks all the time; but, now that they are bound to become greater, we shall still have to conceal them publicly. Shall we not thus have deficiencies and self-deception again? Is there any alternative? You cannot let Russia have the truth on a plate, quite apart from the electorate.

Sunday, 3 March 1957
No more than a steady swell on the North Sea and there is not much wind today. All round there is an impression of vast emptiness, and my life is pleasantly empty too. The Captain lives alone in his sea cabin on the bridge. When I make my way up there to get a blow of air (and to get a feeling of being associated in some degree with what's going on) he usually appears with some comment for the officer of the watch or a question for the navigating officer who is frequently hovering around. The rest of the officers appear in the wardroom or for meals, but otherwise are never seen. I suppose that they fuss a bit around their own parishes, but they don't give the impression of being busy.

Sunday, 10 March 1957
Half past six and we are in calmer waters under a frosty sky as we approach the fjord leading to Oslo. It has been a week, I suppose, of the kind of weather to be expected: grey skies, heavy swell and force six to eight winds with a good deal of pitching and rolling. Tyne stuck all this well; and, with the aid of a daily marine pill, so have I.

I've had a full programme for seeing all parts of the ship. Main features:

- the earnestness of number 1 (Lt Cdr John Keir) in demonstrating examples of out of date and uneconomical design;

- tea in the Chief Petty Officer's Mess (The ancient C.P.O. steward to the Captain getting at me about one law for officers and another for ratings; a cheerful debate about the future of the navy);
- sharing the early morning watch, from 4 a.m. to 7 a.m., with Lt Cdr Frank Oates, glad of all my borrowed cold-weather clothing;
- a chat with the national service man, who told me he intended to be a film director, with the chief cook, who obviously lacked praise and for whom nothing was right, with the stores C.P.O., who said he had no use for the sea: clambering up and down steep hatches with the supply officer in order to show an interest (as if anybody could!) in refrigerators and electric stores;
- going round with the senior engineer who insisted that he was not mechanically minded;
- listening to a long personal bleat from the senior medical officer;
- arguing about life in the service compared to life outside with the sergeant major of the Royal Marines detachment; a sharp discussion about government policy with the master-at-arms and his staff over tea and bread and jam;
- a long and interesting chat with the padre, who expressed the view that officers today were frightened of their men because they didn't see enough of them apart from duty and didn't know how to make proper contact with them;
- drinking 'bandmasters' of sherry for dinner.

Main impressions:

The navy is impatient at the out-of-date and uneconomical design of living spaces in ships. Gadgets – hoovers, polishers and the rest – help, but cannot save much cleaning time when every ceiling is a dust-collecting mass of ventilation trunking and electrical leads . . . The navy blame the present design defects on the naval constructors ('Who are not naval officers and don't live at sea') and don't always recognise that part of the blame should go to the enthusiastic naval officer in the Admiralty who introduces further technical refinements into ships.

The navy loves its 'caboosh' system – the small, tucked-away living space in store or office or wherever, in which one or two ratings can sleep separate from the bustle of the Mess-deck. Associated with this is the love of the small Mess and, with some people, of the broadside messing system. This outlook leads to a dilemma. Complaints about the lack of space for hammock-slinging and about the cold food on the Mess-decks point to the introduction of bunks and cafeteria-messing. But will not these go against the homeliness of the 'caboosh' system? . . . Most people accept that we should, as it were, do away with the slum-houses and put up new blocks of flats: but the new arrangements must, in large ships, try to soften the cold atmosphere of an institution.

The former long-service navy should be regarded as some-thing of the past. In general, only the C.P.O. and perhaps P.O. will regard re-engagement as worthwhile. The pension can probably never be more than a small subsidy; and at the age at which a man can get it he is poorly placed for any civilian pension scheme, and sometimes even for a job. For many men the sensible course is to leave after twelve years. In any event wives are almost certain to encourage their husbands to leave, whether after twelve or after seven years in the service. They naturally dislike the disturbance and they see their brothers, brothers-in-law and friends' husbands coming home every evening and doing spare-time jobs at the weekend and per-haps drawing more pay than their own husbands . . . The Admiralty should not waste unnecessary time and money trying to solve the insoluble.

*

Good morale depends on the navy feeling it has a purpose. The Tyne is a depot ship not a proper warship.* Showing the flag, especially with the commander-in-chief embarked, involves large parties on board for which some of the ships' company have to prepare. For many men life can boil down to a tedious business of cleaning up. They did not join the navy for that. The disturbance and discomfort of sea life will be accentuated by a feeling that their service at sea serves no useful naval purpose. It is therefore most important that all ships should work their men hard on jobs relating to the fighting task in war. Not always easy to arrange . . .

Many other things could be mentioned. The navigating officer thought his charts and equipment good, but most people, such as the electrical offices on the radio side, regarded their equipment as coming out of the Ark, compared with equipment they had seen on the USS Northampton.

Friday March 15 1957
The last pages are dated 10 March, but parts are written later. Now we are approaching the coast of Holland. I can hear a lighthouse fog-horning; and at 12:45 we shall fire our salutes on reaching the Hook of Holland.

Our visit to Oslo was fun. First impression is of a small, rather dishevelled city, and the four days' thaw leaving thick slush on the streets and the pavement soaking wet did not improve it. But gradually its charm has effect. The sun comes out and the snow gleams on the roofs and on the pale blue, fir-dotted hills in the distance. Groups of people in scarlet and blue ski clothes stand with their skis by the tram stops, on their way to skiing half an hour away. Everywhere there are children in bright trousers and tasselled woollen hats, and the feeling is conveyed that nobody is

---

* HMS *Tyne* was refitted and recommissioned as the Home Fleet flagship in mid-April 1958, serving also as depot ship for the Second Submarine Squadron. For HMS *Tyne*'s history, see: http://www.royalnavyresearcharchive.org.uk/BPF-EIF/Ships/TYNE.htm#.XBkiuvzgpbU; accessed 18/12/18.

very poor nor very sad nor very hard-worked. I saw some of the sights. The park alive with Vigeland's statuary of the human race; nude statues full of vigour and inventiveness; but too many of them, too close together: the mind cannot stand it.*

———

28th February 1958

I have been at home since last Friday. Finishing up my 1957 quota of leave and taking a rest after a strenuous six weeks at the Admiralty. Last July I moved from Political Section II of Military Branch to be head of the shore organisation section: from International law, Middle East, South America and Antarctica, Burma and Indonesia, and the rest of my countries, to dockyard planning, reduction of shore establishments, w/c stations, Malta and Singapore politics, the nuclear submarine, ranges, weapons and warfare policy.

It has been a very busy six to seven months. A year or so ago Duncan Sandys became Minister of Defence and his White Paper of April 1957 spelled out the determination of the present government to cut defence expenditure in order to stimulate and stabilise the overloaded economy. The navy's Vote A was to be cut by about 25 per cent; navy votes as a whole to be reduced. This policy led to the '80 plan': a navy of about 80,000 men. The plan envisaged many reductions ashore between now and 1962 including several dockyards. It was a superficial blueprint – the broad brush, as people like to say.

First Lord loosed it into Whitehall in mid-June, complaining loudly in a cover note of the effects on the security and influence of this country if it were put into effect. Months of gestation: that is, argument in the Defence Committee, ministerial letters, Admiralty memoranda.

———

* Frogner Park includes some 200 bronze and granite sculptures by Gustav Vigeland, installed by him as a project for the city of Oslo.

Finally, early this year what has been called the 80+ Navy emerged (a Vote A of about 88,000), and this is being worked out in greater detail now. It may stand as the basis of planning for two to three years. Meanwhile, so far as is possible in step with the discussions on the size and dispositions of the long-term Fleet, we examined the future of all the dockyards more thoroughly. This is a task which I very largely had to run. A ghastly memorandum had to be written in July. This was addressed to the Minister of Defence and others. It led to the setting up of an inter-departmental committee of officials under Nigel Birch, economic secretary to the Treasury, which sat, with [Sir Clifford] Jarrett and [Vice Admiral Sir Gordon] Hubback as members, during July. The urgency of deciding on the terms of integration for Malta highlighted the critical issue of the future of the Malta dockyard. The Cabinet considered this in November; and shortly afterwards the Defence Committee took the report of the Birch Committee. They did not settle the whole business – too many conflicting interests for that – but they did endorse our decision to close Portland and Sheerness Dockyards.

My chief task then became that of seeing through the announcement of this decision. How easy it appears! But it involved the population locally and scrutiny by the many Admiralty departments concerned about rundown and closure plans, and strict secrecy was a necessity and an anxiety. To Portland and Sheerness were added three other major decisions (for it is the oldest political rule to announce a number of nasty decisions at one and the same time): the abolition of the Nore Command and the closure of Chatham Barracks and other fleet establishments, the transfer of the Torpedo Experimental Establishment from Greenwich to Portland to complete the concentration there of the underwater R&D establishments, and the reorganisation and reduction of the Home Air Command, including the closure of Donibristle Aircraft Yard and five other air establishments.

Three main aspects to the business: the submission of plans for the approval of the Board; the clearance of the parliamentary and local announcements with commander-in-chief of the local naval authorities; getting the authority of the Cabinet and the agreement of all ministers directly concerned. Perhaps the hardest week was the one in which I had to prepare two Board memoranda: on Portland, where a substantial reorganisation is taking place under a rather critical board eye; and on Nore, Chatham and Sheerness, about which feelings were running hot in the Second Sea Lord's departments. But I had several very late nights at the office producing revised versions of the parliamentary announcement. On the evening of the day on which it was decided to change the presentation from a longish announcement and a statement circulated with the official report to a short announcement and the publication on the same afternoon of the First Lord's Explanatory Memorandum. I just caught the last train by seizing a taxi on the Embankment. If I had not had the assistance of overnight typing by the War Registry, time might have defeated us once or twice. Up to the last I was exposed to critical suggestions by the commander-in-chief of the Nore, questions and amendments from the Secretary of State for Scotland (Mackie) and eleventh hour fussing by Lord Selkirk (First Lord) or the Hon. Tam Galbraith (Civil Lord).* But it all turned out well on the day, or at least well enough.

On The Day – Tuesday, 18 February – a busy programme:

Going over possible questions in Parliament with the Civil Lord, on the basis of the 'Bible' of Notes to supplementaries and for dealing with press enquiries, which we coordinated and edited from all corners of the Admiralty;
    At lunchtime a last-minute note to commanders about the time of their press releases because the First Lord had meekly given in to the Chief Whip's insistence that his announcement in the Lords should be put back to 3:30 p.m. so that the time gap between both Houses should not be too great;
    3:30 p.m. in the House of Commons: Civil Lord sandwiched

---

* The Conservative peer the 10th Earl of Selkirk served as First Lord of the Admiralty from January 1957 to October 1959; Sir Thomas Galbraith, KBE, known as Tam was a Conservative MP who served as Civil Lord of the Admiralty in the same years.

between the Chancellor of the Exchequer (announcing increases in National Health contributions) and the Foreign Secretary (making a short statement on Cyprus). Me in the box with Philip Moore (principal private secretary) and other private secretaries; Civil Lord halfway through his statement by the time we got in, a loud buzz all round before he had got through; then MPs getting up all over the house; Tom Steele (whom I heard fixing his questions with Civil Lord in the morning by telephone) got called in his capacity as the Opposition naval spokesman and made a bungle, drooling on in a plaintive way while MPs of the constituencies affected tried to get their questions in. Galbraith, white and nervous in the crowded house, did not answer well; he said afterwards that the Prime Minister, sitting beside him, did not help by whispering 'Too many damn questions: don't answer them';

4:15 p.m. Press conference in Room 60, West Block: First Lord, First Sea Lord, and Secretary answering questions. Unimpressive. First Lord follows a clever, egotistic appeal from Mountbatten addressed, through the press, to the navy, with an emotional apologia for the painful decision on the Torpedo Experimental Establishment, Greenock. Dudley Pope of the *Evening News* tries to get First Lord to be lucid about the role of the aircraft carrier, shakes his head and gives up in despair, and then publishes article two days later: LET'S FACE IT, IT'S A FOURTH-CLASS NAVY;

5:15 p.m. TV cameras in Room 70, West Block. Interviews of First Sea Lord and First Lord together by ITV, BBC and Gaumont British News. Selkirk tired and muddled, Philip Moore masterful: 'Don't think that will quite do, First Lord, do you?' The Secretary and Chief of Naval Information and I stand by and watch. Amusing, but a little pathetic, except for film star Mountbatten;

Finally, at 6:30 p.m., First Lord meets all MPs affected in the Moses room of the Lords. This is a useful occasion. About fifty MPs arrived and Selkirk was good with them. No question bowled us out completely.

At 7:30 p.m. I raced by taxi to the Piccadilly Theatre to join Penny, the Cleverlys and their friends, the Vulliamys, in a theatre party, for Benn Levy's *The Rape of the Belt* (John Clements, Constance Cummings, and Kay Hammond who turned out to be away with flu). Amusing but not brilliant; I smiled but did not laugh.

This account of the dockyards business leaves the impression that I did it all. Of course I did not. I looked after the wider implications of dockyard policy and of closing Sheerness and Portland dockyards; I also held all the strings (as one man had to do) of the announcement and associated statements and messages . . .* As usual with the Admiralty, the task was one of initiating and coordinating action, of kicking the ball to the right people and keeping it smoothly in play. That's the job of the Secretariat Man.

Lord Selkirk with the navy in the Mediterranean, Pat on the right, June 1959.

---

* The dockyard at Sheerness at the mouth of the River Medway was founded in the 1660s and closed in 1960; a commercial port remains. The Royal Navy Dockyard was established at Portland Harbour in the mid-nineteenth century and closed in 1959, although the Naval Base remained. Both dockyards were historic locations in which the navy had been able to build or repair ships, but cuts in government expenditure necessitated their closure.

13

Novembers – *1959–1966: With the First Lord and the Secretary of State*

NOVEMBER 1959

The new government brought Lord Carrington to the Board of Admiralty as First Lord and, in yet another November, I found myself accepted by him as his principal private secretary – as I had been, since December 1958, to his predecessor, the Earl of Selkirk.

For me it was another important moment. The principal private secretary to the ministerial head of a government department holds a key appointment, involving the unqualified trust both of the minister and of the officials of the department. Peter Carrington had been High Commissioner in Australia, from which he had been about to return when offered by telegram the post of First Lord. From the moment I met him at Heathrow (as he mentions in his autobiography) I developed a good working relationship with him – a man only two or three years older than myself. We also became and have remained personal friends, partly because when, eleven years later, he became Secretary of State for Defence, I was in the departmental post of Deputy Undersecretary of State (policy and programmes) and so constantly engaged in Defence business with him.

Sixteen years were to pass before November became significant once again. They were exciting and exacting years. Our twin sons, James and Andrew, were born in February 1960; their prospective

Lord Carrington, First Lord of the Admiralty (extreme left), pictured at Portsmouth with Rear-Admiral Hamilton, Mr. Nairne and Admiral Unwin (right).

NOW YOU'RE ALL
WRONG, JACK!

ALL was ship-shape at Portsmouth as the Navy waited to greet the First Lord of the Admiralty, Lord Carrington, aboard the minesweeper HMS Sheraton.

Then as the Very Important Person was piped aboard, Admiral John Unwin, superintendent of the dockyard, stepped forward to greet him. . . .

So did the minesweeper captain, Lieutenant-Commander George King, who acted as guide on a tour of his ship.

The scene was photographed and filmed and then the VIP was piped ashore.

All seemed to have gone well—until pictures of the "First Lord" appeared in a local newspaper and on television.

Then, as red-faced offi- *The VIP—who wasn't*

Daily Mirror, January 1960, reporting an incident in which Patrick Nairne had apparently been received on board HMS *Sheraton* in Portsmouth Harbour, and given a tour, as if he was the First Lord of the Admiralty, Lord Carrington, who followed behind.

arrival identified by X-ray and communicated to me when Penny had arrived, rather late, for lunch in the House of Lords, which Peter and Iona Carrington had specially arranged in order to meet her. Margaret was born – at home in South Lodge – in May 1961.

Clockwise from top left: Sandy, Fiona, Kathy, Andrew, Margaret and James,
South Lodge, 1962.

1965: WITH THE SECRETARY OF STATE FOR DEFENCE

In January 1965, initially to my horror, I was again appointed
principal private secretary. The post was accorded more senior
rank in the now reorganised Ministry of Defence, and I was personally selected by Denis Healey, Secretary of State for Defence in
the new Labour government of 1964. Another rewarding partnership and lasting friendship were established.

1966: DEFENCE REVIEW TOUR – LETTER HOME

*Written on Qantas airletter paper – headed 'About to cross the
International Date Line, 29/30 January 1966'*

Darling Pen – How are you? We were 'grounded' at San Francisco
last night and lodged in the St Francis hotel & I miss you when I

South Lodge from the garden with Margaret Nairne, 1964.

am alone in a hotel room. It is now 2:40 p.m. Fiji time, but 6:30 p.m. (or thereabouts) San F. time. Five hours to go to Fiji, & it already feels as if it has been a long day. But not a bad one. We have just spent an hour refuelling at Honolulu: hot sun, light sun, light breeze, Japanese girls in bright dresses, small children . . . and watching them I thought of the chickenpoxers at home. I wonder how they are.

Things have gone fairly well so far . . . As we approached Washington, we ran into heavy snow & our pilot made a splendid landing in a blinding snowstorm. Next morning the sun shone on a brilliant snow, and Washington – a lovely city – looked its best.

I sat in on the talks all morning: a few feet away from Rusk, McNamara & co. When it came to lunchtime Healey found that he was invited to lunch alone with McNamara & his two senior ministers, Vance and McNaughton.* 'Hey, I think I'd better have somebody with me; I'll take Pat.' So I dropped out of my lunch with the whizz kids & found myself with the Great, at a small table in McN's Conference Room. Further talks in the p.m.; then the usual rush of Press Conference, business talk, telegrams, & dictation before dining . . .

I then had to correct the record of the morning's and afternoon meetings until 12:30–1 a.m. I get to bed, at the end of these long days, worn out, but then wake up very early (i.e. British time!). We all find the same. However, I feel pretty well so far – & we've got a nice party with us (tho' far too many, as I always said) . . .

Early this morning I had a telegram from Richard about the Defence White Paper, quoting advice from No. 10 about the length of our tour; & as of this minute, we've decided to arrive home on Sunday evening, 6 Feb . . . A nuisance to drop out of the Borneo trip; but I dare say I shall reconcile myself to it!

I am writing rather uncomfortably on my knee. Best love, darling. I don't think that this is much of a letter. And I don't know when it will reach you . . . All my love to you all – from Pat

---

* David Dean Rusk (1909–1994) was United States Secretary of State under presidents John F. Kennedy and Lyndon B. Johnson from 1961 to 1969; Robert McNamara (1916–2009), an American business executive, served as United States Secretary of Defense from 1961 to 1968; Cyrus Vance (1917–2002), lawyer, served as Secretary of the Army and Deputy Secretary of Defense; John McNaughton (1921–1967) was United States Assistant Secretary of Defense for International Security Affairs and a close advisor to McNamara.

With Denis Healey, Secretary of State for Defence, on Defence Review Tour, 1966.

Painting while on Defence Review Tour, 1966.

CIVIL AND PUBLIC SERVICE: 1967–1981

Introduction

If you simply ask civil servants on any given subject what they think about it, you are apt to waste everybody's time. They form little ad hoc committees and propose papers of the on-the-one-hand-but-on-the-other sort. If instead you say what you want done, they are likely to find a good way of doing it.

Lord Egremont, *Wyndham and Children First*, 1968

Commonplace book, entry no. 521

Various senior civil servants of my father's generation are thought to have been sources for the TV sitcom *Yes Minister* (written by Antony Jay and Jonathan Lynn, and broadcast initially on BBC2 from 1980 to 1984). Others may, like him, have received copies of the published scripts with appreciative dedications. My father knew that the series might be significant for public perceptions and referred to it as a brilliant satire, but thought, 'Like all satires it is streaked with truth but it is not a reliable guide to the partnership between ministers and Civil Servants which the complexity of government and international relations necessitates [*see Chapter 17*]. My father pursued long-term interests both in the improvement of the Civil Service and in how its crucial work could be better understood. And he contributed to a positive riposte titled, *No, Minister*, a sequence of BBC investigative radio programmes made by Hugo Young and Anne Sloman in 1981.

In 1951 his early interest in promoting better management skills in the Civil Service is evident in his review of T. A. Critchley's book *The Civil Service Today*. His own article, 'Management and the Administrative Class', published in *Public Administration* in the summer of 1964, asks if a 'Science of Management [*should be*] superseding the Art of Administration'. He discusses the relationship between inspired leadership and determined management, linked to public accountability, and the vital maintenance of public trust. These interests were reinforced in this period by contributions to professional conferences and talks given at the Royal College of Defence Studies and elsewhere.

On the occasion of his promotion to become Assistant Undersecretary of State (Logistics), after working together on the extensive Defence Review reductions, Denis Healey sent an appreciative letter to my father, in which he wrote: 'Management has always been uniquely a Nairne forte – here again you showed extraordinary ability to follow through a decision and programme the handling of a problem so that the solution was achieved on time. What little I have learnt about administration – a closed book to me in 1964 – I owe overwhelmingly to you.' (*See Appendix 1 for complete letter.*)

After a second period of working with Lord Carrington (Secretary of State for Defence from 1970), my father left Defence in 1973 for the very uncertain world of the Cabinet Office. He ran the Civil Contingencies Unit with the unexpected crisis of the Three-Day Week in early 1974. He also headed the European Unit as a new Labour government decided to renegotiate Britain's terms of membership of the European Community, and then put the result to the test in the first national referendum in 1975. Two decades later in 1996 as chairman of the independent Commission on the Conduct of Referendums he was to muse on the outcome, successful as it had been for the Government. Writing in 2019 amidst the uncertainty of Brexit, I can imagine what my father's sharp analytical response would have been to the outcome of the 2016 European referendum and its effects on political and public life.

Promotion in November 1975 to become permanent secretary at the huge Department of Health and Social Security was a genuine surprise. My father had always thought it more likely that he would be posted back to Defence. Some analogy was made in the Civil Service about relations (and conflicts) between professional and managerial leaders in the fields both of health and the services. At home we teased my father unhelpfully on his latent hypochondria and this making him the perfect person for the job. As with strategic defence and Civil Service reform, improving the management, resources and ethics of health care were matters to which he would bring a focused and critical mind.

SN

14

Resources for Defence, 1973

*Excerpt from a lecture given at the Royal College of
Defence Studies, 22 March 1973*

With defence resources, enough is never enough. When is national
security 'secured'? It is a matter of judgement; and the judgement
of today may not be right for tomorrow. What we have to do is
to judge: first, what share of national resources defence must be
allocated – *what* the defence slice of the national expenditure cake
(that well-known 'cake') should be; secondly, how it will be best
to allocate, plan and manage the resources given to defence – *how*
the defence budgetary slice should be cut up and consumed within
the defence programme.

All this involves choice for government ministers and for the
chiefs of staff – *choice*, one of the most painful of human activities.
[. . .]

The cake of the gross national product (GNP) of this country
has to be shared out between the competing claims of four broad
areas – capital expenditure, private consumption, public expenditure and exports. The Defence Budget has to be provided from
the third area – the total of public expenditure, which covers
central government (that is Whitehall), the local authorities
(throughout the country), and capital expenditure in the national-
ised industries. In this country – and this would be true of most
other countries – the scale of public expenditure has risen substan-
tially since the beginning of the century. In the second half of the

nineteenth century, public expenditure in Britain accounted for about 10 per cent of the GNP (and the average for defence was 2 per cent of GNP); it is now around 50 per cent. This is a measure of the extent to which government today has had to deploy the resources of the nation to meet the requirements of governing.

The gross national product amounts today to nearly £60 billion. Of this over £29 billion is devoted to public expenditure. What of this can be made available for defence? This question takes us to the problem of choice.

I suppose that one should start with the larger questions of political policy or philosophy. A nation has to decide – or its chosen government has to decide for it – what kind of life it wants to live; what its priorities are; and how its resources should be allocated. But every independent nation needs a defence policy because a first charge is to protect the security of its own people.

A simple enough statement – but it is only the starting point for a complex analysis of what threatens national security, leading to an assessment of the part which defence policy must take within external policies as a whole, and of the roles which the armed forces must play in order to carry out defence policies. That analysis and that assessment rapidly bring us to the question of defence resources – and to the major factors governing it: the economic prospects of the country; national manpower trends; and the technological resources and character of our industrial base.

It is no good having a defence policy which ruins the nation it is designed to protect – just as it is no good sacrificing security to economic prosperity. A balance has to be struck. Britain has had some experience of the problems in recent years: following devaluation in 1967, the coat of our external and defence policy had to be cut to meet the cloth available; and now that, with a Conservative government, the policy has been to let out the coat a bit, we are having to find the cloth we need for the purpose.

[. . .]

We are a country which is irrevocably committed to a substantial level of social services, which has a rising scale of higher education and which is expressing a growing concern about what

is known as 'the quality of life' or environmental measures. This trend was perhaps first marked by the words of Mr Denis Healey in the 1969 Defence Debate: 'Education for the first time in our history is getting more money than defence . . .' Under the present government almost all the major social and environmental programmes are planned to grow faster than defence; and this reflects a situation common throughout North America and Western Europe. Only a serious increase in the threat to our security would change this trend.

[. . .]

However, the real cost of defence expenditure has been, broadly speaking, doubling in succeeding generations. But the gross national product has grown at half that rate or less. So, if we assume (and I would not take a more optimistic assumption, since we have been taking a diminishing share over the last twenty years) a constant share of GNP for defence, then the scale and pace of re-equipment will progressively diminish. There is also a responsibility towards the industry that builds the ships and tanks and aircraft. A wide range of industries benefit from defence expenditure. Twenty-six industries devote more than 2.5 per cent of their output to meeting defence needs, four more than 10 per cent and two – shipbuilding and aircraft – more than a third. Defence employs of the order of 700,000 people, service and civilian, directly; but it provides employment to about the same number again in industry. This is of considerable importance when the level and pattern of unemployment is a major preoccupation of government.

[. . .]

Can we hope that the cake of national expenditure will get larger? Perhaps we can; but Britain will *certainly* need to improve her economic performance. Without that, the screw on defence will be bound to tighten. Even if it does improve, it may still be necessary to restrict public expenditure, including defence, as a condition of sustaining that improvement. The fact is that this country's economic performance has been bad – in absolute terms and in relation to other countries – for a number of years past.

There is, of course, no 'right' share of GNP to spend on defence but unless we can achieve a sustained GNP growth rate higher than 3 per cent, nothing less than a 5 to 5.5 per cent share is going to be adequate to carry out our present defence policy.

We shall have to make our case for that 5 to 5.5 per cent. Here are the main political elements:

NATO. Our fundamental security rests on the strength of the North Atlantic Alliance. We believe that, compared with our European allies, we are making a very adequate contribution to the Alliance . . . and have a higher rate of defence expenditure per head than any other European country except Germany . . . At the same time, we recognise that the Europeans must be ready, in the years ahead, to take a larger share of the defence burden; and we must continue to make an adequate contribution to this.

British Dependencies. We still retain specific defence obligations for the protection of British territories overseas – for example, Hong Kong and Gibraltar. We must continue to provide the resources to enable us to discharge those obligations in a sound military way . . .

Contributions to Stability. The Government is also concerned 'within the resources available' to bear a share of the responsibility for the preservation of stability in the world outside Europe . . .

British Polaris Force. Finally, there is the British Polaris Force – a valuable contribution to the Western strategic nuclear deterrent at under 2 per cent of the defence budget at present. But can we maintain its effectiveness without spending more?

These political/strategic factors are the primary and most important elements in the argument . . . So how do we translate them into long-term plans – for all three Services – *within* our resources? How do we translate our assessment of the quality and character of the Soviet threat into equipment programmes for the Services –

within our resources? How do we translate – again, *within* our resources – the threat to security in Western Europe and to stability outside Europe into peacetime deployment plans and into contingency plans for an emergency? And, if the main purpose of all our forces – not on our own, but within the framework of our alliances – is to *deter*, what are the yardsticks by which to settle what we must spend, and what we must forgo, in making our contribution to an effective deterrent?

With defence, enough is never enough. Our forces are stretched now by the tasks which they are required to perform – particularly by the requirements of Northern Ireland. There are defence tasks at present that we would like to do better or more fully. And our resource difficulties are going to grow in the future as equipment and manpower costs grow.

But there is no point in bellyaching. We must go on arguing the defence budget case as vigorously as we can. In addition, we must plan to make the best of the slice of the cake we get. In the next financial year this will total £3.365 billion. Its component parts are 47 per cent on manpower expenditure (USSR, 30 per cent); 37 per cent on equipment; and 16 per cent on the rest, the works programme, fuel, food, and so on. A most important point . . . is that over the last ten years the proportion taken up by manpower has *increased* and equipment *fallen* by about the same amount.

[. . .]

My concluding thoughts:

First, compared with the spending of the superpowers, Britain's share of world defence expenditure is very small (about 3 per cent); but in the light of our economic situation, and within our public expenditure programme as a whole, we are still giving a more than adequate share of resources to defence . . . It is worth bearing in mind that almost all of our European allies – without the burden of overseas expenditure, and in some cases with much stronger economies – devote a significantly lower proportion of their resources to defence; and also that our US allies devote a far lower proportion of their GNP to housing, social security and health. This is the old chestnut of 'burden sharing'. Is this an international problem we ought to try and solve? Or is it insoluble? President Nixon does not appear to be forgetting about it.

Secondly, should Western Europe give new thought to it? . . . There is the problem of *manpower*. Shall we be bidding for budgetary resources only to find that we have not got the men to fulfil our plans? There are the *technological* problems: can we hope to do better in planning and monitoring major equipment projects? Do we go too far in seeking the best technology can offer? There are *political/strategic* problems: how does one assess what is adequate in terms of quality and quantity – for example, in the size of the navy – when the object is to deter and never to fight?

Thirdly, I have concentrated on the policy aspects of resource planning; but should we be doing more to develop effective systems for managing our resources? Could we go further in adopting the efficiency criteria of industry? Should we give greater responsibility to our service managers and make them more accountable for their performance? What does the concept of 'productivity' mean, if anything, in Defence?

These are some of the main questions we all need to think about. It is not a matter of blaming the politicians. It is not a question of blaming the Treasury. It is the responsibility of all of us to understand the pressures on resources; to argue well the case for the Defence share; and to make really good use of the share we get. One side of the coin is to take the long-term view . . . The other side of the coin is to remember the wise saying: any damn fool, with time, can produce a beautiful long-term planning picture – what really requires character and skill is darting from one day-to-day crisis to the next as one tries to make plans work.

15

Novembers – *The 1970s*

Written and edited in 1999–2000

By the mid-1970s three further promotions had followed and I had completed two and a quarter years as second permanent secretary in the Cabinet Office and head of the new European Unit to which I had been appointed, instead of, as first suggested, to the Civil Service Department, since Peter Carrington had insisted that 'the Civil Service Department post would be too incestuous'.

I had a testing time in the Cabinet Office. The exacting task of coordinating the policy issues and objectives of all government departments engaged on European Economic Community business was seriously aggravated for me in the winter of 1973 by the coalminers' national strike – since, probably on the assumption that major emergencies at home were likely to be rare, the head of the European Unit was also required to chair the Civil Contingencies Unit. That unit found itself with the central responsibility for handling, under the Cabinet, the Whitehall discussions and Cabinet business in the unprecedented circumstances of the widespread industrial action which led to the introduction of a three-day week in early 1974, the calling by the prime minister, Edward Heath, of a general election in February of that year, and the fall, by the narrowest margin of votes, of the Tory government.

The Labour government, under Harold Wilson, quickly settled with the miners, but proceeded to create a new and entirely different dispute of its own by declaring to the European Economic

Community that it intended to renegotiate our terms of entry into the Community and, in the light of the outcome, 'to consult the British people' on whether the United Kingdom should remain a member. The hearts of officials, especially those of my Foreign Office colleagues, sank at the prospect. It fell to the European Unit, working closely with the Foreign and Commonwealth Office, to coordinate the renegotiation, which was effectively concluded at an EEC summit conference in Dublin in March 1975. The next and unprecedented step was to organise the first national referendum to which the Government had been committed since January. It was held on 5 June 1975 on the ballot question: 'Do you think that the UK should stay in the European Community (The Common Market)?' I shared in a moment of unqualified rejoicing and relief – unique, I think, in all my years in the Civil Service – when the overwhelming response, 67 per cent, by the electorate was 'Yes'.

DEAR VOTER

This pamphlet is being sent by the Government to every household in Britain. We hope that it will help you to decide how to cast your vote in the coming Referendum on the European Community (Common Market).

Please read it. Please discuss it with your family and your friends.

We have tried here to answer some of the important questions you may be asking, with natural anxiety, about the historic choice that now faces all of us.

We explain why the Government, after long, hard negotiations, are recommending to the British people that we should remain a member of the European Community.

We do not pretend, and have never pretended, that we got everything we wanted in those negotiations. But we did get big and significant improvements on the previous terms.

We confidently believe that these better terms can give Britain a New Deal in Europe. A Deal that will help us, help the Commonwealth, and help our partners in Europe.

That is why we are asking you to vote in favour of remaining in the Community.

I ask you again to read and discuss this pamphlet.

Above all, I urge all of you to use your vote.

For it is *your* vote that will now decide. The Government will accept *your* verdict.

Harold Wilson

YOUR RIGHT TO CHOOSE

The coming Referendum fulfils a pledge made to the British electorate in the general election of February 1974.

The Labour Party manifesto in the election made it clear that Labour rejected the terms under which Britain's entry into the Common Market had been negotiated, and promised that, if returned to power, they would set out to get better terms.

The British people were promised the right to decide through the ballot box whether or not we should stay in the Common Market on the new terms.

And that the Government would abide by the result.

That is why the Referendum is to be held. Everyone who has a vote for a Parliamentary election—that is, everyone on the Parliamentary election register which came into force in February 1975—will be entitled to vote.

First European Referendum, 1975, pamphlet delivered to all UK households.

But the excitement was over by the autumn. I did not know what my own next step was likely to be, but I assumed that I would probably return fairly soon to the Ministry of Defence. But Sir Douglas Allen, head of the Civil Service, asked to see me and, most unexpectedly, told me that he wished me to move to the Department of Health and Social Security as first permanent secretary. I was to take up the appointment – but, of course – in November.

NOVEMBER 1975: FINAL WHITEHALL YEARS

This was another formidable prospect. November 1975 – nearly twenty years after the Suez disaster – was also a notably difficult month for the country, and certainly for the DHSS and myself. My new appointment put me in the highest ranks of the Civil Service but I could not help feeling a marked sense of strain when I arrived in the DHSS at Alexander Fleming House, Elephant and Castle – where, from my seventh floor window, I could survey so many of the homes of the department's more deprived clientele. The Secretary of State for Health and Social Security was Barbara Castle. Her published diary and autobiography reported my arrival, as successor to Sir Philip Rogers, at a time of acute problems for the National Health Service: industrial action by both doctors and nurses; the British Medical Association's resistance to the abolition of private-pay beds in hospitals; the dispute about the hours of junior doctors; dissatisfaction over the recent reorganisation of the Health Service; and, not least, the threat of severe reductions in expenditure as a consequence of high inflation and the Government's economic difficulties. In the much-quoted remark of Anthony Crosland at the time, 'The party was over.'

I had negotiated for myself a gap of a fortnight between leaving the Cabinet Office and assuming full charge in the DHSS and I had filled it with a visit to the West Midlands where the university, the hospitals, the social services and the social security offices gave me some insight into the best and the worst of the DHSS's huge field of responsibility. It was the start of more than six and a half demanding years – under three secretaries of state, Barbara Castle, David Ennals and Patrick Jenkin, as the country moved from some turbulent times under a Labour government to the beginning of eighteen controversial years of Tory government under Margaret Thatcher and John Major.

16

Reflections on Retiring, 1981

New Window, *DHSS Staff Magazine, August 1981*

It is commonplace to give, as I have done, more than thirty years' service. But that is a long span – longer than the disclosure ban on official papers at the Public Records Office. Were the ways of Whitehall and the Civil Service very different when I joined the Admiralty in December 1947?

BUILDINGS CHANGE

There was a coal fire alight in the tall narrow room where I began as an assistant principal. The Principal, whose room it was, came downstairs from the resident clerk's quarters in his bedroom slippers between half past nine and quarter to ten. He occasionally had disturbed nights with naval signals and Foreign Office telegrams because the Admiralty was an operational HQ for the navy as well as a service department in Whitehall – occupying the building which houses the Civil Service Department today.

The buildings of Whitehall have certainly changed, reflecting the reorganisation of departments in the 1960s. As I have regularly sat in the head of the Civil Service's room above Horse Guards Parade, I have sometimes reflected that I was in the room which David Beatty occupied when, as the youngest rear admiral in the navy, he was naval secretary to Winston Churchill in 1912–13. The room has a connecting door with what was once the room of the First

Pat in his office at Alexander Fleming House, Elephant and Castle, as permanent
secretary, Department of Health and Social Security, 1977.

Lord of the Admiralty – in which I remember being present, as the
principal on the Middle East desk, while the First Sea Lord, Earl
Mountbatten of Burma, rapidly outlined the dispositions of the
Fleet on the morning after Nasser announced the nationalisation
of the Suez Canal in July 1956.

UNCHANGING TEMPO

One thing which has not changed during my time in the service
has been the pressures and the tempo. They were hectic for the
service departments during the summer and autumn of 1956, but

so they had been at other times – for example, only a few months after I joined the Admiralty when it looked as if I might have to postpone my wedding leave because of the Soviet blockade of Berlin in the summer of 1948. In that same year – according to Jennie Lee's book *My Life with Nye* – Nye Bevan was seriously worried by the tempo in the Ministry of Health and Housing and by the extent to which the tasks of the post-war housing programme and the launching of the National Health Service were over-straining the health of senior civil servants in the ministry.

There have been testing periods in plenty since then. The climax of a major policy initiative or of a round of negotiations, the timetable of a bill or some kind of sudden administrative crisis hitting the headlines, can strike the civil servant like a sharp attack of flu or sciatica – raising one's temperature, putting one out of action for all other business, and leaving one exhausted when things return to normal.

My own experience of the negotiation of a new defence agreement with Mr Mintoff in Malta in 1970–71 and of the renegotiation of the terms of the United Kingdom's entry into the European Community helped to prepare me for my arrival in the DHSS in the late autumn of 1975. Within a few days of taking over from Sir Philip Rogers I was caught up in negotiations with the British Medical Association during which I quickly learned that consultants discussing the future of DHSS pay beds could be as suspicious as the Prime Minister of Malta and that the junior doctors after a better deal could be as exacting as the French.

Over the last five years at the Elephant and Castle office, parliamentary and other official business have imposed severe and unremitting strains on ministers and officials at the 'top of the office'. As I have done my best to cope with the unceasing flow of memoranda, submissions and letters, I have often felt like a batsman who is always at the crease: some balls can be allowed to go past the wicket, but on many it is necessary to offer a shot, and on a few it is essential to use one's bat effectively and score some runs – chipping in with advice or some other action of one's own. It has been an experience which has made me sympathetic to the

words of a former permanent undersecretary of the Foreign Office
[*Sir Ivone Kirkpatrick*], who wrote:

> To a tired man, who has to plough through a pile of complex files at
> a sitting, the aspect of one untidy file is so repugnant as to inspire
> positive hatred of the perpetrator. Moreover he would not be human
> if his first impulse were not to question, if not to reject out of hand,
> the department's advice. It is a fact borne out by long experience that
> tidily presented advice often goes through without delay, whilst the
> same advice untidily presented leads to questions or misunderstandings
> which eventually involve the department and higher authorities in
> much avoidable work.*

The spirit underlying these words had a share in stimulating my
sponsorship of *Our Business* – 'a guide to the conduct of business
in DHSS Headquarters'.

A SHIFT IN BALANCE AND STYLE

The first chapter of *Our Business* begins with these words: 'The
tasks and organisation of the department change, as government
policies and changes in ministerial responsibilities require; but
there is a basic and relatively unchanging framework for the conduct of business.'

That is true of the 'framework' but not of the Civil Service's
approach to the business within it. During my time there has been
a significant shift in balance and style.

At the higher levels of the service there has been an important
change in the balance between advising on policy and managing
departments. In 1951 I had to review a book called *The Civil
Service Today*.† No section of the book was devoted to management; the word 'management' did not even appear in the index.

---

* Commenting on drafting standards in the Foreign Office, *c.*1949, in *The Inner
Circle: Memoirs*, Macmillan & Co., 1959.
† Review of T. A. Critchley, *The Civil Service Today*, with an introduction by Lord
Beveridge, Gollanz, *Public Administration*, 1951.

Thirty years ago governments were as closely concerned as they are today with the size of the Civil Service and 'the numbers game'; but O&M [*Organisation and Methods*] was still regarded as a radical new technique; management services had not been developed in their present form and the computer age lay many years ahead. The Civil Service has still quite a long way to go down the road of better management, but the scene is very different from what it was. Our computer complex at Newcastle bears witness to the scale of our investment in modern technology. The time devoted by the permanent secretary, as chairman of the Department Management Board, to staff numbers, administration costs, management services and techniques, and industrial relations reflects not only his own close concern with management business, but also the greater involvement of ministers in managerial responsibilities.

There have been changes in style too. Operational business in the Admiralty had to be handled fast as signals buzzed to and fro, but normal policy business was dealt with (for better or for worse) in a more formal and leisurely way than is the practice in at least the upper reaches of the Ministry of Defence or the DHSS. Views and advice were minuted on files known as dockets which, when policy proposals were complex, could often circulate between naval and civilian branches for many months before, eventually, the coordinating civilian branch made what was known as a Board submission. The submission would then move upwards – usually through several undersecretaries and the secretary of the Admiralty (or the single deputy secretary) until it reached two or sometimes three naval members of the Board and ultimately a junior minister or the First Lord of the Admiralty himself. It was a laborious process and its traditional character was marked by green ink for the First Sea Lord's initials and red ink for the First Lord's; but it did expose clearly the arguments at every level. And it also made possible the occasional moment of glory for the junior official, enshrined in the story of Lord Curzon, who, attracted by the advice of a young first secretary on a bulky file submitted to him, wrote: 'I prefer the advice of the man with a signature like an umbrella handle.'

ACCOUNTING TO PARLIAMENT

Much of my time in the DHSS has had to be devoted, very properly, to responding to critical reports by the comptroller and auditor general, and to preparing for my annual appearances before the Committee of Public Accounts. My Admiralty background taught me how Samuel Pepys had to account to Parliament. Witness his diary for 22 October 1667:

> 22 October. Slept but ill all the last part of the night, for fear of this day's success in Parliament: therefore up, and all of us all the morning close till almost two o'clock, collecting all we had to say and had done from the beginning touching the safety of the River Medway and Chatham. And having done this and put it into order we away, I not having time to eat my dinner . . . We come to the Parliament-door, and there, after a little waiting till the Committee was sat, we were, the House being very full, called in . . . I had a chair brought me to lean my books upon, and so did give them such an account, in a series of the whole business that had passed the Office touching the matter, and so answered all questions given me about it, that I did not perceive but they were fully satisfied with me and the business as to our Office. My discourse held till within an hour after candle-light, for I had candles brought in to read my papers by . . . At last the House dismissed us, and my cozen Pepys did come out and joy me in my acquitting myself so well, and so did several others; and my fellow-officers all very brisk to see themselves so well acquitted, which makes me a little proud. So, with our hearts very light, Sir W. Pen and I in his coach home, it being now near eight o'clock, and so to the office, and did a little business by the post, and so home, hungry, and eat a good supper; and so, with my mind well at ease, to bed . . .

PLUS ÇA CHANGE

I too have experienced Pepys' feeling of relief after a long and exacting hearing before the Public Accounts Committee.

My random reflections suggest – what I believe to be true – that, though buildings, technology, and methods and style of business have changed, many features of the Civil Service and pubic administration remain essentially the same – and, not least, the professional integrity and friendly character of the Civil Service. My deep appreciation of that is my message to my colleagues as I go.

FAREWELL WORDS

I came, as a stranger in a strange land, to Alexander Fleming House in the autumn of 1975, and I shall always be grateful for the support and kindness I have received. I have visited the Central Offices more than once, as many local offices as I could, and almost every branch of Headquarters. The impression I take away differs from the image of the service which the media tends to present. It is an impression of intelligent, conscientious, kindly and devoted men and women – getting on with the job of supporting ministers and serving the public under the pressures of turbulent times. The tasks ahead will be no less exacting; but I am confident that the department will cope with them as effectively as in the past.

17

An Unplanned Career

Talk given at the University of Essex Convocation,
10 September 1988

Your chairman conveyed her invitation with what seemed to me to be the generous suggestion that I could choose any subject. But you may have memories of the teacher at school who, somewhat at a loss, instructed the class to write an essay on any subject it chose – and one then spent a worried half an hour flitting mentally from one alternative subject to another. I also recall the schoolmaster in Evelyn Waugh's *Decline and Fall* who, even more at a loss and desperate to keep order in the class, offered a prize of ten shillings for the longest essay on any subject irrespective of any merit.

After brooding uneasily, I decided to consider a theme that might at least interest me – the theme of myself – what I have called 'reflections on an unplanned career'.

I wonder how many people feel they plan their lives? At least any philosophers reading this will understand the qualifications attached to free will. There is an ancient saying: 'Man proposes, God disposes . . .' And that is sometimes irritably illustrated today by the remark that: 'Man is born free, but everywhere he is in traffic jams . . .'

For my part, I have made a few choices in my life – of my wife (or did she choose me?), the place of my home (but circumstances narrowed the options), curtains and carpets for the living room (the most difficult choice of the lot), and so on; most of them have

Chancellor of the University of Essex, 1983–1997.

been shared choices and I feel that, for most of my life, I have responded to the choice or decision of others.

Since other people's childhood memories are usually as boring as other people's dreams, I do not intend to describe my boyhood years in Hampshire during which my father, who had taken early retirement from the army in the defence cuts of the late 1920s, sought without success to find a job until, during the 1939–45 war, he was employed to teach painting and drawing at Winchester College. I was what used to be called a scholarship boy, which gave me the mixed experience of boarding school, teaching me, among other things, that reading can be the opium of the unhappy child, and that an addiction to reading is the most rewarding of life's addictions.

I was from the outset a conformist, a *collaborateur* – paying the price for being able to live my own life with the minimum of interference. As it seems looking back, the years may have been slowly moulding me into a prospective member of the Establishment. I can – for better or (you may think) for worse – illustrate that. In March 1935 I sat nervously on a school settee alongside another small boy of thirteen. We had never met before and we were candidates for the scholarships on offer. We both won awards and so spent five years together moving upwards in the school. We both left school and virtually never met until, later, we sat side by side again. This time we were on a settee in Muscat; my former school fellow [*Donald Hawley*] was now Ambassador to Oman and I, a deputy secretary in the Ministry of Defence. We were sitting on the settee because we were both in support of Lord Carrington, then Secretary of State for Defence, during his official talks in 1973 with Sultan Qaboos, ruler of Oman.

Escaping from school as soon as I could, I was allowed to take up an Oxford place at the age of eighteen for the summer term of 1940. But I did not stay long. There is nothing more effective than a world war in putting a stop to personal career planning. I can remember seeing the survivors of Dunkirk, black in the face from the sun, with nothing to do but stroll up and down the streets of Oxford. I can visualise the sunny day on which I saw the Fall of France announced on the newspaper placards. Academic study was not for me – the college agreed to my leaving the university and joining the army.

I share the view of historians that the last world war could have been prevented but I can understand why the generation of my parents failed to take effective steps to do so. The League of

Nations at Geneva could not have prevented it as the League had even greater limitations than the United Nations Organisation in New York has today. The principal nations of Europe, with the political backing of the United States, could have prevented it if they had based their attempts to achieve collective security not simply on physical superiority in defence (and they were slow to re-arm), but (much more important) on a clear collective political will to act together against Germany. And that was lacking.

My concern for my children and grandchildren is that they should not lose sight of that lesson. It is the essential basis for the collective solidarity of the North Atlantic Treaty Organisation which for more than thirty years has effectively demonstrated the political will to resist aggression against Western Europe on the part of the Soviet Union. But I do not wish to be misunderstood. The collective political will of military allies depends on more than public words and public treaties. The horror and the fear of nuclear weapons – and there must continue to be a worldwide understanding of the horror and the fear – have proved to be the ultimate deterrents because they give the backing of military force to NATO's political will – a will which would be seriously weakened if it could depend only on conventional forces inferior in quantity and, in part, quality to Soviet forces. The Soviet ice is still hard and thick on the defence front.

I worked closely with Denis Healey when he was Defence Secretary and I was impressed by what he used to call the Healey Theorem. It explains why defence forces and expenditure cannot easily be reduced, and goes like this: to the Soviet Politburo there may need to be only about a 5 per cent risk that an all-out attack on Western Europe would lead to a full military response by NATO forces; on the other hand, the countries of NATO, if they are to retain confidence in deterrence, need at least a 95 per cent reassurance that their forces would respond effectively to any form of attack from the Soviet Union.

No sophisticated considerations of defence policy were in my mind when, after a period in the ranks, I was commissioned in a Highland Regiment, the Seaforth Highlanders, at the age of nineteen. That was 1941 and I find it difficult to believe now that I spent four and a half years as an infantry officer in this country, North Africa, Sicily and North-West Europe. I had my share of bad moments, and I was fortunate to survive, but I escaped the terrors of those in London and other cities who were exposed to the German Blitz, and I had none of the anxieties of my friends who were married with young children at home.

In short, I was expendable. There may be nobody here this afternoon who shares my experience of war and military service. It has left me very critical of those today who appear to think that conventional war could be tolerable in a way that nuclear war is certainly not. It also gave me a perspective, or perhaps a philosophy, of some value, derived from harder times. If you are deprived of bread for many months, as we were in the Western Desert, and required to take a turn of watch at night when short of sleep over many months, you value bread and sleep a great deal more for the rest of your life. If you see your friends killed and are forced to recognise that it may be your turn next within a matter of hours or days, you find it impossible to believe that a man's life can be perfectly planned.

I was the only officer in the battalion who hoped to return to university and it was therefore assumed that I knew how to hold a pen. In the desert and Sicily I was battalion intelligence officer; in North-West Europe I was its adjutant. In early December 1945, I was dealing with the battalion's mail just east of Cuxhaven in Germany when I came across a succinct War Office letter conveying the glad news that temporary Captain P. D. Nairne was to be released under the Class B scheme so that he could return to Oxford University. So in January 1946 I was back in Oxford, feeling very old at the age of twenty-four and entirely uncertain about what my future should be. I had had, I came to realise, more personal responsibilities for other men's lives than I was to have again at any time in my life. At the same time, I had acquired no qualifications to offer other than experience and, after five years away from academic work, I doubted whether I could get the good degree I wanted.

As I was to learn on return to Oxford over thirty years later, every university generation is a vintage of its own; and I think that the post-war generation to which I belonged was what the wine merchants call 'a slightly heavy, dry wine'. There was some disenchantment. The post-war years were austere – with rationing, damaged buildings and one of the coldest winters ever. It was a feature of that vintage that there was a competitive wish to enter the public service. That may have been a reflection of the experience of the unemployment years of the 1930s or it may have been a feeling that those who had survived the war should give something back in return. Be that as it may I joined the ranks of those who applied for what was then called the Administrative Class of the Civil Service. I nearly failed to get in. There was then, as now, a qualifying exam and, not surprisingly after my war years, I did poorly in it; but I scraped through to the selection board stage and, helped by achieving a better degree than I had expected, I was offered a place; and it must have been my years as an infantry officer that led the Civil Service Commission to appoint me to the Admiralty.

My formal education was at an end – which meant, to my relief (a relief you may all understand) that I would not have to sit again with pen and paper in an examination hall. I was left with an ambivalent feeling about education which many may share. It would be untrue and churlish to say that I gained little from a total of six terms at Oxford. And brooding on how little I can remember of my early Latin and Greek I have sometimes quoted on degree days here at the University of Essex that 'education is what is left when we have forgotten everything that we have learned'.

On the other hand, I am a committed academic elitist, firmly convinced that the intellectually enquiring mind of man must be both free and disciplined – free in the pursuit of knowledge without constraints from government, and disciplined by the high standards of academic integrity that good research requires. As to fields of research, I was impressed last year by a remark from that great contemporary engineer, Sir Monty Finniston, chancellor of another university, who said that universities must continue to push back the frontiers of science, but that, while we usually found a solution to many of the problems of science and technology, we seemed to be incapable of solving the problems of living in our own society. That was a task to which the universities and their research students should devote themselves. The University of Essex is playing a valuable part in that direction.

As we know, universities have the aim of producing not a book or a computer product but a man or a woman with intellectual and moral values. I have learned, during my recent years as chairman of the Oxford University Careers Service, that it does not matter a great deal what most people study at university. Few Essex graduates can count today on the kind of vocational training in addition to a degree which an Essex student secured in the past.

I spent the first seventeen years of my Civil Service life working with the navy in the Admiralty – then, as now, no place for a disenchanted sceptic, as Mr Clive Ponting found a year or two ago.* I was thirty-four years altogether in Whitehall – twenty-five in the defence field; just over two years in the Cabinet Office; and six years at the Department of Health and Social Security. If there are any civil servants here today they belong to a different generation from myself and they may not nod approval when I say that I commend a career in the public service. I commend it not because it offers secure, reasonably paid, and pensionable employment; it is now less secure, less well-paid than most jobs in the private sector, and its index-linked pensions have been constantly under challenge. I commend it because it offers, at least to those in the administrative group, week in and week out, the stimulus and enjoyment of difficult and different administrative and management tasks in a changing political environment.

The political climate has been changing further, somewhat disagreeably, since I left the service. How do I see the Whitehall scene?

---

* Clive Ponting was a civil servant accused of leaking sensitive documents in 1984 relating to the sinking of the ARA *General Belgrano* in the Falklands conflict: https://en.wikipedia.org/wiki/Clive_Ponting; accessed 03/04/17.

I think that there is a serious risk today of devaluing the Civil Service. I can understand the reason why. At the junior levels of the service – for example, in the 500 social security offices for which I had some responsibility at the DHSS – there are many staff who find it difficult to understand, and so administer, the statutory policies and regulations that they are required to apply – and today, understandably, many of the public are thoroughly dissatisfied with the benefits which government policies offer.

There is also a widespread tendency to look more critically than in the past at the upper reaches of the service. The politicians sometimes view senior civil servants as the servants of a big country house. They welcome ministers of a newly elected government as the new tenants of the house and, while acknowledging that it is their role to serve the new tenants as they wish, they do everything possible in practice to ensure that the house continues to run very much as they, the Civil Service, wish it to run . . . In my own experience, the higher levels of the British Civil Service offer something which is virtually unique in the world – a non-political continuity of effective administration service in partnership with the ministers of whatever political party is elected to power.

At different times in my career, I myself was private secretary to Lord Carrington and to Mr Denis Healey; later on I worked with them both at a much more senior level. They have both become personal friends, and neither has ever cared, nor asked, what my own political views are. *Yes Minister* is a brilliant satire. Like all satires it is streaked with truth but it is not a reliable guide to the partnership between ministers and Civil Servants which the complexity of government and international relations necessitates.

But what I have said is not intended to imply that I take a complacent view about the efficiency of government. On the contrary, I believe that we should be constantly searching for new ways of running the country that may prove more efficient and also more acceptable to all of us.

The impact of information technology and our role in the European Community beyond 1992 are two obvious factors with a potentially large impact on the operation of government. But there are wider factors than that. Those who are most critical of White-hall tend to underrate the parliamentary factor. We pay a fairly high price in government efficiency (or inefficiency) for the valu-able commodity of a vigorous parliamentary democracy; and it may be essential for Parliament to change its ways – as the tele-vising of Parliament may gradually bring about.

As a member of the Franks Committee examining events leading up to the Falklands invasion, I learned how exceptionally difficult it is to define and apply sound criteria by which to judge the oper-ation of government [see Chapter 20: Franks and the Falklands, 1982]. The House of Commons, not surprisingly, came down on the Government like a ton of bricks when the Falklands were invaded. But the House of Commons came down like a ton of bricks on Mr Ridley when he attempted, a few years earlier, to present a solution to the Falkland Islands problem.* My experience in Hong Kong left me with unqualified admiration for what that extraordinary city – the freest, but least democratic, city in the Commonwealth – had achieved with its urban and financial devel-opments while coping with the constant influx of immigrants from Communist China. But I also realised that it was the absence of parliamentary democracy, and the associated adversarial relations in the House of Commons, which had enabled Hong Kong to apply a coherent and consistent economic strategy such as the UK had failed to pursue [see Chapter 22: A Monitor in Hong Kong, 1984].

I had a ringside seat for a sudden change of government, with a radical change in policies, in 1974 – during my anxious, though fascinating, short period in the Cabinet Office. That experience underlined for me the importance of a partnership of trust between officials and ministers. The Labour Party unexpectedly won the election of February 1974 at the time of the miners' strike. It had committed itself to renegotiating the terms of entry into the

---

* Nicholas Ridley, later Lord Ridley, was appointed in 1979 as Minister of State at the Foreign and Commonwealth Office in Margaret Thatcher's government and had been responsible for the Falkland Islands.

European Community and then consulting the wishes of the British people on the result. When it came into office, it was far from clear about the implications of either objective. The task of renegotiation was tortuous; FCO officials in particular were fully committed to membership; the Prime Minister and Foreign Secretary had to trust them when they pointed out the renegotiation problems. What helped most at the time was the realisation, particularly by James Callaghan, that, by the grace of its enlargement and historical evolution, the European Community was becoming the kind of community of which this island member of the Commonwealth could eventually be an effective member. Not that anyone can know what kind of Community it will eventually become. It seems unlikely to be the kind of Community that Jean Monnet originally envisaged when the membership was only six countries. We need to look for further evolution over a period of at least a hundred years.

A partnership of mutual confidence was also essential when it emerged, in autumn 1974, that the Prime Minister and the Cabinet had no clear idea of what they meant by the commitment to consult the wishes of the British people about the outcome of the renegotiation. It turned out that that commitment had to mean the first referendum in Britain, but that raised for us a range of difficult questions about the organisation and operation of a referendum which had to be considered separately, and for the first time in British history, by the Labour Cabinet of the day. I still do not know how the Government would have acted if the result of the referendum in the summer of 1975 had been exceedingly close – one way or the other. The Cabinet had not committed itself beyond the idea that a majority would do. But could the country have lived with a majority of, say, only a few hundred votes in favour of staying within the Community? Or, even more difficult, in favour of coming out of the Community? We shall never know.

I remember the evening before the result was known. The Cabinet Secretary (later Lord Hunt) and I were due to have a discussion with the Prime Minister and Jim Callaghan, the Foreign Secretary, about the contingency planning we had done on the assumption that the referendum would take the United Kingdom out of the European Community. We found that our political masters had no interest in what we had to say. They were clearly convinced that the vote would be in the opposite direction. James Callaghan said that he had met an old woman in his own constituency of southeast Cardiff who had said to him: 'I don't like this European Community, Mr Callaghan, but I have voted for my grandchildren and I think that they would wish to be part of it.'

Lastly, I should say something about my six unexpected and difficult years at the Department of Health and Social Security.

Whatever political view you take, one has to give credit to the present government for an inflation rate which is reasonably steady at about 4 per cent. It is an extraordinary memory that some twelve years ago, in the mid-1970s, inflation was over 25 per cent. In the autumn in which I joined the DHSS it had become clear to a reluctant Labour government that inflation must be gripped, and that that meant severe cuts in public expenditure. As the late Mr Anthony Crosland put it, 'the party is over . . .' My responsibilities as first permanent secretary related to the running of the DHSS (around 100,000 strong in those days) as a whole, and to being the principal adviser to the Secretary of State on policy relating to the National Health Service and the personal social services. We lived under a perpetual drizzle of external criticism, not least from the NHS itself.

So what do I take away from that experience? First, a hope. It is that the Government, with its instinctive wish to make a radical change in every institution, will avoid making radical changes in either the organisation or financing of the National Health Service. The National Health Service is open to improvement in many directions and from the contacts I continue to have with many of those working within it I am confident that many improvements can be made within a working environment where demand will always be infinite and resources will always be finite.

Secondly, I take away a recognition that the relationship between central government and local authorities, whether local elected authorities or local health authorities, will continue to be a source of difficulty and change. The present Conservative government came to power in 1979 committed to a policy of standing back and avoiding interference at the local level. But it has turned itself into one of the most interventionist of governments we have ever had. It is a paradox that a government that wishes to bring about change within the short period before the next election is compelled to take the lead itself if action is to follow with reasonable speed.

I have not touched on freedom of information, a campaign to which I am an adviser, nor on the intelligence world, where I have a close interest in the final judgement from the Law Lords on the *Spycatcher* case.* Nor have I trodden directly on political ground, and it would probably have been wrong of me to do so. But I cannot resist adding that I deplore the disenchantment about politics that I have found, for the most part, among the students whom I have come to know in Oxford. This disenchantment seems to reflect, in part, a distrust of politics and the political scene (political is a 'dirty' word), but primarily a failure on the part of our political leaders to create a convincing and appealing picture of how they wish to help the multiracial people of this overcrowded island to develop a happy and prosperous social environment for themselves and their children. To mention one aspect: it was [*William*] Beveridge himself, not the present government, that emphasised the obligation to work – but forty years ago there were no jobs. What is the obligation of the Government when for so many there can be no jobs?

Disenchantment is not, however, the word I would use to describe my impression of the generation of students I have come to know well as head of an Oxford college. I have been struck by the talented and hard-working character of virtually every member of my own college student body. If the problems of the end of the 1960s related to turbulence among students, the problems at the

---

* *Spycatcher: The Candid Autobiography of a Senior Intelligence Officer* (1987) claims to reveal spying techniques by ex-MI5 officer and Assistant Director, Peter Wright, with co-author Paul Greengrass. Although the British government attempted to prevent publication, it was first published in Australia and then in the United Kingdom following a final judgement in the House of Lords in 1988.

end of the 1980s relate to turbulence affecting the future of the universities themselves.

I have talked on the themes of my own career but I have tried to avoid saying too much about myself. For my part, I do not think that I could have achieved anything or have survived some of the strains I have experienced if I had not had a personal Christian faith to support me. And I am deeply convinced of the importance of fundamental Christian values to our society.

Portrait by Andrew Festing for the University of Essex.

I believe that society in Britain needs more than that. It needs a confident conviction that it can resolve, or at least mitigate, the difficulties and problems that are with us today. It is characteristic of the generation of my lifetime to talk in terms of 'problems'. Perhaps younger generations can drop that word? My experience of my American friends is that they do not always talk of 'problems' in the way that we do. One of the valuable features of all good universities is that they offer many opportunities to develop self-confidence and talents in a positive way.

Finally, they offer something else of true value, which is often of greater importance than academic results, and greater personal significance than the issues about which I have spoken – the opportunity which a university gives to develop friendships that may last a lifetime. My last words are my favourite quotation from an unfashionable poet of sixty to seventy years ago, Hilaire Belloc, [from 'Dedicatory Ode', 1923]:

> From quiet homes and first beginning,
> Out to the undiscovered ends,
> There's nothing worth the wear of winning,
> But laughter and the love of friends.

18

A Christian in the Public Service

An edited version of a talk given on 21 October 1982

It is not a routine expression of modesty that makes me start by writing that during my time in the public service I could have been described as the Unknown Christian.* I have never opened my mouth to bear witness for Christ in Whitehall. I have rarely known whether my Civil Service colleagues were practising Christians or not. The Civil Service allows a man a large measure of private life and there has always been a clear dividing line between my public duties in Whitehall and my personal life in a Surrey parish.

My own Christian faith has, over many years, become increasingly important to me – and I will return to that. But in reflecting on my position as a Christian in the public service, I have been driven to ask the question: 'Why was Christianity, why was my own Christian faith, *not* more relevant to my life and responsibilities in the public service?'

That begs, I think, a more fundamental question. Why *should* the Christian faith have any direct relevance to the functions and tasks of government, the Public Service, and the public sector as a whole?

---

* This talk came about, as my father put it, because of 'the irresistible force of Dr Wallace Haine's power of persuasion'. Pat said, 'How honoured I feel to be first in the queue to address such a distinguished audience (including some old friends) in accordance with naval practice by which the most junior and least important member of the service boards the boat first.'

Oxshott church, Surrey, Christmas card, 1967.

Nobody suggested it to me that it *had* when I became a civil servant. As religious toleration gradually became religious indifference in this country, nobody cared what faith a government servant had or what church, if any, he attended. When I joined the army, I had to make a routine declaration: I declared that I was C of E, and I wore an identity disc round my neck to prove it on death in battle. When I entered the Civil Service the only formality required was a signed declaration under the Official Secrets Act; and during my time the only faith that signified in government was Marxist, Trotskyite, or Militant Tendency.

Our Christian heritage as a country and the existence of an established Anglican Church, have not appeared to me to have any noticeable impact on the conduct of government in Westminster or Whitehall. For my part, I have often argued that some proposal

Pat's Second World War dog-tags.

might not be negotiable or could not be afforded or would not work, but I never argued that what was proposed would be against my Christian principles or morality. The question of whether we needed to consult the Treasury on something that the department wished to do was almost always a relevant question; I have never heard it suggested that we needed to consult God.

We often fussed about the extent of backbench support when our Minister came to introduce a bill in the House of Commons but we never stopped to ask whether we were likely to have Christ with us. I know that I am saying nothing new in quoting the words of Canon Henry Scott Holland of the Christian Socialist Movement around the beginning of the [*previous*] century. He said that Christianity:

> ... has been allowed to lose its grip on the real facts, so that the big affairs of the world go on their way as if it were not there. In the world of diplomacy, of international relationships, it does not count.

In trade and industry it has hardly any place. Over the dominating motives and aims by which our enormous wealth is created it has little or no control. In many departments of business it is openly denied. It exercises no authority over the wealth, after it has been made. It established no overruling conscience, no paramount sense of responsibility ... So men do *not* see that we, churchmen, contribute an ideal element to solid affairs ... Politics are not changed by our taking part in them. We take our colour from them, not they from us.

So where does this string of negatives by a strong Christian leave us? I doubt if the early Church regarded Christian faith as relevant to politics and business. The first Christians did not think in political terms, regarding all life as, in effect, a waiting for the Kingdom of God – a state in which the practical or political considerations of this life were of little account beside the hope of salvation which all Christians shared. Is it a fact today, going far beyond my personal experience, that a civil servant's Christian faith *is* no more than a private matter – relevant to parish and family life, but *not* to public life?

I find it difficult to let it go at that when I consider in particular the major public issues of poverty, unemployment, nuclear weapons, and the Third World and reflect on the moral questions that they pose. Governments are concerned with many matters that deeply concern Christians. Is it naïve to attribute to Christian doctrines or commitment such action as governments have taken to mitigate, if not resolve, these problems in the world? It is not part of my theme to discuss politics but I should make this point. It goes without saying that the Christian motivation of a politician can count: professed Christians such as (in the past) Wilberforce, Gladstone or Lord Halifax have been influential as Christians as well as politicians. But I believe that what they achieved in government has depended on their political skill, not on their Christian faith.

For the public servant, required to serve politicians in power, what is good in government is to be welcomed; and, if Christian motives lie behind it, the Christian public servant will rejoice. But for him a more pertinent question is whether the pragmatic pressures of government place his Christian conscience under unacceptable strain.

Whitehall in my time has not been Berlin in the 1930s or South Africa today. Governments under which I served have been denounced loudly enough for their policies and some of those policies have had little appeal to the civil servants who have helped to formulate and implement them. But that is not to say that civil servants – required to serve loyally successive governments of a different political colour – have also been required to be agents of evil measures offending Christian morality or formally condemned by the Church. I can speak only for myself; and I must – with humility – confess that my conscience survived intact.

I am well aware of the disagreeable aspects of immigration policies but I have never had to apply offensive racial measures. I

Pastel portrait of
Pat by Melissa
Dring PS, 1983

understood the moral and emotional conflict to which the Suez Crisis of 1956 subjected some of my colleagues but I did not personally feel as they did. I have spent a lifetime in a department responsible for the nuclear defence of this country and I respect but cannot support the CND [*Campaign for Nuclear Disarmament*] movement. More recently I cannot say that I have been troubled as permanent secretary of a department committed to supervising abortion laws.

I would be ready to sympathise with the Christian critic who chose to condemn what I have said as bureaucratic blinkers. But I would think him or her wrong to be condemning.

First, I would say to them that it is an imperfect world – a world in which the individual Christian should sustain Christian values as they see them but also a world in which the Christian public servant must play their part in government by dealing with problems as they are. If that means compromise, I welcome compromise if that spells good in the hand rather than perfection in the bush.

Secondly, while I felt it right to join the army and fight in the last war, I share a hatred and dread of war as a means of resolving international issues. Equally, while the thought of using nuclear weapons appals me, I am convinced, as an overriding political judgement, that the nuclear weapons of the West have so far helped to deter major war against the free nations of the West.

But, thirdly, we have to recognise that different Christians take different views on political matters. Some Christians are pacifists and some civil servants cannot be happy to work in Defence. I know one public servant who is so opposed to nuclear weapons that he has left the public service. He has my respect.

I have not been concerned with a choice between Christian and non-Christian policies – even less with service under Christian or non-Christian governments. My Christian faith is a personal matter for me. If I should find myself handling business or discussing problems with fellow Christians I should like that. It may lead sometimes to the easier resolution of difficult government problems but not necessarily so. I do *not* think that Christian faith in itself can offer a key to the problems confronting government in a largely non-Christian society and non-Christian world.

But that conviction does not weaken my view of the importance of Christianity to me as an individual. Some Christian consciences will be more tender than others in handling the business of daily life. But no Christian should leave his conscience in the church pew at home. Christians have no right to claim some kind of monopoly for decency, honesty and fair dealing but there *can* be circumstances in which a Christian may be able to do better, or perhaps behave better, than a non-Christian. What I believe, in short, is that a Christian can and must bring his own Christian faith and spirit into his daily life in the public service – as a support for moral values and a source of inner strength.

I had a conventional Christian upbringing: a grandfather who was a parson; a father who did not care for the Church and a mother who sang in the church choir; compulsory chapel at school; an ingrained habit of regular Communion. And I recognised that many people whom I respected were stronger Christians than I.

The War shook the faith of the schoolboy. The experience of sudden and apparently random death made it impossible to believe that there was a planned or ordained destiny for each of us in this world. I came to accept the wise saying of the Reverend Sydney Smith: 'Whether we live or die is a great deal less important than most people think.'

But rather more important, if I was uncertain about the hand of God in my life, I was also quite certain that there were strict limits to my own capacity for shaping my destiny. When I returned to Oxford after the war, my Christian belief stimulated a more conscious effort to put myself in the hands of God. I had begun to recognise the Christian faith as an infection rather than an argument and that Christ is a source of strength on which each of us can draw . . . I have had to do many things that I was not sure whether I could do. I have consistently found that my prayers for strength and guidance have received an answer.

In short, feeble Christian that I am, I have been conscious of the perpetual gift of grace. It has not been what I, as a Christian, have been able to give to the public service: it has, on the contrary, been what Christ has been able to give me to sustain me in the public service. I would hope that that had perhaps rubbed off in several ways – for example, in a readiness to recognise the individual worth of one's colleagues, at whatever level in the organisation; in a consciousness of my own relative unimportance by the Christian's scale of values; and in a sense of perspective that always helped me to remember that there are more important things in life than government.

I have tried to say that, for me personally, what has mattered most has been the strength I have received from a faith in Christ, as a source of spiritual support which has helped sustain me over many exacting days and during many busy days.

I have often felt that many Christian public servants should echo the well-known prayer of Charles I's major general (Sir Jacob Astley) before the Battle of Edgehill: 'O Lord, thou knowest how busy I must be this day. If I forget Thee, do not Thou forget me.'

ST CATHERINE'S, THE FALKLANDS AND HONG KONG: 1981–1988

Introduction

What other blessings of life are there save these two, fearless rest and hopeful work? Such rest and such work, I earnestly wish for myself and for you and for all men: to have space and freedom to gain such rest and such work is the end of politics: to learn how best to gain it is the end of education: to learn its inmost meaning is the end of religion.

William Morris, 1877
Commonplace book, entry no. 379

After overseeing the vast edifice of the DHSS, the switch to the intricacies of Oxford college life in a Master's Lodgings was a considerable shift for my parents. My father admired St Catherine's as a modern college (built between 1964 and 1966 to designs by the Danish architect Arne Jacobsen), and with the great figure of Alan Bullock as the founding and preceding Master, this was a delightful challenge. A move of the family house to Chilson, just outside Charlbury, was also effected. And the Evenlode valley emerged as a perfect subject for the attentive eye of a watercolour painter. Here family gatherings were expanding with the appearance of an increasing number of grandchildren (twelve over fifteen years).

In a short piece written in 1985 for the *Oxford Magazine*, my father probably holds back when calling for change: 'The institutions of Oxford are not inept, and the university is certainly not incapable of change. But major criticisms from within the university remain as valid as they were in the 1960s; and the "big business" which colleges have become would gain from management arrangements adapted to match them.' Much has changed but much, perhaps, remains the same.

A post-Civil Service life was likely to involve much continued public service and while devoting time to leading and fundraising for St Catherine's, my father took on a wide range of responsibilities, including trusteeship, of the Joseph Rowntree Memorial Trust and the National Maritime Museum, a non-executive directorship of the West Midlands Board of Central TV and the Chancellorship of the University of Essex. Two major appointments about which he wrote later were to the Franks Committee (technically The Falkland Islands Review Committee) in 1982 and as a government monitor in Hong Kong in 1984.

Letters to *The Times* offered an occasional outlet for his views in this period – subjects ranging from the Civil Service, the Policy Unit, Health Service reforms, Hong Kong, to the Official Secrets Act. When my father aligned himself as an adviser to the Campaign for Freedom of Information (specifically the repeal of Section 2 of the Official Secrets Act), some were surprised. One newspaper commentator wrote, 'When Sir Patrick Nairne, who is a distinguished ex-permanent secretary and the head of an Oxford college to boot, recommended a Freedom of Information Act on TV, I heard one senior civil servant talking about him as if he had started wearing a grass skirt and seeing UFOs.'*

In 1987 he was appointed chairman of the Institute of Medical Ethics Working Party on HIV/AIDS and also became a founding trustee of the National Aids Trust. He made an increasing commitment to exhibit his watercolours (including at the Clarges and Oliver Swann galleries), and he became chairman and then vice president of the Society for Italic Handwriting.

---

* Katharine Whitehorn, 'Whitehall's New Wave', *Observer*, 16 March 1986, p. 19.

Continued contact with students in this period made him worry about what he saw as a growing disaffection with the political world. While he admired the creative energy of many students, he was concerned about whether politicians offered a sufficiently imaginative vision for the future of the country.

SN

19

Novembers – *1981: St Catherine's College, Oxford*

Written in 1999–2000

NOVEMBER 1981

In July 1981 I retired from the Civil Service after thirty-four years in Whitehall. At the start of the year I had been – another most surprising turn of events – elected Master of St Catherine's College, Oxford. The normal course would have been to take up the appointment at the start of the new academic year of 1981–82 but we had settled for a late holiday in October, arranging to rent an apartment owned by friends near Uzès, west of Avignon. The college agreed to install me, as its statutes required, at the Stated General Meeting on the first Friday in October, and to allow me to postpone my arrival until after we had returned. Thus occurred another significant November occasion – the beginning of a complete change of life for Penny and me, as I became head of an Oxford college.

We had been fortunate in selling South Lodge: now we had to pack up all we had, put most of our furniture into store, order and direct removal vans, clean and sweep the old Victorian house from top to bottom, and then drive separately – in our VW van and Ford Fiesta car – to Oxford. We arrived at the college, worn out, in the early hours of a dark November day. As strangers in an alien land, we felt somewhat isolated in the lodgings. The college buildings were only a few yards away but unknown territory

Pat with Lord
Alan Bullock, his
predecessor and
Founding Master
of St Catherine's
College, Oxford,
1982.

for us both. I could simply walk in and establish myself with my
secretary in the Master's office near the college lodge but Penny
was left uncertain about where to turn for the practical help which
she needed in the lodgings. It had, in fact, been left until after my
arrival to settle the day on which I should effectively become
Master. The Acting Master, Derek Davies, the senior law fellow,
and I quickly decided that it might as well be straight away and
on that first evening we attended a college concert in the hall. I
recollect a most delightful performance of Weber's bassoon concerto and that one of the fellows announced that Penny and I were
present. A glass of wine followed while we chatted to the students

standing around us: the natives were encouragingly friendly. It was the earliest of days, but, as we walked back to the lodgings, I felt that we had been presented with a good heritage.

Sketch of St Catherine's College, 1986.

The Fellowship of St Catherine's (with Tiddles the family cat), 1987.

20

Franks and the Falklands, 1982

Written in 2001

A head round the classroom door over sixty years ago.

'Nairne, you're wanted.'

Such words rarely foreshadowed good news. Today it would be a telephone call or a carefully crafted letter – no more initially perhaps than an invitation to lunch or the suggestion of a talk, accompanied by a hint of the subject or business which lay behind the approach. The tone would be entirely different from that of the classroom summons, but the unspoken message would be the same: trouble ahead or the proposed imposition of some new commitment and an unforeseen intrusion into one's life.

Nobody can be free from intrusions. After retiring from Whitehall in 1981, I was exposed to many sudden and unforeseen requests (not orders or instructions, but more pressing than invitations) to undertake commitments, some of them substantial, unrelated to St Catherine's while I was Master, or unconnected with other commitments after I had left the college. It was, I suppose, to be expected. Retirement for many people can mean a shift from an orderly and exacting, though efficiently supported, job in a more or less single field of responsibility to a range of different, some equally exacting, commitments handled by oneself in the spirit of 'do it yourself home maintenance'. There is, however, one important difference: in retirement one can say 'No'.

I did not wish to say 'No' to the first unexpected intrusion into my life after Whitehall. It occurred on 30 June 1982 when I was lunching at the Garrick Club as the guest of Lord Vaizey (I cannot recall why). I had just been handed a gin and tonic at the bar when a member of the club staff came up to my host and then passed a slip of paper to me. A telephone message from the office of Sir Robert Armstrong, Secretary of the Cabinet: 'Could you manage to look in to see Sir Robert before returning to Oxford?'*

I rather doubt whether I guessed what he wanted, though I recall surprise at the note of urgency. As I later sat in his office, well known to me from my Cabinet Office years, I was taken aback by his question. Would I be willing to be a member of the small committee which the Government was establishing to review – and Robert broadly indicated what became the committee's terms of reference – the way in which the relevant responsibilities of successive governments had been discharged in the years leading up to the Argentine invasion of the Falkland Islands on 2 April? It was to be a committee of privy counsellors because of the sensitive security factors relating to the decisions of successive prime ministers and governments of different political parties. Lord Franks had agreed to be chairman and four former Cabinet ministers had been invited to make up the membership of the small committee. If I agreed to serve, I would have to be admitted to the Privy Council.

It would have been difficult to refuse such an invitation – and I was excited to be asked. After discussion with Penny and consultation with key members of the college governing body, I wrote a letter of acceptance. I was, however, concerned about the likely disruption of our holiday in Pembrokeshire arranged for early July, and also about the potential impact on my college responsibilities in the months ahead. But, as it turned out, Lord Franks had just had a cataract operation and required three weeks in which to recover, and, as I was courteously informed by letter, I was not to

---

* Robert Armstrong, now Lord Armstrong, was Cabinet Secretary from 1979 to 1987, through Margaret Thatcher's period as prime minister, and head of the Home Civil Service from 1981.

be admitted to the Privy Council at Buckingham Palace until 30 July 1982.

I am puzzled that I can remember so little about what was, in its small way, a unique and historic event in the annals of the Nairne family. My Oxford engagement diary for 1981–82 shows no more than a small, scribbled entry, 'Privy Council . . . Vacation guest night'. I must have found the occasion a strain, but memory suggests that it all went smoothly. In his published diaries, Richard Crossman described his own experience of what takes place:

> October, 1964: Undoubtedly the most fantastic episode . . . was the kissing of hands and the rehearsal . . . I don't suppose anything more dull, pretentious, or plain silly has ever been invented. There we were, sixteen grown men. For an hour we were taught how to stand up, how to kneel on one knee on a cushion, how to raise the right hand with the Bible in it, how to advance three paces towards the Queen, how to take the hand and kiss it, how to move back ten paces without falling over the stools – which had been carefully arranged so that you did fall over them. Oh dear! . . . we drove to the Palace and there stood about until we entered a great drawing room . . . We were uneasy, she was uneasy. Then at the end informality broke out and she said, 'You all moved backwards very nicely', and we all laughed. And then she pressed a bell and we left her. We were Privy Councillors [*sic*]; we had kissed hands.*

Barbara Castle, in her autobiography, *Fighting All The Way*, added a tailpiece about the same occasion, on which she had also been admitted to the Privy Council, referring contemptuously to 'the clumsiness of public schoolboy Crossman of Winchester, who almost fell off his stool'.

After two Ministers of State had 'kissed hands' before me, I was called forward by the Lord President of the Council, The Right Honourable John Biffen MP, and I did not trip up or fall off the

---

* Richard Crossman, *The Diaries of a Cabinet Minister: Volume 1: Minister of Housing 1964–66*, Hamish Hamilton and Jonathan Cape, 1975, p. 29

stool. I do not remember the Queen saying anything personal to me (though she had met me at three investitures and two private audiences when I was permanent secretary of the DHSS), but she was relaxed and friendly towards everyone present. The ritualistic royal approval of bills and orders in Council, rapidly read out, was given by the Queen. She then exchanged a few words with John Biffen and departed. So then did we all, I now holding the small copy of the New Testament, inscribed and dated by the Lord President, which is traditionally given to new Privy Counsellors, and formally entitled 'The Rt Hon.' to which my brother James's meticulously written envelopes bear witness.

That, as people say, was it. Since then I have been required to play a modest part in two appeals in the academic field of London University, of which the Queen Mother was then Visitor (and so delegated any appeals to the Privy Council); and in 1998 I attended the grand Privy Council Dinner in the House of Lords for the Queen and The Duke of Edinburgh in celebration of their Golden Wedding.

Oliver Franks was the doyen of independent chairmen of major investigations, as his *Who's Who* entry showed. Argentina's successful invasion had brought severe criticism of the Government, and the recapture of the Falkland Islands with some heavy casualties could not diminish that. Only a man of Lord Franks's stature – in the chair of a small committee composed of those with relevant experience in government – could be expected to command the confidence of Parliament and the country. But he was seventy-seven years old and I suspected that it had needed the personal interest of the Prime Minister and a visit by the Cabinet Secretary to persuade him.

Back to what was quickly referred to as the Franks Committee. Formally named the Falkland Islands Review Committee, it met for the first time on 26 July 1982, in a small room on the first floor of the Civil Service Department situated in the old Admiralty building. This was to be our base until Christmas. Sitting round the table, with Franks in the chair, were Lord Barber, then chairman of the Standard Chartered Bank and a former Tory Chancellor of the Exchequer; Viscount Watkinson, formerly a Tory Minister of

Final meeting of the Falklands Committee: from left, Lord Lever, Sir Patrick
Nairne, Lord Merlyn-Rees, Tony Rawsthorne (Secretary to the Committee),
Lord Franks, Viscount Watkinson and Lord Barber, 29 December 1982.

Defence; Lord Lever, formerly a Labour Treasury Minister and
Chancellor of the Duchy of Lancaster; Merlyn Rees (a life peer),
formerly a Labour Home Secretary and a Minister of State for
Defence; and myself. My own qualifications? A former second per-
manent secretary in the Cabinet Office and previously Deputy
Undersecretary of State (Policy and Programmes) in the Ministry of
Defence, prior to my six years as permanent secretary of the Depart-
ment of Health and Social Security.

The head of our secretariat of four staff was Anthony Rawsthorne, a civil servant seconded from the Home Office.

Lord Franks was a firm chairman who did not allow committee
members to stray off the point. We got to know each other over
lunch, provided in a private room next to the Civil Service Department restaurant. Franks presided. When the committee met for the
whole day, most members, sometimes all, attended; and there was
frequently general conversation in which Harold Lever often took
the lead by telling us entertaining stories from his political life.

Neither Barber nor Watkinson knew me – the former friendly, quick, and breezy in manner, the latter a man of few words, conveying the impression that he was a reluctant member, strongly supportive of the Government, and impatient to get the task quickly and satisfactorily finished. Harold Lever remembered me from my Cabinet Office years: warm, humorous, generous in spirit. He had once given me lunch at his London home where I admired his Impressionist paintings and also, since he went out of his way to show it to me, a photograph of his young and beautiful wife. I had come to know Merlyn Rees in the 1960s when he was Minister of State for the RAF and I was private secretary to Denis Healey. He and I became close to each other on the committee, developing a friendship which has been kept alive by occasional meetings until the late 1990s.

A modest amount of wine was provided at lunch. I was uncertain how the Chairman would respond to this. He was a Quaker and brought up, I understood, as an abstainer. But there was also a story that when, as a young fellow of Queen's at Oxford, he and his wife had moved into college accommodation, they had found a half-full bottle of sherry in a cupboard and, on the countervailing principle of 'waste not, want not', finished the bottle – and never looked back. The committee was reassured when he led the way with a glass, sometimes two glasses, of the wine on the table. But he was certainly a modest drinker. He remarked one day that, when he was the British Ambassador in Washington, he had learned to protect himself at interminable diplomatic receptions by saying quietly to his host that he had a slight heart condition and would prefer a soft drink. The fact was that Oliver had mellowed in old age if the accounts of the younger Franks were true. While the committee was meeting, I happened to meet a former fellow of Queen's who enquired after Oliver and added that he remembered him as provost of the college thirty-five years earlier: 'He was not at all an easy man to get to know and when at last the ice was broken, one found that the water was distinctly cold.'

He was kindness itself to me, consulting me frequently as the committee's work proceeded. He and his wife usually stayed in the

Stafford Hotel during the week, at least in the early days, but quite often we travelled back to Oxford together and I cycled once or twice to Charlbury Road to discuss matters with him at home and quickly joined the army of his admirers around him. I was, I felt, to be a temporary close colleague rather than a new friend. I was surprised by one feature of his chairmanship: contrary to the practice of most chairmen of important committees, he never drafted a first draft of the report himself. I mentioned this at the time to Bill (Sir Edgar) Williams, Warden of Rhodes House, whom I would meet occasionally in Oxford.

'Oliver is lazy,' he replied. 'He purveys wisdom but does not feel a need to write it. Look at his entry in *Who's Who* – no mention of anything published.'

The charge of laziness is very much open to question but I soon learned why it had been so important for Franks to have been right in his choice of secretary – as indeed he was: Tony Rawsthorne proved to be a skilful drafter. When drafts were tabled, however, they stimulated lengthy discussions and some disagreement. As expected of the Civil Service member, I volunteered some revisions to the succession of drafts and was specifically asked to try my hand at others. Other members occasionally did the same. Franks's role was to appraise and adjudicate, to say firmly when he judged that the right words had been found, in a quiet and authoritative voice, which discouraged any further argument.

His principal strength, however, lay in the two directions which had established his outstanding reputation as a chairman. These were his masterly grasp of the inquiry – identifying the essential facts and arguments, and enabling all members of a committee to share a continuous, collective and coherent view of where the inquiry was leading; and his magisterial technique in questioning witnesses – courteous, precise, penetrating – and summing up what they had said – either to confirm their evidence, or occasionally to encourage them to think again, and more carefully, to state what it was that they had really wanted to say. These capabilities made him uniquely suitable for handling the Falklands inquiry.

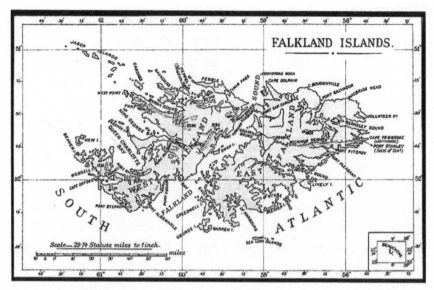

Map of the Falkland Islands, from 'The Colonial Office List', 1898.

Argentina was then a country with some 80,000 British passport holders, an Anglican Church, and a long history of friendly diplomatic and trade relations with the United Kingdom. The sudden invasion of the Falkland Islands on Friday 2 April 1982 was a dramatic and humiliating shock which had produced a widespread reaction of emotional anger in the country. The popular press had been in full cry. A remote British territory with a small and loyal British population had been captured. Our NATO-based defence strategy towards the USSR appeared to have blinded us to a threat of which, it was claimed, the Government had been warned.

As prime minister, Margaret Thatcher was confronted with a political challenge on which her personal future crucially depended. I listened in the Master's Lodgings at St Catherine's to the passionate House of Commons debate on the morning of Saturday, 3 April – the only Saturday morning debate during my long Whitehall years, possibly the only one since the 1939–45 war. As I listened, I imagined myself back in the Ministry of Defence and thought of the acute strains on the Prime Minister and former Whitehall colleagues. I admired her courageous leadership, right or wrong, ever since the horrifying moment three days earlier when she had to confront the alarming fact that it was too late to take any military action which could prevent the impending Argentine invasion reported through intelligence channels.

As the committee's report described it in a day-by-day account of the days leading up to the invasion:

> In the early evening of Wednesday 31 March, Mr. Nott [*Defence Secretary*] sought, and obtained, an urgent meeting with the Prime Minister, which took place in her room at the House of Commons. It was also attended by Mr. Atkins, Mr. Luce [*both FCO ministers*] and Foreign and Commonwealth and Ministry of Defence officials. The Chief of Naval Staff [*Admiral Sir Henry Leach*] was also present, having gone to the House of Commons to brief Mr. Nott.

Lord Carrington, the Foreign and Commonwealth Secretary, was visiting Israel. The Chief of Defence Staff, Admiral of the Fleet Sir Terence Lewin, was on an overseas tour prior to his retirement. The only naval vessel in the South Atlantic, HMS *Endurance*, a small and lightly armed converted icebreaker, had recently been diverted from the Falklands to South Georgia. The Argentine government had chosen a particularly awkward week in which to invade.

In May 1982 the Foreign and Commonwealth Office published a pamphlet, 'The Falkland Islands – The Facts'. Its final paragraph pointed a finger of serious criticism: 'The Argentine invasion is an act of unprovoked aggression. History provides many examples where the international community's failure to take action over such acts by aggressive powers led to much graver crises later.'

Those words, following the strong reactions of Parliament and the press, underline the reasons why Lord Carrington, Mr Atkins and Mr Luce all resigned from the Government, and why the Prime Minister decided to establish a committee of inquiry of the composition and character of the Falkland Islands Review Committee. But it was a wise political decision not to launch the committee publicly until the end of June – after the Falklands War, which through good fortune matched by bravery and military skill, had been won.

The committee's task has often been misunderstood. It was *not* asked to examine either the Government's role in the diplomatic period between the invasion and the landing of our forces on the Islands or the way in which the Government conducted the war that resulted in the Argentine surrender. Our terms of reference were:

> To review the way in which the responsibilities of the Government in relation to the Falkland Islands and their Dependencies were discharged in the period leading up to the Argentine invasion of the Falkland Islands on 2 April 1982, taking account of all such factors in previous years as are relevant; and to report.

To put it bluntly, to consider whether the Government at the time should and could have prevented the invasion and whether the relevant decisions and actions of the present and previous governments were open to criticism.

Our Report (Cmnd. 8787) was published in January 1983. It sought to make clear, at least to the careful reader (and some of the Report's critics were not so careful), the particularly difficult character of the committee's task. An objective approach required us to set aside things known with hindsight and avoid criticism of the Government for failing to act in a particular way when later events showed that it would have been better had ministers acted in another way. Was the action which had been taken entirely reasonable and defensible in the light of the circumstances and available information at the time? But this approach depended on being certain that the committee understood correctly the circumstances and could fully review the 'available information' at the relevant time.

There was a further inescapable complication. If the committee were to assume that the Government could, and should, have acted in a particular way at a particular moment, and was open to criticism because it did *not* act in that way, would it be right to assume that other 'parties' (in this case the Argentine government) would have acted as they did rather than have reacted in some different way? Lord Franks was concerned to impress on the committee the complex consequences of setting aside hindsight. At the same time, it was important to keep in mind the wise words of Bishop Butler: 'Things are what they are, and the consequences of them will be what they will be: why then should we desire to be deceived?'

But 'things' can change, and change quickly. When the British government announced its decision to withdraw HMS *Endurance* completely from the South Atlantic – the only naval vessel which regularly visited the Falklands – one important consequence would certainly have been a message to the Argentine government that Britain would be less concerned in future about the defence of the Islands. The hidden and timely move to the South Atlantic of a nuclear submarine might have quickly reversed the previous 'message'.

Our Report began by describing how we had set about our task. The Prime Minister had made clear on 8 July, when its establishment was debated in Parliament, that the committee should have 'access to all relevant papers and persons'. Franks insisted on personal and formal written assurances from the Cabinet Secretary and the appropriate permanent secretaries that all the relevant papers, including all the most secret intelligence material, had been sent to us. At Franks's suggestion a large part of August and September was devoted by committee members to reading individually all the papers made available, and to presenting in writing a brief summary of their initial reactions. The period from the end of September until the beginning of November was then largely devoted to what turned out to be thirty sessions of oral evidence from all those principally involved over the past years in matters relating to the Government's policy towards the Falkland Islands. The witnesses included all the former prime ministers in the years since 1965, the year in which the dispute over the Islands between the UK and Argentina was (as the Report put it) 'first brought to international attention'. It was laborious and absorbing work.

Our Report went on to describe the evolution of policy relating to the Islands and the exact sequence of events leading up to the Argentine invasion. The accuracy of our account was never challenged at the time – though it was necessarily based on what evidence and information were available to us. It could not include any study of Argentine papers. All aspects of the South Georgia incident, for example, and the intentions and activities of the Argentine scrap-metal merchant, Signor Davidoff, were never completely clear to us. These qualifications did not, however, affect the main conclusions of the Report nor the way in which they were welcomed nor the extent to which they were criticised. Perhaps it was inevitable that the conclusions – succinctly stated at the end, after setting out the key issues and the committee's judgement on each of them – should be challenged by the Opposition in the House of Commons and by parts of the press. The heavy casualties and the cost of the war and opposing political views in Parliament saw to that.

But was it also inevitable that the critics failed to consider, carefully and objectively, the important last two paragraphs of the Report's introduction – drawing attention to the crucial factor of hindsight?

> In our review we have taken particular care to avoid the exercise of hindsight in reaching judgments on the development of policy and on the actions of ministers and officials. We have sought to judge on each important issue whether the views expressed and the action taken by those concerned were reasonable in the light of the information available to them and the circumstances prevailing at the time, and not to substitute our judgement of what we might have done in those circumstances.
>
> We have also borne in mind that our task required us to focus exclusively on the Government's responsibilities for the Falkland Islands and the Dependencies, whereas those concerned, both Ministers and officials, had to deal with many other major and pressing preoccupations.

The date of the invasion, 2 April 1982 – specifically mentioned in the committee's terms of reference – was also a significant factor. In 1981–82 it was clear to all concerned in Whitehall that the

Argentine threat to the Falklands had increased. But, as the Report put it: 'What stands out is the dilemma to which successive governments were exposed by their policy of seeking to resolve, or at least contain, the dispute by diplomatic negotiation on the one hand and their commitment to the defence of the Falkland Islands on the other.'

Some of the critics, determined to identify a culprit, appeared at times to suggest that it was the British government and in particular the Foreign and Commonwealth Office rather than the Argentine junta which had caused the invasion of the Falkland Islands. The committee for its part expressed some important criticisms, including:

- failings in the intelligence machinery;

- a failure by the Cabinet to review, collectively and regularly, the growing Argentine threat;

- the decision to announce the planned withdrawal of HMS *Endurance* from the area at the end of her 1981–82 tour;

- slowness in preparing any contingency plans and, more particularly, the failure of the Foreign and Commonwealth Office to alert the Cabinet effectively as the crisis deepened in March 1982;

- the somewhat inadequate response to the Argentine landing in South Georgia;

- slowness by the Ministry of Defence in finally sending a nuclear submarine to the South Atlantic.

But even if there had been no grounds for any of these criticisms would the Argentine invasion on 2 April have been prevented? Or, to put it in another way, were these British failings, in aggregate, the prime cause of the invasion?

Before answering those questions, the Report should be read as a whole. The committee stressed several key factors:

- the Argentine determination to secure the Falkland Islands ('Las Malvinas') in 1982 through increasing diplomatic pressures, possibly leading to more drastic action, including invasion, later in the year (when the South Atlantic winter would have prevented any British military response);

- Argentina's rapidly deteriorating economic situation in March 1982, with demonstrations in the streets against the dictator, General Galtieri, creating strong political pressures to divert public attention by exploiting the confused developments in South Georgia;

- the last-minute decision (as intelligence reports had shown) to invade at the beginning of April – when it would have more militarily prudent to have waited until nearer the winter and HMS *Endurance* had been finally withdrawn.

The committee also recognised that the British Government had to act within important constraints:

- the strong wishes of the Falkland Islanders – with some strong support in the House of Commons – which limited diplomatic room for manoeuvre with Argentina;

- the strategic and military priorities resulting from our NATO commitments;

- the active diplomatic policy of seeking to bring the Argentine government back to the negotiating table – a policy which overt British deterrent action seemed likely to frustrate.

These considerations led into the final and most important paragraph of the Report, the conclusion of the Review:

Against this background we have pointed out in this chapter where different decisions might have been taken, where fuller consideration of alternative courses of action might, in our opinion, have been advantageous, and where the machinery of government might have been better used. But, if the British Government had acted differently in the ways we have indicated, it is impossible to judge what the impact on the Argentine Government or the implications for the course of events might have been. There is no reasonable basis for any suggestion – which would be purely hypothetical – that the invasion would have been prevented if the Government had acted in the ways indicated in our report. Taking account of these considerations, and of all the evidence we have received, we conclude that we would not be justified in attaching any criticism or blame to the present Government for the Argentine Junta's decision to commit its act of unprovoked aggression in the invasion of the Falkland Islands on 2 April 1982.

I accepted at the time, and, approaching twenty years later, I accept now, that the committee's conclusion was justified. I had contributed to the wording of the paragraph, but the final text belonged to the committee as a whole. Oliver Franks was determined to secure an unqualified unanimous view, and the text formally agreed round the table almost certainly reflected consultation with individual members. But I recall feeling uneasy about the words 'we would not be justified in attaching any criticism or blame' when the criticisms that we ourselves had expressed would have most likely influenced in some degree the sudden and bold decision by the Argentine government to invade the Falklands. It would have been difficult, however, to have qualified the committee's words, even if the committee as a whole had been disposed to formulate some qualification. More to the point, there was no case for qualifying the Argentine government's responsibility for its decision to invade, made in the last few days of March 1982.

In a personal letter of thanks, dated 2 January 1983, which I received from Margaret Thatcher, the prime minister, she wrote:

'In a matter which is of concern to a very wide public, and particularly to those who served in the South Atlantic campaign and their families, it is of the greatest importance that the conclusions of the committee, whatever they were, should have been unanimous.'

The committee had aimed to complete its work on the inquiry within six months and we had succeeded in doing so in time to break up before Christmas. Tony Barber entertained the committee to lunch at the Standard Chartered Bank; Oliver and Barbara Franks invited the small committee secretariat and also Penny and myself to lunch at their home in Oxford. We parted as a committee, never to meet together again. Franks required us to hand in all our working papers as committee members, made clear that he did not intend to hold a press conference when the Report was published, and placed upon us the injunction that we too, as individuals, should avoid speaking to the press with information or comment relating to the committee's task and Report.

I was delighted to think no more about the Falklands until the Report was published in mid-January after Parliament had returned from the Christmas recess, being presented there on 18 January 1983. The Prime Minister, who had postponed writing to committee members until after she had seen the Report, ended her letter by saying: 'I am afraid that St Catherine's will have seen little of its Master in the second half of 1982.'

Not quite true, though my thoughts were usually more with the committee than with the college. I did my best to be around in the college on the days when I was not in London, and I had learned on arrival that a wise head of a college never fails to be in the chair at governing body meetings.

The Government and especially the Prime Minister were deeply relieved on reading the Report's conclusions and ready to take in its stride the criticisms expressed by the committee. James Callaghan, an impressive voice, supported by Denis Healey, in the Parliamentary Opposition, expressed a derisive general reaction: 'For 338 paragraphs the Franks Report painted a splendid picture, delineating the light and shade. The glowing colours came out.

When Franks got to paragraph 339, he got fed up with the canvas that he was painting and chucked a bucket of whitewash over it.'

Drawing on his own experience of dealing with Argentina as prime minister in the late 1970s he made a number of detailed, critical, and cogent comments. So did Denis Healey, a former Defence Secretary, whose speech in the debate on the Report included one carefully judged paragraph:

> As the report says, no one can be certain on this matter. In the end General Galtieri invaded and the Government acted as they did. If they had acted differently, no one can be certain what the situation might have been. I believe that the report provides enough evidence to suggest that the Government's sins of omission and commission were serious enough to raise the possibility that different actions could have led General Galtieri to reject invasion.

He was reflecting the misgivings I have mentioned. Referring approvingly to a particular paragraph of the Report which emphasised, by way of criticism, the value of collective ministerial meetings, he made a friendly remark in passing about his former private secretary: 'In a report, in the drafting of which my ex-private secretary Sir Patrick Nairne had a hand, those are quite tough words.'

Some leading figures of the press criticised the committee, notably Simon Jenkins of *The Times* and Max Hastings, who had gone to the Falklands as a war reporter. In 1983 they published jointly a well-written book on the war, *The Battle for the Falklands*.*

Franks was unmoved. He resisted – as he had told the committee that he would do – all requests for interviews. He told me personally that his considerable experience of previous inquiries had taught him that it was best to leave reports to speak for themselves, and that exchanges with the press could easily lead to media comments which distorted or confused a report's judgements and conclusions.

---

* *The Battle for the Falklands*, by Max Hastings and Simon Jenkins, Michael Joseph, London, 1983.

On the tenth anniversary of the invasion Simon Jenkins returned to the charge. He published a damaging piece in *The Times* of 2 April 1992, headed 'A very British Cover-up'. I felt strongly that the article should not go unchallenged – in particular, this paragraph about the committee's conclusions:

> What have ten years done to that conclusion? It was written in the heat of victory and the authors saw no virtue in puncturing military glory. It took its evidence on Argentine motives and strategy only from the British Foreign Office. This evidence indicated, ludicrously, that the invasion was dreamed up by the junta overnight on March 30 or 31. Thus Franks was able to present it as a bolt from the blue, unpredictable and unpreventable. Seldom can a committee have so wilfully decided to fool itself.

I feel a sharp pang of resentment as I quote that paragraph today – in January 2001. What it says, and what some other parts of the article say, are inaccurate and unbalanced. The committee did not find the drafting of its final paragraph an easy task, knowing that Parliament, the press, and other commentators would pick on it in isolation, however much the Report stressed the need for it to be read as a whole. When, as I have said, I myself felt somewhat ill at ease with that paragraph in December 1982, possible alternative and better words eluded me and still do today. I had great respect for Oliver Franks's judgement and, after all the members of the committee had had their say in a thorough discussion of a formulation of the concluding paragraph, he had indicated firmly that he was satisfied and that no more should be said.

The quotation from Denis Healey's speech points to the core of the problem which has nagged at my mind. Would it be right to assess the cumulative effect of the failings or misjudgements in the Government's performance over the relevant years, and particularly in the early months of 1982, as giving to the British government, rather than to the Argentine junta, responsibility for the invasion of the Falklands on 2 April 1982? In spite of my misgivings I remain strongly convinced that it would not – and Healey, for his part, spoke only of the possibility that different actions could have deterred General Galtieri. The important fact to be emphasised again is that a critical review of events based on setting hindsight aside is an unusual and exacting task. In general, inquiries do not set that condition since they are primarily concerned to identify and then report on the lessons to be learned from the mistakes which have been made. What the Franks Committee had to do was different.

I drafted an article for Franks to send to *The Times* in response to Simon Jenkins's article of April 1992. I had no hope that it would change Jenkins's mind. I had happened to meet him at a Ditchley Foundation meeting some time in the mid-1980s when he had sought a brief chat in the hope, I think, that I privately shared his view. He remained unpersuaded by mine. I can understand his feelings. He and Max Hastings were acutely conscious of the cost in casualties of the Falklands War, and of how easily Britain might have lost it. He felt angry, in particular, that the committee had, as he saw it, let off so lightly Foreign Office officials and intelligence staffs of whom the committee had expressed some criticisms.

On 5 April 1992 Oliver Franks wrote in reply to my draft:

Thank you for your letter and the admirable draft you enclosed with it. I have thought a great deal about your suggestion. On the one hand the implication that the committee was at best slipshod in dealing with the evidence and the assertion that we covered up the truth are both false and offensive. On the other hand the practice I have followed throughout the various commissions and committees on which I have served has steadfastly been never to explain, advocate or defend a report or what was in it. After full reflection I have decided that I should stick to my practice. I should be uncomfortable if I did not as I believe it to be an important practice. Therefore I am very sorry I can't do what you suggest.

That was effectively the end of the matter. *The Times* might well have been ready to publish an article by me, but to submit one myself was unthinkable, not only because I had consulted Oliver and he had refused, but also because of the undertaking to avoid public comment which the committee had all made. But, later in April 1992, there was an unexpected and welcome development. A short book was published which put matters into much better perspective than the Jenkins article. Franks foreshadowed it in his letter to me:

> By pure coincidence the Report is being republished on 9 April with a twenty-page introduction by Professor Alex Danchev which goes some way to counter Simon Jenkins's assertions. As you will see he is very clear, for example, about our avoidance of hindsight. It begins to be the answer.

I met and had been impressed by Alex Danchev of Keele University, and by his grasp of the events, and of the Government's action, leading up to the invasion; and it was good news that our Report was to be re-published in full in his short book.* When it emerged, I found that it had on the back cover a flattering quotation from a piece written by David Watt of *The Times*: 'The Franks Report is marvellous – a miracle of lucid narrative, detached argument and precise, economical prose.'

In his introduction, Danchev quoted from a letter which I had written to him in 1990 in response to some questions which he had put to me:

> As always Franks stuck strictly to his terms of reference. Put crudely, the report blamed General Galtieri rather than Mrs Thatcher (or Lord Carrington) for what happened on 2 April 1982. No explicit conclusion was drawn about what had happened earlier or what might have happened later. As Sir Patrick Nairne has explained:

---

* Alex Danchev (1955–2016) was brilliant as a political chronicler and an art historian; I got to know him through my work at the National Portrait Gallery, and particularly when we were first planning an exhibition of Cézanne's portraits, and he was writing a new biography of Cézanne. He went on to edit a new edition of Cézanne's letters. Sadly he died unexpectedly in 2016.

'We were not asked to review the discharge of the government's responsibilities in relation to the general deterrence of Argentina from invasion. Of course, the Report says a lot about deterrent action, and we criticised the government for some inadequacies and failings, but here the second and third sentences of paragraph 339 are crucial – and we might perhaps have given them greater emphasis. If the strategic deployment by successive governments of our naval forces had given the South Atlantic a higher priority, and if in 1981–2 we had not been trying to persuade Argentina to "cool it", Argentina *might* have been deterred from invasion; but, in the actual circumstances, the committee could not conclude that the Thatcher government should be blamed for Galtieri's dash for the Malvinas.'

The last word on the events which culminated in the invasion of the Falkland Islands may perhaps be found in a well-known diplomatic dilemma. In dealing with a potential aggressor, how can a government succeed in striking the right balance between the pursuit of a peaceful solution and the display of deterrent action? It is usually a subtle problem of timing. A government can easily continue to show self-restraint and patience, and then, as Professor Danchev points out, time can abruptly run out. His own last words are a quotation from F. M. Cornford's *Microcosmographia Academica*: 'Time, by the way, is like the medlar; it has a trick of going rotten before it is ripe.'

21

Novembers – *1984: Hong Kong*

Written in 1999–2000

NOVEMBER 1984

Is that the end of the notable Novembers? Not entirely. In the Autumn of 1984 the Foreign and Commonwealth Secretary, Sir Geoffrey Howe, appointed me as one of the two government monitors with the task of overseeing the consultation of the Hong Kong people about the draft agreement governing reunification with China. I flew alone to Hong Kong in the third week of September to join my fellow monitor, Mr Justice Simon Li Fook-sean, the senior Chinese appeal judge in the territory. The lack of a fully democratic constitution in Hong Kong ruled out the possibility of holding a referendum, and a wide range of processes – by way of the media and meetings at every level of society – had to be employed by a specially established assessment office. The task of Simon Li and myself was to observe and, where possible, participate in everything that was done, and then to report to the Foreign and Commonwealth Secretary on the integrity and effectiveness of the consultation. November proved to be the significant month.

Penny boldly decided to fly to Hong Kong, arriving on 14 November and staying for about a week. She quickly shared my rapidly acquired addiction to Hong Kong and we had a day trip together, via Macau, to China. At the same time, the Foreign and Commonwealth Office instructed me to return, mission completed, by the end of November so that the House of Commons could debate the draft agreement before the Christmas recess, in the knowledge of Hong Kong's reaction to it. Geoffrey Howe and the Foreign Office were content with the monitors' report in which I had been determined to go beyond our brief by including a short summary of our own on the response and outlook of the Hong Kong people. I arrived back at the college on 28 November and was greeted warmly in the crowded hall when I spoke at the annual St Catherine's Night Dinner on 29 November 1984.

22

A Monitor in Hong Kong, 1984

Written in 2001

Time would run out for Hong Kong. Successive British governments were fully aware that it would. But that did little to help
the Government decide, in the early 1980s, how best to plan for
the prospect that the leases for (what were known as) the New
Territories and part of Hong Kong across the harbour from Hong
Kong Island would run out in 1997. Unsuccessful attempts had
been made to negotiate their renewal; but the Chinese government
had made clear that they could not be renewed. Hard facts of
territorial sovereignty confronted the Governor, the Foreign and
Commonwealth Secretary, and the Prime Minister. They could not
be ignored.

Hong Kong was not in my mind at all until the summer of 1984
when a surprising letter marked 'Personal and In Confidence'
arrived from the Foreign and Commonwealth Office. It was from
Mr Richard Luce MP, Minister of State:

> I am sorry that it has not been possible to speak on the telephone as I
> had hoped, and this letter will therefore come to you rather out of the
> blue.
>
> My purpose in attempting to get in touch on the telephone was in
> connection with our talks with the Chinese on Hong Kong. Specifically,
> it was to ask you whether you might be willing to serve as the UK
> member of the Monitoring Team to be appointed by the British

Government, as part of arrangements to test the acceptability in Hong
Kong of an agreement with the Chinese Government on the future of
the territory.

Richard Luce had added in his own hand that Geoffrey Howe,
the Foreign and Commonwealth Secretary, would have written
himself had he not been on holiday, and that Howe much hoped,
like himself, that I would accept.

I had no doubt that they did. The notice was short. I suspected
that I was not the first choice and that one or two more obvious
choices had declined the invitation. I naturally hesitated myself. I
had first to meet the Minister and hear more about the scope and
timing of the commitment. Quite apart from the personal considerations of Penny and myself, I had also to check whether the
college governing body would agree to my leaving the college for
a period to undertake a major government task in Hong Kong.

I had a meeting with Richard Luce at the Foreign Office on the
afternoon of Tuesday 14 August, the day before my sixty-third
birthday. I had qualms about my ability for the task, but while
Penny and I did not welcome the prospect of being apart for at
least two months, we agreed that I should not decline such a fascinating commitment if the college agreed . . . and it was settled
that I should see the Foreign Secretary on 6 September and fly to
Hong Kong on the 25th.

Briefing talks in the Foreign Office with Sir Percy Cradock,
former ambassador in Beijing and the diplomatic guru on China,
and Anthony Galsworthy, then head of the Hong Kong Department (ambassador himself in Beijing in 1997) gave me a summary
of the Revolution and economic reformer, Deng Xiaoping. Deng
fully appreciated China's strong position in relation to Hong Kong,
recognising in particular that the water supply and other facilities
on which Hong Kong Island depended were in the territories leased
from China. The Hong Kong economy was heavily dependent on
property development, and sufficiently long leases required the
stability that could be provided only by a negotiated agreement
with China about Hong Kong's future beyond 1997. Negotiations

had, therefore, been started and by summer 1984 an agreement was in sight. Hence the prospective need to consult the views of the Hong Kong people with independent monitors to oversee the task and report to the British government.

In May 1984 there had been a debate in the House of Commons in which Geoffrey Howe had reported good progress in the negotiations with China. He also said that he was considering how best to consult the people of Hong Kong about the outcome of the negotiations with China, envisaged as a draft treaty of reunification with China. It was an unprecedented and difficult question since Hong Kong was not a parliamentary democracy. Only just over half its population had an entitlement to vote and many of those entitled had not been interested enough to register as voters. A fair and valid referendum was, therefore, judged to be impracticable. But a politically acceptable form of consultation had to be found and on 18 July Geoffrey Howe announced special ad hoc arrangements in order to 'test the acceptability in Hong Kong' of whatever agreement was reached with the Chinese Government about the future of the territory.

As for much else in dealing with Hong Kong, the arrangements were unique. Their key features were:

- the establishment of an Assessment Office in Hong Kong under a commissioner, Mr Ian Macpherson, the Acting Secretary of Home Affairs in Hong Kong;*

- terms of Reference which required the Assessment Office to receive all views expressed on the draft agreement, directly or indirectly, through established channels or through the media in all its forms; to collate, analyse and assess such views; and to submit a report to the Governor which

---

* Ian Macpherson CBE joined the Hong Kong government as a civil servant in 1962 and rose to the rank of secretary, government secretariat in 1986. He later held a number of senior positions including commissioner of the Assessment Office, Secretary for Transport, and Secretary General, Planning Committee for the Hong Kong University of Science and Technology (HKUST).

should include an overall assessment of the extent of the acceptance of the draft agreement by the Hong Kong people;

– the appointment of an independent monitoring team with the task of observing all aspects of the work of the Assessment Office and then submitting an independent report to the Foreign and Commonwealth Secretary on whether the team was satisfied that the Assessment Office had 'properly, accurately, and impartially' carried out its required tasks.

This was where I came in. The monitoring team was composed of the Hon. Mr Justice Simon Li Fook-sean, the senior Chinese Appeal judge in Hong Kong, and myself, rather elaborately described as the Rt Hon. Sir Patrick Nairne, GCB, MC, MA.*

The pair of names looked respectable enough: a venerable local appeal judge and a Privy Counsellor from the United Kingdom. But why did the Foreign Office – and, for that matter, I myself – think that I should be a suitable and effective monitor? What did I know about Hong Kong? My knowledge of this unique territory – not an independent member of the British Commonwealth, but of higher status than a colony – was mainly derived from as few as three visits to Hong Kong during my years in Defence. I visited first, in 1966, as principal private secretary to the Secretary of State for Defence, Denis Healey, and then again in 1970 and 1973 with the Tory Secretary of State, Lord Carrington, when I was Deputy Undersecretary of State (Policy and Programmes) in the Ministry of Defence. The fact that I had had some experience of the evolution of Hong Kong over the years but was far from being a Hong Konger may have been a factor in the choice of myself. But I am

* Simon Li Fook-sean retired in 1987 at the age of sixty-four as the colony's most senior Chinese judge; he was appointed by the Beijing government to many positions during the transition period, including being deputy director of the preliminary working committee of the Preparatory Committee for the Hong Kong Special Administrative Region.

inclined to guess that the reasons for my choice were less subtle. I was fairly well known in the Foreign Office and had been prominent in Whitehall. Being head of an Oxford college carried, rightly or wrongly, a superficial badge of independent integrity.

On my first visit in 1966 relations with China over Hong Kong were strained. The Healey party was taken to a hill about a couple of miles from the frontier between the Hong Kong New Territories and China. Some exotic butterflies floated around as, under a blazing hot sun, we surveyed from a distant hill the Chinese railway line and a sparsely populated part of the large province of Guangdong. By the time of the 1970 visit there had been considerable development beyond the railway line and the political circumstances allowed us to drive much closer, though not too close, to the frontier. In 1973, however, we walked right up to the frontier crossing point and watched a few Chinese soldiers on duty at the small railway station only a few yards away. [*See colour illustrations for sketches of Hong Kong from these visits.*]

I travelled first class from Heathrow and my own arrival at 3:45 p.m. on Tuesday 26 September was certainly not a routine occasion for me. I briefly described it on 27 September in the first of my many letters to Penny:

> I've virtually recovered from the flight – which went smoothly and comfortably. Simon Li and the administrative officer (Mrs Carrie Willis, HK Chinese) met me; batteries of cameras and an innocuous statement by Nairne; VIP treatment over baggage and passport. Everything made easy. Have met one or two old friends, including the Governor (Sir Edward Youde), with whom I lunch on Monday, whose presentation of the White Paper on the Agreement has been remarkably well received.*

---

* Sir Edward Youde was a very experienced British diplomat who had served four tours of Foreign Office duty in China, including as ambassador from 1974 to 1978. He had also served in Washington as a member of the British mission to the United Nations between 1965 and 1969. He was appointed as Governor of Hong Kong from May 1982 and undertook key negotiating work on the Hong Kong Agreement with the People's Republic of China. He died in office in December 1986.

Mrs Carrie Willis was, I learned, the Chinese head of the monitors' small office. She settled me into a suite high up in the Hilton Hotel. Outside the window of the sitting room I could see the concrete jungle of the high-rise office buildings between the Hilton and the harbour. The huge illuminated words 'Bank of America' dominated the sky. If I could have craned my neck round the corner, I might just have seen Norman Foster's bold new Hong Kong and Shanghai Bank.

On the very day of my arrival the Governor, Sir Edward Youde, returned from Beijing carrying the draft agreement negotiated by the British Government with the Government of The People's Republic of China. My first duty that same evening was to attend the meeting of the Legislative Council at which the Governor made a general statement about the outcome of the negotiations. What he had to say was, as I wrote to Penny, as well received as he could have expected, and the reaction of the Hong Kong papers the next morning was generally favourable. As *The South China Monitor* put it, TWO CHEERS . . . for what had been achieved.

I quickly became conscious of two outstanding features of the situation – first, although the Governor personally was a member of the negotiating team, China had insisted that the negotiations were to be conducted exclusively between the British and Chinese governments, and Hong Kong had been carefully kept in the dark as negotiations proceeded. The result was that Hong Kong had feared a much worse outcome: hence immediate relief when the text of the draft agreement (in over 3 million copies) was published. Secondly, the Foreign Office officials and the Governor, and particularly Sir Percy Cradock, who had been directly engaged in the negotiations, were very pleased with themselves at securing, after many months, as good a draft agreement as they could have expected. Hence there would be no British Government disposition – confirmed by Sir Geoffrey Howe to the House of Commons – to contemplate as either desirable or practicable any change in the substance of the agreement, whatever views might be expressed by the people of Hong Kong.

I noted straight away, in my notebook, that there was an immediate 'tendency (by British correspondents?) to question the value of
the assessment task since it is a "take it or leave it" agreement'. On
Wednesday 27 September, I watched the Governor's press conference
on television and noted: 'Governor speaks v. confidently; but he
dodges question: What if outcome of assessment task is negative?
His simple and firmly stated line: "I strongly commend the agreement . . . The alternative: handover without an agreement."'

Simon Li and I were fully conscious of our rather awkward
position. For the House of Commons in London we provided an
essential independent oversight of the only practicable way of fulfilling the Government's commitment to consult the Hong Kong
people. The inescapable first step was to find out, as far as possible,
how the Hong Kong people at every level of society and their
institutions in all their variety, were reacting to the terms of the
draft agreement. This seemed sensible enough to Westminster and
Whitehall. But what stood out prominently in the minds of Hong
Kong itself, with every reason to distrust China, were the alarming
consequences of being handed over to Communist China in thirteen years' time. It was not surprising that there were many in
Hong Kong, including parts of the press, who took a cynical view
of what the British government was presenting as genuine consultation and independent monitoring.

A well-known journalist on the *Sunday Times*, Simon Winchester,
a St Catherine's alumnus whom I had regarded as a friend, published a hostile and unpleasant piece.* I wrote to Penny: 'It is the
kind of piece that has given S. W. his particular reputation in the
FCO. It is cleverly written; it contains many sentences of truth, but
its main thrust is an unbalanced and ill-informed comment on the
agreement and the consultation of Hong Kong.'

There was much more in the article and I was particularly irri-
tated at S. W. mentioning some unnamed 'colleague' as 'admitting'

---

* Simon Winchester OBE is a distinguished journalist and author who had recently
covered the Falkland Islands conflict and at this point was based in Hong Kong and
working for the *Sunday Times* as a freelance correspondent.

that 'Nairne's role is essentially redundant'. But I had not been over thirty years in Whitehall without learning that some journalists do not wish to spoil their eye-catching stories by exposing themselves to true facts.

A more serious critic in Hong Kong was Emily Lau, whom I met, and liked, over lunch on 12 November.* She wrote, on 27 November, in the *Far Eastern Economic Review*, in terms which other correspondents had broadly expressed earlier:

> Hong Kong should have learned its lesson. In September we were presented with a fait accompli in the form of the Sino-British joint declaration on the territory's future. Although the British Government had consistently promised the Hong Kong people throughout the two years of secret negotiations with China that any agreement must be acceptable to us, shortly before the initialling we were told that we had got to accept the accord in full or reject it at our peril. Not one word or comma in the document could be changed.

Emily Lau was given to expressing her views in strong, sometimes extreme, terms as a passionate opponent of Communist China; but there was some sense in what she went on to write:

> Even before the initialling of the draft agreement, many Hong Kong people had already accepted that it could not be changed, and hence decided that it would be pointless to comment on it. The real battle, they say, is in the drafting of the Basic Law. Such an attitude is, to say the least, defeatist . . .

It was not realistic, in the autumn of 1984, to regard the amendment of the text of the draft agreement as a serious possibility, but its translation into what the Chinese called the Basic Law – that

* Emily Lau worked as a journalist in this period but went on to become an important politician and the first woman directly elected to the Legislative Council of Hong Kong. In an extensive Wikipedia entry, she is described as a 'politician with strong convictions on the promotion of democracy, human rights and equal opportunities in Hong Kong'.

is, a Chinese government text covering the full terms of the agreement as a basis for political endorsement in Beijing – lay ahead as a crucially important task; and, as I learned from the work of the Assessment Office, Chinese was a language which was open, in subtle ways, to changes of meaning. But Emily Lau, in looking ahead, in a general way, to what a determined and more politically active Hong Kong might do to strengthen its position in the years up to 1997, took little or no account of the many detailed transitional arrangements which still had to be negotiated in the Joint Liaison Group – a group in which Hong Kong would be directly represented. At the early stage of autumn 1984, however, she was not to be persuaded about the value of the Assessment Office or of the monitoring team:

> For the purpose of the [British] parliamentary debate in December, an Assessment Office was set up in September to collect and collate Hong Kong public opinion. Since then it has been thoroughly discredited, being labelled as a 'charade to mask a diplomatic defeat', a 'farce', and 'a sick joke'.

Understandable words from a young and forceful political journalist who could not bear the prospect of 'free' Hong Kong being handed over to totalitarian Communist China.

There were moments in September and October 1984 when I wondered whether I had allowed myself to become the stooge of the Foreign Office, required to play a pre-scripted part in a public diplomatic demonstration for the benefit only of the British Parliament and world opinion. But I had no real difficulty in convincing myself that this was not so. The British government had publicly promised consultation; this had been arranged in the only practicable form, as accepted by Parliament, as the House of Commons had to have some independent check of the efficiency and impartiality of the consultation process – *essential* for the purpose of finding out what Hong Kong people did think about the draft agreement. It would clearly be wise to await the fulfilment of this commitment before writing it off as a futile and costly exercise. The reports, published at the end of November 1984, by the Assessment Office, and independently by Simon Li and myself, did not bear out Emily Lau's premature judgments.

The Assessment Office was headed by an impressive team. Simon Li arranged a small dinner party on the evening of 27 September, as I wrote to Penny:

> I'm just back from Mr Justice Simon Li's dinner party at the Hong Kong Club (Western food, Mayfair décor) to enable me to meet socially the members of the Assessment Office I met in a conference room this morning. The boss of the A.O. (Commissioner) is Ian Macpherson, married to a Chinese wife with two step-daughters, identical Chinese twins, at Sevenoaks School. His deputy, who was sitting on my right, is Mrs Elizabeth Wong, mother of teenage children; former teacher, failed novelist, up and coming civil servant; and on her right none other than a former Catz graduate student, Wilfred Wong (no relation!).

I was driven everywhere in a car allocated to me together with a delightful and knowledgeable Chinese driver who proved to be an invaluable support. The new Supreme Court building for the senior judiciary provided house-room for both the Assessment Office (at the bottom of the building) and for Simon Li and myself (near the top of the building).

A typical day for me:

- Breakfast at about 8 a.m. – either in my room or in the Hilton's cafe – having listened to the World Service news while getting dressed.
- Walk to the Supreme Court building – not far, but route noisy and atmosphere disagreeable from relentless traffic and bulldozers at work for a city of ceaseless economic growth requiring ever more new buildings.
- 9 a.m. – Simon Li and I attend the Assessment Office's

morning meeting. The office's senior team, under the chairmanship of Ian Macpherson, would go through all the representations and general comments on the draft agreement received in the previous twenty-four hours in response to the widely publicised invitation to say specifically whether the draft agreement was acceptable and to express any other views. It was at these meetings that I learned, from the occasional genial argument between Ian and Simon Li, how the Chinese language could be open in translation to significant differences of meaning.

- The remainder of the morning would be devoted to some discussion with Simon Li, to talking individually to members of the Assessment Office in order to understand and inspect how they were carrying out their functions (for example, the particularly difficult task of monitoring the media in all its forms) and often paying a personal call on one of the many key people in Hong Kong inside or outside the Government.

- Lunch. Probably in the Judges' Mess if I had an early commitment after lunch – often to attend a meeting of one of the fourteen District Boards at which the agenda included a discussion of the draft agreement. There were two or three special lunches each week – with the Governor, for example, on 1 October after a private talk in which he was careful to say nothing that might influence our own impression of Hong Kong's views; with an elderly Chinese friend of Larry Bachmann (a Domus Fellow of St Catherine's) who smoked throughout lunch in the Mandarin Hotel and was at pains to impress on me that Hong Kong Chinese were not interested in politics, caring only for business and their family; and with the directors of Jardine Fleming.

- Afternoon. Attend our principal monitoring meetings – including ten of the fourteen District Boards, debates in the Legislative and Urban Councils, and some fourteen meetings with other institutional bodies. If I was not sitting in on a meeting, there was usually another visit – for example, to see Hong Kong's new housing programme beyond Kowloon (where I was particularly impressed by a system which placed primary responsibility for looking after each housing block on the families resettled there) or to visit the impressive Chinese New University in the New Territories (Hong Kong boldly proceeded to build a third university in advance of reunification in 1997).

- Before leaving the office there would be letters to be dealt with, including correspondence with Tony Galsworthy at the Foreign Office.
- Back to my room in the Hilton (hoping to find, as I often did, a letter from Penny), before – two or three times a week – going to a dinner party, in which I found myself the chief guest – for example with the Attorney General, Michael Thomas QC (whom I heard make a brilliant speech in support of the agreement, and who later married the rich and glamorous Chinese member of the Legislative Council, Miss Lydia Dunn). If I was not dining out, I would eat modestly alone in the Hong Kong Club or in the hotel.

There were also, however, some important, though more informal, monitoring occasions in the evening – for example, sitting at the back of the room in a primary school in Kowloon, with an interpreter whispering into my ear, whilst District Board members conducted an open consultation meeting with local residents; meeting a group of trade union representatives to listen to their views; attending a Public Affairs Forum at which the draft agreement was discussed.

An extract from my letter to Penny in mid-October:

Friday 12 October – Weather has not been especially good, but the sun shone consistently today. The car came to the Hilton at 9:45 (just after Cicely Mayhew rang – would I come to see them at their son's flat on Monday evening?) and we drove through the harbour tunnel to Kowloon and then NE along the coast, past the many islands, to the new town – all tower blocks, unfinished roads, and bulldozers – of

Tuen Mun where I sat in on the District Board meeting. The very young District Officer opened the discussion of the White Paper [*the draft agreement*] and went round the table securing views of members. The agenda item was finished in half an hour. The Board was unanimous in support of the draft agreement. Board members range from local traders and small factory owners to schoolteachers and social welfare officers. It was impossible not to be impressed by the assorted readiness to trust China to implement 'one country: two systems'. Forty-five minutes back to the Supreme Court office. At 2 p.m. picked up by the Secretary for Housing David Ford, and taken on a selective housing tour, starting with the most horrific boarding house tenements run by private landlords and ending with the latest very fine housing estates on the edge of Hong Kong. When I got back, I heard that Alf Morris MP and his wife would like a drink off me rather than dinner, so I took them to the Hong Kong Club – after they and I had looked at the TV news available here about the (unbelievably awful) Brighton bomb attack on the Tory Party Conference ... Tomorrow (Saturday) Simon Li and I have a meeting with the Assessment Office at 9:30, then I have a TV and also a radio interview between eleven and one o'clock.

Pat visiting a district in Hong Kong as a monitor, 1984.

At St Catherine's college with
Joanna Greenwood, first
grandchild, 1984

Kathy, Fiona, Sandy, James, Andrew and Margaret Nairne, Mull of Galloway, 1976

Remembering the
Isle of Eriska,
25th wedding
anniversary card,
September 1973

Birthday card for
Penny, May 1984

Easter card for
Penny, 2004

At Casteenovo —
Nr Gubbio.
17. v. '90

Darling Fiona,
I think that I must paint a
card for you : so here is the
mist clearing over the countryside
near Gubbio. Castelnovo is a most
delectable place. We have a small
ground floor apartment with a view
across the valley where Gubbio lies.
& a small & admirable swimming
pool (which we usually have to
ourselves) 15 yards below us. We
find the (beautiful Lancia) hired

car a bit of a strain,
but we just about get by!
It was an exacting drive from
Rome ; since then we've been to
Assisi ; Urbino, we hope, tomorrow.
The weather is superb. This is
the fourth piece of painting I've
done today! All in all, we
might be in another world
— say, Elysium. Too short
a holiday but stunningly good.
We think of you all —
Best love from us both — cb.

Card to Fiona Greenwood from near Gubbio, 17 May 1990

New Territories
from Hong Kong,
1966

Hong Kong, 1973

Hong Kong from
the Peak, 1984

Chilson village, Oxfordshire, winter 1983

Towards Herefordshire, winter 1981

Investiture as Knight Grand Cross of the Order of the Bath,
Westminster Abbey, 15 May 2002

Road to Pudlicote, Oxfordshire, 2007

The stream at Yew Tree, Chilson, 2006

Picnic at Yew Tree, Chilson, 2009

Twelve days after my arrival I wrote in my notebook 'An interim viewpoint': my first impressions of the Hong Kong situation:

9 October:

A. General agreement that:

(1) no better draft agreement could have been negotiated. Many fewer uncertainties than if no agreement;

(2) it requires the HK people to take a lot on trust. It is impossible for anyone to be sure that the PRC [*People's Republic of China*] will implement the agreement faithfully in 1997;

(3) 'faithful implementation' by China will depend on HK remaining prosperous and stable – and for that HK must show confidence in its future;

(4) the build-up of confidence – following the widespread relief at the character of the draft agreement – will depend, at least in part, on the clarification and/or resolution of important issues arising from the agreement.*

B. Perhaps the steering of political evolution, in parallel with sustaining the economic prosperity of HK, is the most difficult problem. Elected Legco [*Legislative Council*] members will need to satisfy the voters. Some business people will abandon HK.

C. (1) No chance of satisfying the Chinese Nationalist Taiwan interest or those who recall, and suffered in, the Cultural Revolution.

(2) No ready way of doing more for the British Dependent Territories Citizens [*BDTCs*] – though government officials might be treated as a 'special case'?

---

* My father's key points were: (a) the Basic Law, including Beijing's good faith in reflecting the text of the agreement; (b) the nationality question: the extent to which the amendment to the British 1981 Act reassures the many British Dependent Territories Citizens; (c) the evolution of representative government; (d) the introduction into Hong Kong of the China's People's Liberation Army; (e) the choice of Chief Executive; (f) handling of land leases and any increase in taxation.

About a month later, on 10 or 11 November, I wrote 'A Further Summary' in the notebook. The significant additional points were:

(1) The detailed character of the agreement – the Chinese, I was told, would have preferred only the declaration at the beginning of the agreement document – was the principal concession secured by the British negotiators after they had had to concede to China the transfer of sovereignty of Hong Kong Island, the impossibility of continued British administration under Chinese sovereignty, and the creation of a *joint* liaison group for implementing the agreement.

(2) Particular uncertainties relating to:
  - election or appointment by the PRC of future HK Chief Executive;
  - the position of BDTCs and their travel documents;
  - the PLA [*People's Liberation Army*] and possible conscription in Hong Kong;
  - the direct involvement of HK in the formulation of the Basic Law (since HK had been excluded from the negotiation of the agreement).

(3) Taken as a whole, the agreement is acceptable to a large majority of people, but it would be premature to estimate a percentage of the total population. For some people it is a matter of acquiescence; for others with communist sympathies it is welcome; complete opposition from Chinese nationalists; bitterness over nationality aspect among many BDTCs.

(4) Success of the agreement on the basis of the Chinese concept of 'One country, two systems' will largely depend on:
  - HK retaining prosperity and stability and that may be affected by the way in which HK develops representative government and succeeds in 'growing' its own Chief Executive;
  - the extent of China's success in developing 'Socialism with Chinese characteristics', and in modernising the country without creating too high a level of inflation or disorganisation.

In spite of all the uncertainties HK must have confidence in itself, as
the business world has confidence in HK now, and recognise that the
degree of unavoidable uncertainty has been significantly reduced by
the terms of the draft agreement.

These reflections sound rather pompous as I write in 2001, but,
with an inescapably uncertain long-term future for Hong Kong,
they could be of some interest in future years. They remained valid
assumptions for the preparation later of our monitors' report. And
now, four years after reunification in 1997, it can be seen that the
Chinese Government is, at least at present, determined to abide
strictly by the agreement and the Basic Law – as it is in its political and economic interest to do so, provided that there is no
subversion threat posed by Hong Kong.

I listened to discussions from the highest to the lowest level in
Hong Kong. I found in them all that a predictable attitude of distrust towards China – given throughout its history to sudden
swings in internal policies and external attitudes – was balanced
against realistic acceptance of what was politically inevitable and
might have been worse. In a District Board meeting far out in
the New Territories, where many present may have welcomed
reunification with China, the discussion of the draft agreement was
surprisingly brief and a more pressing item of business was the
improvement of the bus service into central Hong Kong.

In the Legislative and Urban Councils, however, the debates
were more wide-ranging and sophisticated. Searching questions
were raised on a number of important matters – from issues of
land sales to the likely future of welfare options (questions, in
short, relating to the detailed scope of the future administration
within the Special Administrative Region of Hong Kong). As to the
general policy, Miss Lydia Dunn appeared to speak for a number
of senior Hong Kong citizens. She took the view, in her long Legislative Council speech that 'The agreement is satisfactory as to
intention, content and form' on the basis of six reasons for her
belief that the agreement would be faithfully implemented. The first
three were:

(1) it is a formal and legally binding international agreement freely negotiated between two sovereign states;

(2) the Chinese leadership would surely not have committed so much effort into reaching an agreement if they had no intention of adhering to its terms;

(3) the Chinese leadership have publicly staked their personal prestige and reputation in the eyes of the world.

So far, so good. There remained the old cliché that 'the devil lies in the detail' – and a great deal remained to be clarified and resolved in the thirteen years up to 1997. The official members of the Legislative Council, from the Chief Secretary downwards, were naturally in support of what the British government negotiators – with the Governor closely associated with the task – had achieved. What was most important and especially satisfactory for London was that, with the exception of two abstentions, all the unofficial members of the council voted in support of endorsing the agreement.

I was in Hong Kong for two months. My thoughts were almost entirely concentrated on fulfilling my task as one of the Government's two independent monitors. My days were devoted to listening and learning – combining intellectual detachment with sensitive understanding. How did I enjoy the experience?

In a word, greatly, but my life was often a strain: in effect 'on parade' every day, in the presence of people whom I had never met and who, for the most part, knew nothing about me. In spite of a tendency to claustrophobia I often had to accept being prominently placed in seats and situations from which I could not have escaped without embarrassment. The days were full except at weekends and often exhausting. The pressure of time was strong. I was conscious that, along with the Assessment Office, we, as monitors, had only eight weeks in which to do our job properly if we were to provide a report of the quality required by the end of November.

My fellow monitor, Mr Justice Simon Li, was a quiet man with a friendly face and a sense of humour. He appeared to know every-one of importance in Hong Kong. He had settled there with his family during China's Communist Revolution at the end of 1940s, had had a successful career in law and had become very rich (with a second home in London and a fine Rolls-Royce car, to which he had apologetically introduced me). He apparently had a reputation for somewhat radical political views – possibly judged by the con-servative standards of Hong Kong society – but he never revealed them to me. He could not have been kinder or more hospitable, but (as was apparently the Chinese custom) he never invited me to his own home, and, in our many official discussions, I was always conscious that, in a phrase of today, neither of us ever knew 'where the other came from'. Years later when 1997 approached he made himself agreeable to Beijing and stood (without success) as a candidate for the appointment of Chief Executive.

I had had the advantage of talking to the Minister of State and FCO officials before I left London. It was clear to me what kind of monitors' report the Foreign and Commonwealth Office wanted and I was determined to carry out my task with strict and objective integrity. I could only hope that it would be done in full agreement with Simon Li. It turned out that I quickly established a close partnership with him and also good relations with Ian Macpherson and with his and my own staff. Even so, I felt very much on my own. In spite of all the hospitality I received, I was often lonely.

There was, however, much to enjoy – and it was probably best for me to be on my own at least for the weekdays of the early weeks when I was heavily engaged in concentrating on what I knew I had to do. My arrival became widely known and, in add-ition to what were, for the most part, working lunches and dinners on several weekdays, I was invited out for part of most Saturdays and Sundays. My letters to Penny and my sketchbook bear witness to two or three delightful boat parties on Sundays and on one public holiday, hosted by Sir Arthur Huggins (a retired judge who had been at Radley), by Sir Paul Bryan (an MP, who was a key member of the House of Commons Hong Kong Committee) and by Sir Denys Roberts (Chief Justice of Hong Kong).

Hong Kong picnic expedition, 18 November 1984.

We would sail out of the harbour in the glorious warm sunshine of the autumn weather, anchor in a quiet bay, bathe off the boat, have a picnic lunch aboard and enjoy what was often, for me, useful conversation with other guests. It was all agreeably 'old colonial' – insignificant, but agreeable fruit of what was left of British imperial power.

My notebook also records a final Saturday treat in the form of a helicopter tour, arranged by the Governor, over the whole territory of Hong Kong and up to the Chinese border, beyond which I could see the vast urban development in astonishing contrast to what I had seen during the Denis Healey visit of 1966. At the racecourse I became vividly conscious that the HK Chinese are gamblers by nature – enjoying the excitement of chance at races or in the playing of their favourite game of mah-jong – a factor suggesting that the HK people would not be too dismayed by the uncertainties of their future beyond 1997.

On Monday 29 October, I had just got out of the bath when the telephone rang in my suite. It was Penny ringing at about midnight in St Catherine's. She had decided to come to Hong Kong. Her air ticket was about to be booked; she was proposing to arrive on Wednesday 14 November and to stay for a week. It was only possible to have a few words on the telephone so I was left wondering whether I had sounded adequately enthusiastic.

Earlier, on 30 September, I had written to her with characteristic caution:

> If you were very keen to come out here I would do my best to help arrange it; but I would not recommend it, much as I would love to have you with me. Several strangers (for example, in the boat party) have made welcoming noises in your direction; HK British people are used to visitors ... but the central Hong Kong environment is hideously noisy and ugly, and I cannot think how a wife could enjoy the place on her own, or constantly in the hands of strangers, while her husband beavered away during the day and perhaps on many evenings. But I could, I suppose, be wrong.

My recollection is that I was taken by surprise by Penny's call, but it was an inspired decision on her part. I was certainly conscious that Penny too had been feeling lonely and though members of the family came and went she had experienced difficulties being isolated in the college lodgings. When her letter of 29 October reached me, her plans were fully explained.

The visit was perfectly timed. Simon Li and I had extensive discussions with Ian Macpherson and the senior members of the Assessment Office about the conclusions they had reached, and the reasons for them, on the basis of the large range of representations and evidence which the office had received. We had together produced the final draft of our report. There was further work to be done in our office, and a few more people to see but November 15 (the day after Penny's arrival) was the closing date for responses to the Assessment Office and we had no more monitoring visits to make. Penny happily shared the Hilton suite and joined in the social engagements to which I was committed. She enjoyed seeing a good deal of Hong Kong on her own, including a visit to the

Pat and Penny on a boating expedition, 18 November 1984.

Chinese University and to the Chinese family of Dr Elaine Tam, a graduate student at St Catherine's.

We shared two very special occasions. On Saturday 17 November, Sir Edward and Lady Youde invited us to join them and two other couples for a day out in the Governor's comfortable yacht, the

Lady Maureen; we sailed to the New Territories, and I was able to do a sketch of the coast of China before we went ashore. We visited the Governor's small cottage and then went for a short walk, looking at a temple and being stopped for a moment when an elderly Chinese lady made urgent representations to the Governor on the local issue of a road. It was a unique trip for us. The Youdes – Teddy (who died only a few years later from a heart attack) and Pam (a good Chinese speaker) – were a delightful, unstuffy couple, and I also welcomed the chance of being able to consult the Governor informally about an aspect of the final stages of the monitors' report.

After this sociable weekend we managed to get tickets for one of the regular day trips for tourists to China by way of a seasick-making hovercraft passage to Macau. Even one day in China is a fascinating experience and although we were firmly conducted by an English-speaking Chinese guide, we were able to wander quite freely in the chosen stopping places – an agricultural village with children and elderly people around, a large tourist restaurant and garden for a simple Chinese meal, and the compulsory (I assumed) visit to the birth place of Sun Yat-Sen. The weather was good and the landscape in parts like the lowlands of Scotland in form and colour. In short, a minute glimpse of one of the largest countries in the world, but a glimpse (including a brief passage through the gambling city of Macau) I would hate to have missed.

On Tuesday and Wednesday, 20 and 21 November, I was discussing the final draft of the Assessment Office's report, and working with Simon Li on our own final draft, while Penny shopped around and made the two or three visits without me. We continued to be generously entertained until Penny's day of departure, 22 November.

Penny's short stay was wonderfully enjoyable but I still had to complete satisfactorily my official assignment. On Friday 23 November, Simon Li and I finalised our report. On the Saturday and Sunday, we checked the proofs in English; on the Monday, Simon checked the Chinese proofs. Our report was no more than five pages long; we intended it to be read in full.

We considered it essential to respond in the report, if only briefly, to the public criticism of the value of the Assessment Office's task, even though that office's report had addressed the problem as fully as possible – as these quotations show:

> It is difficult to judge and even more difficult to quantify the scale of response to be expected from five and a half million people invited to express their views about a draft agreement crucial to their own future ... It has not been possible to determine the extent to which the perception that the draft agreement could not be altered affected overall response. Similarly, although assurances were given by the Secretary of State that the views expressed on all points would be of value to the British Parliament and in the continuing discussions between Britain and China, particularly in the Joint Liaison Group, it is not possible to say whether these assurances have affected the response.

But the report went on to state that, in addition to the substantial response through the media, nearly 2,500 direct submissions were received from individuals and from 679 organisations and groups. The conclusion of the office was that 'the views received on every aspect of the draft agreement, taken together, represent and reflect the opinion of a very wide cross-section of the community and provide an effective and credible basis on which to make an assessment.' That conclusion was a crucial factor in enabling Ian Macpherson, the Commissioner, to report that: 'After the most careful analysis and consideration of all the information received, the Office has concluded that most people of Hong Kong find the draft agreement acceptable.'

As monitors we reinforced the words of the Assessment Office by observing from our own experience:

> It was clearly evident that a people traditionally reserved in political matters included many who were also disposed to doubt the value of commenting on the overall acceptability of a draft agreement which was not open to any amendment. Nevertheless, to those who have chosen to call the consultation and assessment task 'a charade' or 'a

farce' we wish to say that their view was certainly not shared by the many Hong Kong people, in different parts of the community, whom we were able to hear discussing, with care and concern, the draft agreement as a whole and all its contents.

Turning to the specific requirements of our terms of reference, and after summarising how we had set about our assignment, we reported that the Assessment Office *had* discharged its duties *impartially*, that it had done so by *properly* and *faithfully* following the procedure laid down for it, and (the most difficult function) that its analysis and assessment of Hong Kong's views of the draft agreement were *accurate*. The Foreign and Commonwealth Office had probably intended that we should leave it at that. But, having shared all the evidence available to the Assessment Office, we decided to add some last words of our own to our endorsement of the accuracy of the Assessment Office's report. Our final paragraph was as follows:

> But the verdict of acceptance implies neither positive enthusiasm nor passive acceptance. The response to the Assessment Office has demonstrated the realism of the people of Hong Kong. They know that their future now lies in their own hands; and the widespread concern to be involved, as the Assessment Office report has highlighted, in the drafting of the Basic Law, is a timely and important token of their wish to stand increasingly on their own feet.

On Thursday 27 November, I flew home and arrived back at St Catherine's at 8 a.m. On the following evening, as Master, I addressed the college at the St Catherine's Night Dinner and received a touchingly warm welcome.

On that same day I had reported to the Foreign and Commonwealth Office and met both Richard Luce, the Minister of State, and the Secretary of State, Sir Geoffrey Howe. The monitors' report had been published in a government paper, Cmnd. 9407, along with the Assessment Office report, and ministers seemed well content with it.

I received a letter from Geoffrey Howe in which he wrote:

I really am grateful to you for taking on the task of Monitor in connection with the assessment of opinion in Hong Kong about the Agreement with China. The report you produced was, if I may say so, a model of clarity and precision. I know that Parliament will attach considerable importance to your view that the Assessment Office conducted its work impartially, and discharged its duties properly.

Yours very sincerely,
[Geoffrey Howe]

On 5 December the House of Commons debated the draft agreement with China on the basis of a motion moved by Sir Geoffrey Howe:

That this House, having considered the views of the people of Hong Kong as set out in the reports of the Assessment Office and the Independent Monitoring Team published in White Paper, Cmnd. 9407, approved Her Majesty's Government's intention to sign the agreement on the future of Hong Kong negotiated with the Chinese Government, which was published in White Paper, Cmnd. 9352.

The debate lasted from 6 p.m. until nearly midnight. Denis Healey, as Shadow Foreign and Commonwealth Secretary, led for the Opposition; he expressed some criticisms and concerns but also emphasised his hope that the House would accept the agreement and that it would then be signed. There was particularly strong support from Edward Heath who had come to know both China and Hong Kong well.

Simon Li and I listened to a large part of the debate from the gallery, especially pleased perhaps to hear Sir Paul Bryan, with his considerable experience of Hong Kong, say, 'I can find no better interpretation of the Hong Kong verdict than the last words of the report of the monitors, Mr Justice Simon Li Fook-sean and Sir Patrick Nairne, to whom we should be very grateful.'

He then quoted in full the final paragraph of our report. The debate was wound up by Mr Richard Luce, the Minister of State. The motion was carried without a division.

Much more could be said. Writing this account seventeen years after my assignment in Hong Kong, I can vividly recall my experience in a variety of ways: the feeling of isolation in my suite near the top of the sky-scraping Hilton Hotel, listening to the World Service on the radio, looking at Hong Kong TV, making notes on the day's work, writing to Penny; my keen interest in the views debated in the Legislative Council and in the questions raised by the different District Boards; the enjoyment of bathing and sketching in a Sunday boat party under the warm November sun; meeting the political barrister, Martin Lee (a passionate opponent of China's policies), Lord Wilberforce, [who was] passing through after visiting Taiwan (whose huge economic success he attributed to the good fortune of possessing no natural resources), Teddy Youde, the impressively calm and relaxed Governor, and the many Chinese, whose names I hardly grasped, whom I met in my daily visits – vigorous, cheerful, and acutely intelligent.

After my return I was asked to give several talks about Hong Kong to different audiences. At the end of what I had to say, I would express the general faith I had acquired in the future of the territory:

Hong Kong has come through troubles enough in the past – the Japanese occupation in the 1939–45 war, the large influx of Chinese refugees after 1949 and the severe riots in the 1960s. As I sat in the traffic jams on Wednesday evenings and Saturday mornings, the days on which as many people as possible in Hong Kong went to the race-course (celebrating its centenary in 1984), I used to reflect on the fact that one of the greatest gambling nations in the world was being confronted with one of the greatest political gambles that the world has seen. This year (of 1985) is the Year of the Ox in Hong Kong – an animal symbolic of the hard-working and indestructible character of the Hong Kong Chinese.

Nearly four years have passed since the last Governor, Christopher Patten, ceremoniously handed over Hong Kong to the People's Republic of China in the presence of the Prince of Wales. Mr Tung Chee-hwa, appointed by the Chinese, is serving as Chief Executive after a prominent career in shipping and many years of voluntary public service to Hong Kong. The Legislative Council is an entirely appointed body and the developments in democratic elections fostered by Chris Patten (and strongly criticised by China at the time) have been halted. Mr Martin Lee and the many who share his distrust of China have, however, behaved with restraint.

The economy has had its ups and downs, but is in general in good shape. China remains a country in which human rights receive little or no respect but on the basis of the established Basic Law it has carefully respected the agreement relating to the Special Administrative Region of Hong Kong.*

Early days still, but so far the great political gamble has succeeded.

---

* My father would have followed closely the protests in Hong Kong through 2019, and would have shared the worries of so many about the future of this special place.

REFLECTIONS: 1988–2013

Introduction

... and we ourselves shall be loved for a while and forgotten.
But the love will have been enough; all those impulses of love
return to the love that made them. Even memory is not necessary
for love. There is a land of the living and a land of the dead and
the bridge is love, the only survival, the only meaning.

Closing words of Thornton Wilder's
The Bridge of San Luis Rey, 1927
Commonplace book (second), unnumbered entry

Following the Mastership at St Catherine's, my father's working
life became less strenuous and time increased for family, travel,
writing and painting. He did take on a few new commitments,
including in 1991 becoming the first chair of the Nuffield Council
on Bioethics for a five-year term. Looking back at the key questions of those years, he wrote, 'Public policy has been developing
slowly while genetic research races on. But how far have screening
programmes been developed? Have the recommended ethical safe-
guards and procedures been adopted? . . . Impossible to know;
perhaps still premature to ask.' Later in a report he emphasises
that influencing government through the council's independent
working groups of experts, set up for particular topics, was the
most effective way of changing national policy.

Even before chairing the Commission on the Conduct of Referendums in 1996, he wrote to *The Times* on 12 May 1994 (just

before the formal establishment of James Goldsmith's Referendum Party) setting out his concerns, and focusing on three issues – the 'terms of the referendum question', whether a simple majority should determine the 'result of the referendum' and how voters could be advised with 'factual information' – which indicate 'the special problems involved if a Cabinet has divided views'.* Although the 1997 Scotland and Wales referendums did not follow the advice of the commission he had chaired, the setting up of the Electoral Commission in 2000, after Lord Neill's report on standards in public life, has produced a system of oversight, though concerns about public information and funding remain.†

My father helped lead the campaign for women to become full members of the Joint Universities Club (finally enacted in February 1996), given it was the chosen location for working lunches for much of his life and he had long wanted it to change. In the arts he was closely involved with the Oxford Museum of Modern Art (now Modern Art Oxford) as a trustee, then as Chair of the Advisory Board from 1988; and then President from 1998 (after my brother Andrew was appointed as director). He was also a trustee of the energetic and successful Oxford School of Drama.

Giving advice took up more time in later years, sometimes within the family, but increasingly across a spectrum of public life; and he accepted taking part in occasional 'hypotheticals' on television. An informal memo to Tessa Jowell (a connection from her

---

* Sir James Goldsmith was a businessman and politician who campaigned in the years following the Maastricht Treaty of 1992 for Britain to leave the European Union and to test the view of the British electorate through a new referendum. In 1994 he was elected to represent a French constituency as a Member of the European Parliament, and he founded and financed the Referendum Party but unsuccessfully contested a British parliamentary seat at the 1997 general election. The Party disbanded later that same year, after Goldsmith's death.

† The Electoral Commission provides independence from government which was the most important recommendation of the 1996 commission; it also provides independent oversight of the processes of a referendum, including how a referendum question is framed and what information is provided to voters. However, as my father predicted, keeping track on what is appropriate information, and keeping expenditure within given limits, has proved very challenging.

work at the Joseph Rowntree Foundation who became a friend) written two days after Labour's landslide election victory in 1997, offers guidance for a new minister.* After emphasising some key points of procedure, and close reliance on a good private secretary, he includes a practical tip that: 'a good driver of your own is an invaluable asset – as is the ability to work without difficulty on papers in a car . . . you will spend quite a large part of your life stuck in traffic'. 'Much of this memo', he ends, 'may strike you as Blinding Glimpses of the Obvious.'

Painting remained important even when arthritic pain and physical restrictions made writing difficult. He was still full of remarkable spirit. Towards the end of his second commonplace book, he includes (twice) the lines from Dr Iannis in *Captain Corelli's Mandolin* by Louis de Bernières (1994), 'Love itself is what is left over when being in love has burned away. Your mother and I had it, we had roots that grew towards each other under-ground, and when all the pretty blooms had fallen from our branches we found that we were one tree and not two.'

As almost his last entry my father included a remark by Jackie Astor: 'The good thing about dying is that you don't have to pack.'†

SN

---

* This may in effect have been a supplement to the editorial he wrote in the spring of 1997, for *Public Policy and Administration* journal, titled 'The Next Government – Agenda for the Civil Service'. In 2012, Tessa Jowell referred to my father as her 'mentor'.

† Quoted in his obituary, 'The Hon Sir John Astor', *The Times*, 12 September 2000, p. 25.

23

Novembers – *1988: Yew Tree*

NOVEMBER 1988

As I approached the age of sixty-seven, I retired from [*the Master-ship of St Catherine's*] College at the end of Trinity Term, 1988. We went on holiday, once again, in October, renting a small house in a village near Siena. The holiday did not prove trouble-free: a sudden ferry strike at Dover and an anxious drive to Calais in order to be in time to load the car on to the train for Nice; the need to fetch all our water for the rented house; the breakdown of the Ford Fiesta and the problem of repair where no English was understood or spoken; the break-in of the car outside our hotel in Florence and the consequent pack of problems; and, on return to Nice, the diffi-culty of finding where to load the car at the station. But nevertheless it was a superb holiday. As we sat, glass of wine in hand, on the terrace of the house, watching the lights go on in Siena as dusk fell across the Tuscany landscape, I felt at peace: no job to return to, no personal responsibility for 'keeping a show on the road', genuine retirement ahead at last – living quietly at Yew Tree, Chilson, just outside Charlbury, from the beginning of November.

It has not turned out to be quite like that. Busy days have remained the driving force for Penny and me, while the months pass more quickly with age. But the month of November no long claims the special place it had reserved for itself in the chronicle of my life – from 1940 to 1988. As I walk on alone down the road to the Evenlode bridge, I continue to reflect on those other

The Methodist Chapel, Chilson, Christmas card, 1986.

Novembers in other times, at other moments, in other places, and with other hopes, joys, fears – with always the unexpected round the next corner. I find it hard to believe that such a variety of experience can have been mine. I am left with a momentary sense of gloom: the thought perhaps of fewer Novembers to come or simply the chill of the November evening across the empty landscape?

I had recently been seeing Charles Wrinch again, whom I had known as the most inspired teacher of English at Radley. He was now ninety-three and near death in a residential home at Shipton-under-Wychwood. I asked him what poets had written about the month of November. He instantly mentioned Robert Bridges. Perhaps he was remembering these lines [*from 'November' published in* New Poems, *1899*]:

> The lonely season in lonely lands, when fled
> Are half the birds, and mists lie low, and the sun
> Is rarely seen, nor strayeth far from his bed;
> The short days pass unwelcomed one by one.

The words reflect rather well the mood of the evening between Chilson and the Evenlode. But they do not reflect my own mood of today. The 'captains and the kings' have now departed from my life, and I am not looking for similar events or occasions to those of the past in whatever Novembers lie ahead. I am where I wish to be, trying to live as I wish to live. I am happy and secure in a partnership of love with Penny, a partnership coincidentally established in Cornbury Park on a bright November afternoon more than half a century ago.

24

The National Health Service: Reflections on a Changing Service, 1988

*Excerpt from a lecture given at Green College, Oxford,
25 January 1988**

I was a short-stay patient at the Department of Health and Social Security, unexpectedly admitted to the Elephant and Castle in autumn 1975 after over twenty-five years elsewhere in Whitehall. My reactions to it were a mix of admiration and concern – particularly concern at the extent to which our finest public service was in difficulties, some of them of its own making.

LAUNCHING OF THE SERVICE

The political architect of the National Health Service, Aneurin Bevan, could not have foreseen all the difficulties; but he forecast their impact. In March 1948 he warned the Institute of Almoners:

> After the new Service is introduced, there will be a cacophony of complaints. The newspapers will be full of them ... I am sure that some doctors will make some irate speeches ... What the Health

---

* A longer version of this lecture was given on 17 April 1988, as the Jephcott Lecture at the Royal Society of Medicine, and published as 'The National Health Service – a Grand Design in Distress', in the *Journal of the Royal Society of Medicine* in 1989.

Service is actually to do ... is to put a megaphone in the mouth of every complainant, so that he will be heard all over the country.

In recent months Bevan's 'megaphone' has become deafening. And the loudest complaints have come from within the Health Service, expressing the frustration of professionals convinced that they could do more and better if they had larger resources. It is relevant to recall some more words of Bevan, speaking to the National Association of Maternity and Child Welfare Centres on the birth of the NHS:

> The new Health Service has been having a most uneasy gestation and a very turbulent birth, but all prodigies behave like that ... This Service must always be changing, growing, and improving; it must always appear to be inadequate. This is the answer I make to some of the Jeremiahs and defeatists who have said to me: 'Why start this Service when we are short of so many things.'

Bevan himself soon learned the truth of his forecast of 'inadequacy' – the initial experience of 'infinite demand, finite resources'. I am convinced that his assertion that the 'Service must always be changing, growing, and improving' represents the challenge and hope to which the NHS must respond if it is to survive as a public service.

CHANGING, GROWING, AND IMPROVING

But how drastic should change be? There is right-wing pressure for a fundamental reassessment of the entire concept of a comprehensive health service free at the point of access. *The Times* has described the Health Service as 'the one great unreformed British institution'. *The Sunday Times* insisted last December that 'tinkering will not do. Forty years on it is time to create a new Health Service to meet the needs of the next forty years.'

But the radical critics appear to forget that ever since the major reorganisation of 1973–4 the NHS has been subjected to constant changes and to the thorough review of a royal commission. It is doubtful whether it should stand for, or can stand, any further large change of organisational structure. I am also sceptical about the wisdom or practicability of fundamental change where many of the critics are now looking – the health service's tax-funded system of financing. As the Royal Commission on the NHS reported in 1979: 'We were not convinced that the claimed advantages of insurance finance, or substantial increases in revenue from charges, would outweigh their undoubted disadvantages in terms of equity and administrative costs.'

The increase since then in the numbers of the unemployed and the elderly reinforce that judgement. The experience of the United States and Western Europe shows the high cost of both medical care and administration in an insurance-based system. A related judgement of the Royal Commission also remains valid: 'No method of financing a part of the national expenditure as large and as politically sensitive as the Health Service was likely to remove it from government influence.'

Whatever change may be made to the NHS we cannot contemplate taking out of politics a service that touches directly on every constituent in Britain. In short, I am convinced that it will be best both for patients and the Health Service to continue to live with the basic organisation and financial structure as it is.

So where do we look for honey?*

There is a widespread cry for more taxpayers' money. And the Government may yet decide to accompany further measures for improvement and change with more generous funding. That may be essential or at least politically unavoidable. I do not know. It is difficult for anyone outside the NHS to know the extent to which it is a crisis of resources rather than a crisis of management. I am convinced, however, that more money on its own will not resolve the major problems.

---

* As far as I can guess my father's use of the word 'honey' is a humorous reference to Winnie the Pooh's endless search; and therefore chimes with the point below that money alone would not be enough to 'resolve the major problems' in the Health Service.

But, recognising its formidable range of problems, how can the Health Service respond to the Bevan imperative of 'changing, growing, and improving' without radical or far-reaching change or reform?

My own answers or reflections relate to three aspects: relations with the public and patients; links with private medicine and local authorities; and cooperation within the NHS.

RELATIONS WITH PUBLIC AND PATIENTS

My first reflection may appear naïve. The NHS must gradually effect a major change in the public perception of the service. It should devote less time to looking upwards to the government that feeds it and more time to looking outward to the public it serves.

The NHS is, for most people, the most important public service. But no public service thinks less about the public than the NHS. The public, as patients, tend to be too subservient to those in the NHS who treat them. The public, as a pressure group, know too little about the Health Service's priority problems. The public, as individuals, are too careless about their own health. The NHS today needs a public with a much better understanding of what the NHS can do and what it cannot do.

Above all, there is insufficient understanding that the most serious difficulties are in the hospitals, largely reflecting the problems of clinical successes. We are allowed to assume that the limits of the comprehensive service are boundless and that new clinical benefits can quickly be available to all.

As the difficulties have increased the media have increased the opportunities for public discussion. But, fairly or unfairly, the impression remains that the Health Service 'goes public' only when it is on the defensive or has specific information to communicate. Public debate has been predominantly political and there has been no sustained information strategy conducted by health authorities. The media channels should be used more positively. In addition, well-organised 'open days', posters and leaflets in surgeries and health centres, and video films in public places should be used to educate local people about their own local health service.

Most doctors are outstandingly conscientious in enabling patients to understand what is wrong with them and what can, or cannot, be done to treat them. But as I recall from my reports from the Health Service Commissioner, of medical cases coming into the courts, and of evidence I have seen as an adviser to the Freedom of Information Campaign, the active involvement of the patient in his or her own treatment, and in the problems it can present, is sometimes indefensibly neglected.

The more rapid turnover of patients, the intensity of hospital and clinical activity, and the consequent pressures on doctors and nurses can contribute to that. I hope that partnership with the patient has an adequate place in medical education today. Hospital authorities should look afresh at patients' handbooks, and they should review through the eyes of patients and visitors the waiting area of casualty departments – the threshold to the NHS – where many people receive their first impressions.

Complementary to all this is the promotion of a healthier life-style. The opening clause of the NHS Act places on the Secretary of State the duty to promote in England and Wales 'a comprehensive Health Service designed to secure improvement in the physical and mental health of the people of those countries'. It is a duty that cannot be regarded as effectively discharged. During my DHSS year there was no satisfactory resolution of the political and economic dilemmas presented by the products of the tobacco and drinks industries. The Government's recent and controversial White Paper *Promoting Better Health* and the role of the new special Health Education Authority reflect good intentions. But I believe that much heavier taxation of tobacco and alcohol and much stronger support for both from government and doctors will be needed if NHS consumers are to think less about what curative medicine must do for them and more about their own responsibility for themselves.

I share the view of Sir Roy Griffiths expressed in 1987 that 'the

interests of the consumer have to be central to every decision'.*
That is the key to promoting a responsible partnership between
the Health Service and a better informed public.

LINKS WITH PRIVATE MEDICINE AND LOCAL AUTHORITIES

A better informed public is likely, however, to be more critical of
the service if it fails to make management changes or to introduce
new arrangements that may increase the overstretched resources of
health care.

Many NHS patients now undergo surgery in private hospitals;
many health authorities contract out their long-term care of
patients; pay-bed revenue is keeping open some NHS wards; about
a tenth of the population now choose to have private health insurance. A mixed economy of health care now exists. What are needed
are a constructive partnership between public and private resources,
a fuller public understanding of how they complement each other,
and conditions established which will effectively safeguard the
interest of those for whom the NHS is the only health service
available.

The last point is of great importance. Private sector medicine,
though relatively small, is growing. It must not rob the NHS of
essential nursing staff nor detract from the responsibilities of NHS
consultants. Patients who wish, and can afford, to see the consultant they want, or to undergo NHS surgery on the date they choose
should be able to do so provided only that it does not put at a
disadvantage waiting-list patients who cannot pay.

It is good that the study by Professor Alain Enthoven of Stanford
University, *Reflections on the Management of the NHS*, published
in 1985, is being further considered. He argued that the Health
Service should buy acute care services from the private sector when
it could get them cheaper than in NHS hospitals. But to apply such

---

* Sir Roy Griffiths was a British businessman engaged in 1983 by the prime minister,
Margaret Thatcher, to produce a report on the management of the National Health
Service. He went on to become deputy chairman of the NHS Management Board
and an adviser to the Government on the Health Service.

competitive criteria as a general practice will require a much fuller and more reliable costing system than exists at present.

The problems of funding have been an obstacle to close co-operation between health and local authorities in community care. Joint financing complemented a valuable feature of the previous structural organisation – the 'co-terminosity' of area health author-ities and local authorities. But few district health authorities are coterminous, and local authorities have tended to have conflicting priorities at the very time when community care for the mentally ill, disabled people and the elderly was being more widely intro-duced. If that policy is to be effectively implemented I believe that the division of responsibilities and the machinery of cooperation between health and local authorities must be improved.

COOPERATION WITHIN THE NHS

My last reflection derives from one of my earliest impressions of the NHS – the extent of the critical distrust that appeared to exist between every level from the DHSS to the hospital.

Twelve years ago there were aggravating factors which differed from those of today. The NHS was convalescing from its first major reorganisation, which had been too cumbersome in structure and too expensive in bureaucracy. A change of government had led to a recurrence of scepticism about the role of the regions and severe inflation had caused a sharp reduction in annual funding after a long period of growth. As another former Minister of Health, Iain Macleod, used to say, 'Money is the root of all pro-gress.'

But the difficulties of the NHS never seemed to me an adequate explanation of its flair for 'rubbishing' itself in public. Clinicians openly criticise the numbers of administrators; administrators respond by criticising waste by clinicians. District teams criticise regional teams and vice versa.

The criticisms were often well-founded, though that is not the point. And the DHSS had its own difficulties. Ministers of both parties always wished to delegate more to the health authorities, but they were compelled, chiefly by parliamentary pressure, to centralise and intervene. A gradual trend in that direction has been consolidated in the establishment of the Health Service Supervisory Board and the NHS Management Board.

What is still needed is a realistic recognition of things as they are. The reality is interdependence – between the Government, on which the NHS depends for its funding, and the health authorities, on which the Government depends for the delivery of services. There should now be a general acceptance of an indissoluble marriage between Whitehall and the NHS – exposed like other marriages to occasional conflict – but a marriage which after forty years should have settled into a relationship of mutual understanding and sympathy.

The philosophy of interdependence needs to be positively promoted between all levels of the Health Service and between the wide range of professionals and trade unions working within it . . . The NHS is the largest glasshouse in the world; it risks its own survival if it cannot resist throwing stones.

I remain a firm advocate of further evolution within the present organisational and financial structure of the NHS. There is still much that can be done to improve the operation and management of the Health Service if there is a positive vision and firm direction on the part of ministers and the health authorities.

The old saying goes that a man grows into his face. After forty years the NHS has grown into its own face. Despite all the problems of policy and finance and of difficulties that seemed as serious as those of today, I look back to an impressively caring face: the face of a health service still dominated by a commitment to aspirations and ideals unequalled in the world. This is a unique strength from which the Government should take heart.

25

Potential Use of Referendums, 1996

Introduction to a Public Policy Seminar at Queen Mary Westfield,
3 December 1996, following publication of the Report of the
Commission on the Conduct of Referendums

Twenty-five years ago I had never heard of referendums. If anyone
had mentioned them, I would probably have said rather priggishly
(and, as I now know, wrongly): 'Don't you mean referenda?' And
I was not particularly conscious of something else which was, and
is, rather more important – Parliamentary sovereignty. But two
years later, in 1973, I was appointed second permanent secretary
in the Cabinet Office with responsibilities relating directly to our
recent entry into the European Community. Through the fits and
starts of uncertain politics, I found myself under a Labour government, playing a major part in renegotiating our terms of entry and
– that done — in organising the first national referendum relating
to our membership of the Common Market.

That referendum, in Lord Callaghan's famous phrase, was 'a life
raft' into which a divided Labour Cabinet chose to climb but there
was, to say the least, little enthusiasm for it as a constitutional
device. And the principal reason for that was Parliamentary sovereignty. In the final volume of his memoirs, *Final Term*, Harold
Wilson gives an account of his announcement to Parliament on 23
January 1975 regarding his government's decision to hold a referendum. Mr Heath, still then Leader of the Opposition, was quick
to point out that 'it cannot be binding on Members of the House

of Commons'. And he went on to emphasise that 'a major constitutional issue was at stake . . . and that Parliament must decide whether this constitutional innovation should take place'. Harold Wilson agreed, saying that it was 'a very special situation not to be taken as a precedent'.

Civil servants like to have precedents to guide them. As we set about organising the conduct of the 1975 referendum, we wished that we had more to guide us than the procedure and machinery for our general and local elections and a quick survey of referendums across the world in countries different from ours, and with entrenched constitutional rules which we do not possess. So, under the skilful political leadership of Mr Edward Short, we had to manage the first national referendum ad hoc, believing that it was not only the first, but also probably the last, referendum we were likely to hold.* At the first sitting of Parliament after the referendum, Sir John Eden asked Mr Wilson: 'Will the Prime Minister keep to his determination not to repeat the constitutional experiment of the Referendum?' And the Prime Minister replied: 'I can give the Right Honourable Member the assurance he seeks.'

But four years later, in 1979, two further referendums were held on devolution to Scotland and Wales. As it turned out, the results caused deep disappointment across the Border and had disagreeable consequences for the Labour Government. But irrespective of the political impact at the time, the fact was that a further precedent for holding a referendum had been set – whatever ministers might choose to say about the avoidance of precedents, and however protective of Parliamentary sovereignty MPs might seek to be. It now seems evident that the earlier Parliamentary reservations have been largely set aside, at least for major constitutional issues on which the electorate is entitled to a direct expression of view. And the reality today, seventeen years from 1979, is that all three main parties have made commitments to the holding of referendums; and

---

* Edward Short MP, later Lord Glenamara CH PC, was in 1975 Leader of the House of Commons and Lord President of the Council, presiding over the Privy Council.

a Referendum Party has been created. The Labour Party in particular, if it were in government, would be committed to giving high priority to various referendums – devolution, once again, to Scotland and Wales and voting reform; and then later economic and monetary union and, very possibly, the English Regions and London, and maybe Northern Ireland.

This does not mean that Parliamentary sovereignty has been thrown out of the Westminster window. We should assume that referendums would continue to depend on Parliamentary legislation; that Parliament would expect to have the last word on the exact wording of the question (even Sir James Goldsmith acknowledges that); and that it would remain open to Parliament to reject the referendum result. But, that provided referendums were conducted efficiently and fairly, and their results accepted in the country as legitimate, the government of the day could be expected to accept the result, and Parliament in the event to follow suit. On that Parliamentary occasion of 23 January 1975, Harold Wilson, as prime minister, expressed the view, difficult to deny, that 'Members would not vote against a clear statement of the nation's feeling through a referendum'.

It was the importance of ensuring the essential condition of the efficient and fair conduct of referendums that led to the joint initiative of the Electoral Reform Society and the Constitution Unit in setting up the Commission on the Conduct of Referendums. Our terms of reference, put briefly, were to prepare for the possibility of referendums in the future by examining the problems involved in their conduct, and by setting out organisational and administrative guidelines. The commission was entirely independent of Whitehall and Westminster. It had no political mandate. Our members were chosen for their experience and expertise.

We were strictly neutral as a body on whether referendums should be held and on what their result should be if they were held. But we were strongly united in the view that – with the prospect of several referendums ahead, and on very different issues – there was an urgent need to establish guidelines for their conduct which would not prejudice Parliamentary sovereignty and would be efficient, fair and consistent, and accepted as such by all political parties and the electorate.

Let me highlight what we have found – the message we wish to convey to the Government, to the political parties, and to all of us, the voters. First, the initiative for holding referendums will continue to lie with the Government and Parliament. But our central, or key, recommendation is that their conduct should be entrusted to a statutory independent body accountable to Parliament. Governments will be seeking to achieve a particular result from some referendums, especially if they are held at the end of exacting negotiations (e.g. in the European Union) and after a full debate in Parliament. In other referendums (e.g. relating to voting reform) MPs and political parties may well have a strong personal interest in the outcome. Referendums should never appear to be a device used by governments for partisan political purposes or take on the character of a plebiscite. I am not suggesting that the ad hoc referendums held in the 1970s were in any way lacking legitimacy. What I am saying is that if further referendums lie ahead, entrusting their conduct to a body *outside* the Government would ensure the maximum confidence in the legitimacy of their results.

Secondly, what would this independent body do? Our report sets out twenty guidelines . . . Some involve political decisions which only the Government can take: e.g. whether a referendum should be advisory, or whether there should be a set threshold of votes to establish a clear majority (there was none set in 1975, but 40 per cent of the electorate was imposed by Parliament for Scotland in 1979). But most of the guidelines involve functions or tasks for which the independent body or commission would be responsible.

To mention the most important ones:

(1)   All voting households should receive a publicly funded leaflet of information; and the independent commission should provide that and should, in particular, ensure that they receive Yes and No cases clearly and equitably prepared.

(2) The referendum question needs to be short and simple. While the final wording should be settled by Parliament the independent commission could advise the Government. It is crucial to avoid bias; a factor that underlines the importance of the commission's information role in the weeks before the poll.

(3) Campaigning organisations, bringing together campaigning groups on each side of the referendum question, and enabling political parties to stand aside, can help promote public debate (as they did in 1975). The independent commission may help such organisations to come together. It would be able to handle the fair distribution of any financial assistance by the Government. It could ensure equitable access to the broadcast media. This role could be particularly important since, as the commission judged, and as government judged at the time of the 1975 and 1979 referendums, any effective control of total campaign expenditure would be impracticable.

(4) Finally, the independent commission would organise the poll, the count, the announcement of the result – the role which the Chief Counting Officers undertook in the previous referendums.

Referendums are now prominent on the political agenda. They will require efficient, fair and consistent rules and guidelines. An independent, statutory body should be established to apply or monitor those guidelines. That body could be an independent Referendum Commission or its functions could be exercised within the ambit of an Electoral Commission. That would be a political choice for a future government.

I am not making a political point if I remind the seminar that if the present government were re-elected there could be *no* referendums in the years immediately ahead . . . Be that as it may, the main aim of the Electoral Reform Society and the Constitution

Unit has been to anticipate an important need which may arise. I believe that the commission's report . . . will meet that need.

I was much encouraged to receive a letter last week from Lord Allen of Abbeydale, to whom I had sent a copy of the Report. He was appointed as Chief Counting Officer for the European Community Referendum of 1975 – a daunting task which broke new ground. His letter said:

> Looking back, it was one of the most interesting assignments I ever had. We had to create our own procedures, and I used to lie awake at night thinking of the things that could go wrong. In the event, it all worked, and we were able to put the papers away and turn to other things. Future operators will now have a lot more to help them!

As an old soldier of the 1975 campaign, I say 'Amen to that'.

26

Handwriting for Life, 1997

Written for the Society for Italic Handwriting Journal*

A few years ago an old friend gave me his copy of a book which I now treasure. It is a bound edition of two tracts on handwriting, edited seventy years ago for the Society for Pure English by the poet Robert Bridges; both are illustrated with plates. 'Two of the plates,' said my friend, 'show the hands of the Nairne family. I think that your family should have my copy.' I was delighted to find facsimile letters from my father to his first cousin and from the cousin to Robert Bridges.

Was it nature or nurture that stimulated my lifelong interest in handwriting? Probably both, but nurture the more important. My father's family had a talent for drawing and painting, and I have inherited a share of it; but that would have come to nothing if I had not been encouraged to work at it and been influenced by the example of my father and his artistic friends. ⸫

My father wrote to his children when they were away at school, and his hand was an attractive model. I never tried to copy his hand – he never suggested that I should do so . . . I was influenced in my early years at school by an exacting teacher who wrote

---

* Also published on the Society for Italic Handwriting website (17 July 2009).

herself in a simple, round, neat hand and did her best to make her pupils learn to form each word carefully and clearly. Not a bad start for the acquisition of a craft.

It was my appointment to the Admiralty on entering the Civil Service in 1947 which introduced me to the craft of handwriting in my working life – and, in particular, to the italic hand. In 1948 I met Alfred Fairbank, then a senior executive officer and civil assistant to the director of dockyards, and encountered impressive examples of his italic hand in routine Admiralty files. He worked in the Admiralty offices at Bath, where I also met Dr Arthur Osley, a close friend of Fairbank. From them I learned that the prime value of the italic hand – though an elegant (in Fairbank's famous phrase) 'dance of the pen' – lay in its being the fastest and clearest mode of handwriting.

Shortly after our first meeting in December 1948 Fairbank wrote me a note which indicates the influence he had on some Admiralty colleagues. I acquired Fairbank's Dryad writing cards, his King Penguin *A Book of Scripts* and his revised *A Handwriting Manual*. Thus inspired and instructed, I set about reforming my own hand: with daily opportunities at my desk for practising the craft and improving my skill during my thirty-four years in Whitehall.

But I have never been able to write as well as I would wish. I am still always hoping that a new pen or a changed nib will enable me to perform better; I was encouraged when Fairbank told me that he frequently swapped pens . . . I seize on each Society journal as a fresh source of inspiration and admire the examples of hands much better than mine. I continue to enjoy the struggle of trying to do better myself – hoping that arthritic fingers may not prove a terminal handicap in the years ahead.

Alfred Fairbank, in the introduction to his *Handwriting Manual*, is fairly down to earth: 'Handwriting is a functional thing, intended for communicating and recording thought . . . How satisfying when something ordinary and commonplace is raised towards the beautiful. Just as speech can be a delightful vehicle of words and thoughts, so too can handwriting; and so language is served.'

at C/o Mrs. Hughes
Bettws
Parrog — Newport
14. 8. 73

Darling Fiona,

    Let me say again how
DELIGHTED I am that you secured a 2nd.
Warmest congratulations. You made a splendid
thing of your Oxford time. I am full of
admiration. And (who knows, dear girl?)
it might even prove of some practical use
— if, say, you wanted to turn a penny with
a little A level or Oxford entry tutoring.
I enclose a thin book bought to mark
the announcement in 'The Times'.

    I write at 7.25 pm. We were due to meet
your elder sister at Fishguard at 10 pm.; she
has rung from Paddington to say that she
has missed the train: I must now drive to
Carmarthen, an hour away, to meet her at 9.30
pm. I'm sucking my teeth (those new ones

P.S. Did you see the experts (but pompous!) review of Vanessa Jones's acting in 'R + J' in last week's Sunday T.'?

A letter to daughter Fiona, 1973.

I was telling you about) with irritation. But all I can do is to say cheerfully that I was put out, but that it doesn't matter. And, of course, it won't matter. But, at this moment, after a round of golf, a bathe, 2 watercolours & the fits & starts of Nairne family life, on one of the hottest days of the year, I'd give a great deal not to have to drive along the Pembrokeshire roads on my own to Carmarthen. The rest of the family will be watching the fireworks... But it's Excellent that K. comes tn.

We have had the most dazzling weather so far. Cloudless skies since Sunday. I've nearly finished all my Cobalt. JAM had a pony lesson this morning, preparing for a pony trek on Friday. Andrew felt the pony was practising him in turning right (left & stopping, not vice versa. M. has her friend Sally, who (like the Japanese) is flower-like, a passive specimen of nature more than a member of the human race. Mummy is looking wonderfully sun-burnt. I'm trying to forget about Europe, but not quite succeeding. Thank you so much for yr. of Tarbert. Much love to you both. Don't let Romans demoralise you! Daddy —

27

James–Jan: A Triumph of Courage, 1996/2006

*Drafted in the year of Jan Morris's seventieth birthday in
October 1996 and expanded into a longer version in 2006*

An Admiral of the Fleet and a Chiswick antenatal clinic brought
James (later Jan) and myself together. It was 1951. My wife, Penny,
met James's wife, Elizabeth, in a local antenatal clinic and it
emerged that we were close neighbours in Hammersmith Terrace.
The wives brought the four of us together one evening and James
and I met – I nearly thirty, a junior civil servant in the Admiralty
and James, some five years younger, on the staff of *The Times*. It
was the start of a long friendship.

At the outset our friendship was fostered in an unexpected way.
We found that we shared a fascination for a sailor who had
become a powerful and famous personality in the previous century,
Jacky Fisher – Admiral of the Fleet Lord Fisher. I do not think that
I began to understand Morris's curious obsession with Fisher until
I read Jan's book, *Fisher's Face*, published in 1995. But the extraordinary Admiral may well have come up at an early – perhaps our
first – meeting when I was talking about my job in the Admiralty.
I suspect that I would have mentioned my small collection of Fisher's books and papers and have shown off a piece of vintage Fisher,
which an Admiralty colleague had generously given me on his
retirement. This was a Fisher letter, dated 22 September 1914, to
a junior Admiralty minister, written in his large domineering handwriting, signed (in words he often chose to use) 'Yours till Hell

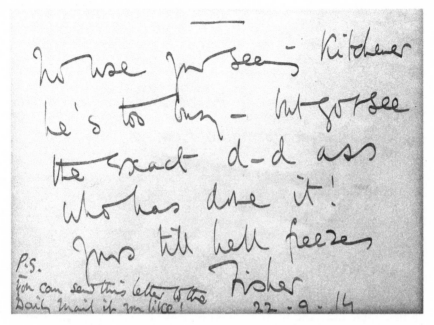

Detail of a 1914 letter by Admiral Lord Fisher, belonging to Pat.

freezes'. Another of Fisher's favourite phrases was 'Think in Oceans'. That suited James who gave me the immediate impression of having a worldwide outlook appropriate to a future foreign correspondent.

I have surfed the large Morris collection on our shelves – *Coast to Coast, Coronation Everest, Pax Britannica, Oxford, Sultan in Oman, Venice* and *Spain* are just a beginning and I cannot be sure of their order – quickly starting to doubt whether the dates of publication were a reliable guide to the letters and cards from James–Jan that fell out as I took the books from the shelves – intermittent tokens, over many years, of a friendship sustained. Did the dates of the correspondence mark year and place? Not so. Scarcely a letter nor a card carry a date, and the postmarks are faint and faded.

One early letter is dated: an air-letter, written on '15 June '53', from 'a hotel of unparalleled awfulness' in Kathmandu – written, at a moment of rejoicing for both James and Elizabeth, to congratulate us on the birth of our son. But it was, of course, the messages, not the dates, that mattered. A card from the historic Raffles Hotel, Singapore, simply saying 'Where else?'; a card, post-marked 1990, wishing us 'a smashing *fin de siècle*'; a card criticis-ing my 'whistlephobia'; a letter ending 'I'm off to Canada (on Imperial business)'; a letter about Hong Kong, concluding 'I shall look out for you in Statue Square in 1997'; a card from 'the 2nd Severn Crossing', after unexpectedly seeing me in a television pro-gramme: 'What a delight to find you in my lonely hotel room here last night . . .'; finally a card remarking, 'What a long time you, Fisher and I have known each other!'

I could not, however, have foreseen the character of his first exploit abroad.

I have been reading again *Coronation Everest* [1958], James's gripping account of the ascent of Everest at the end of May over fifty years ago. He had had none of the exacting experience of mountains of Brigadier John Hunt's carefully picked team but he tells how he had succeeded in completing the exhausting climb to Camp IV. Here he had joined Hunt and the other expedition mem-bers anxiously waiting for news of the success or failure of Hillary and Tenzing, the two men chosen to make the final ascent to the summit.* James vividly described their sudden appearance.

> I rushed to the door of the tent, and there emerging from a little gully, not more than five hundred yards away, were four worn figures in windproof clothing . . . I could not see the climbers very clearly, for the exertion of running had steamed up my goggles . . . But I watched them approaching dimly, with never a sign of success or failure, like drugged men . . . Soon I could not see a thing for the steam, so I pushed the goggles up from my eyes; and just as I recovered from the sudden dazzle of the snow I caught sight of George Lowe, leading the

---

* Brigadier John Hunt, later Lord Hunt, KG, CBE, DSO, was a British Army officer best known as the leader of the 1953 British Expedition to Mount Everest. Tenzing Norgay GM OSN, often referred to as Sherpa Tenzing, was an outstanding Nepali-Indian Sherpa mountaineer who died in 1986. With Tenzing at the summit was Sir Edmund Hillary KG ONZ KBE, an outstanding New Zealand explorer and mountaineer.

party down the hill. He was raising his arm and waving as he walked! It was thumbs up! Everest was climbed! Hillary brandished his ice-axe in weary triumph; Tenzing slipped suddenly sideways, recovered and shot us a brilliant white smile, and they were among us; back from the summit . . .

In the final chapter of *Coronation Everest* James wrote of his urgent and frightening descent of the mountain, motivated by a determination to get the news to London in time for the day of the Queen's Coronation. It was the afternoon of 30 May 1953, the day after the summit had been reached. There were only three full days to the Coronation and James wrote:

I realised that I must start down the mountain again that very afternoon . . . This time there would be no night's rest at Camp III. I must go straight down the ice-fall to Base Camp that evening. My body, still aching from the upward climb in the morning, did not like the sound of this at all . . .

James accepted Michael Westmacott's generous offer to accompany him and, reading his vivid account of the descent, it is hard to believe that he would have reached Base Camp when he did without Westmacott's support.*

The finale is vividly described. By the light of a flickering hurricane lamp, James tapped out a coded message on his typewriter: 'Snow conditions bad stop advanced base abandoned yesterday stop awaiting improvement.' Which, being interpreted, meant: 'Summit of Everest reached on May 29 by Hillary and Tenzing'. James added two words: 'All well'.

A day or so later, spending the night in a village on his way to Kathmandu, James erected the aerial of his radio receiver and on the following morning – 2 June – the day of the Coronation – he heard the news that he had been hoping to hear.

---

* Michael Westmacott was a prominent British mountaineer. Educated at Radley College, he later became President of the Alpine Club.

A few crackles and hisses; and then the voice of an Englishman. Everest had been climbed, he said, The Queen had been given the news on the eve of the Coronation . . . This news of Coronation Everest (said that good man in London) had been first announced in a copyright dispatch in *The Times*.

More than fifty years of travel and adventure were to follow but I believe that this Everest achievement, complementary to that of the Expedition team, was Jan's 'Finest Hour'. She has demonstrated on many occasions the other outstanding qualities which have been uniquely hers – notably, a superb talent for writing, well beyond the normal ability of a good travel writer or a first-class professional journalist; and a capacity for making friendly and reassuring contact with whomever she meets, whether – to mention two perhaps surprising examples – a party of sherpas on the slopes of Everest or a group of slaves in the household of the Sultan of Muscat and Oman. But the quality which stands out in the Everest story and especially in the account of the descent from Camp IV is different. It was Jan's courage: courage of a particularly high order.

There have been many other occasions on which Jan's courage must have been put to the test in all her years of travel across the world. But I believe that there has been only one other experience which matched the Everest exploit in its demands on Jan's physical courage and spirit of determination. It was wholly different in kind from the experience of Everest. It took place in Casablanca where, in the summer of 1972, James became Jan.

Conundrum, published two years after Casablanca, tells the story.* The first words of the first chapter show what a long, and often painful, road it was to be from the beginning to the end: 'I was three or perhaps four years old when I realised that I had been born into the wrong body, and should really be a girl . . . What

---

* Jan Morris's *Conundrum* was the first book under her new name and gives a very moving account of what led to her decision to have a sex-change operation. Such an operation was at this point exceptional and previously much misunderstood.

triggered so bizarre a thought I have long forgotten, but the conviction was unfaltering from the start.'

That remarkable insight marked the first step on the long road to Casablanca. It is rather hard to believe that it was that small child who grew into a young officer serving briefly in a cavalry regiment and then, after Oxford, into *The Times* correspondent who carried down the mountain the news that Everest had been climbed.

Chapter 5 of *Conundrum* tells of 'the long, well-beaten, expensive and fruitless path of the Harley Street psychiatrists and sexologists'. 'None of them in those days,' Jan wrote, 'knew anything about the matter at all, though none of them admitted it.' Eventually she went to New York to see an endocrinologist, Dr Harry Benjamin, who emerged as the first person to understand something of her predicament. Jan quoted him as saying: 'If we cannot alter the conviction to fit the body, should we not, in certain circumstances, alter the body to fit the conviction?'

This was what James (as she still was) had hoped for, but he accepted Dr Benjamin's advice that to change the body in order to effect a sex change should be regarded as a last resort.

So where did my wife and I come in? Jan explained in *Conundrum* that, between 1964 and 1972, she swallowed at least 12,000 pills prescribed by Dr Benjamin and it must have been sometime towards the end of that span of years [*1967*] that we received an unexpected invitation to borrow the Morris home, Trefan, at Llanystumdwy, while James and Elizabeth were abroad. I could get away only at weekends, but Penny readily decided to stay for the fortnight with our three younger children.

I could not stay in anyone else's house without inspecting the books on the shelves, and especially the shelves of a library like James's. Reading, some years later, chapter 13 of *Conundrum*, I found that I had had the same experience as Mark Morris: 'My eldest son, Mark, tells me that he first guessed the truth by discovering in our library a shelf of books on trans-sexuality – carefully placed there, as it happened, so that he would guess.'

Photograph by Fiona from visit to Trefan, North Wales, summer 1967.

Could those books have been, at least partly, an explanation of our sudden invitation to be temporary tenants of the house? While on holiday in Wales a few years later we visited the Morris family for the day. James displayed some obvious physical changes which even our young children noticed. But not a word was said on either side. And we knew nothing later of James's visit to Casablanca in 1972.

Jan has written that everybody in her predicament knew of a Dr B in Casablanca and of his skill as a surgeon. She did not know his address and, in the relaxed Morris way, simply travelled to Casablanca and looked it up in the city's telephone directory. His clinic turned out to be in one of the grander modern parts of the city and Jan describes Dr B himself as 'exceedingly handsome' wearing 'a dark blue open-necked shirt, sports trousers and games shoes'. The doctor examined James, mentioned the matter of the fee and referred him to his receptionist who required payment of the whole fee in advance. James was conducted to his room by Dr B's wife, who combined a luxuriant caftan with a nurse's uniform.

She led him down a spiral staircase to the end room in a corridor of 'clinical austerity'.

Jan's description of what followed sounds distinctly alarming, more than enough to test any man's courage. But Jan wrote that she 'felt no tremor of fear'.

> It was dark by now, and the room was uninviting. Its lighting was dim, its floor was less than scrupulously clean, and its basin, I soon discovered, never had hot water. Outside the window I could hear a faint rumble of traffic, and more precise street noises from the alley below. Inside the clinic seemed to be plunged into a permanent silence, as though I was shut away and insulated from all other life – not far from the truth, either, for the bell did not work and there was no other patient on the floor. Nobody came. I sat on the bed in the silence and did *The Times* crossword puzzle: for if these circumstances sound depressing to you, alarming even, I felt in my mind no flicker of disconsolance, no tremor of fear, no regret and no irresolution. Powers beyond my control had brought me to room 5 at the clinic in Casablanca, and I could not have run away even if I had wished to.

It was the same spirit of determination and courage which had carried James down from Camp IV to Base Camp on Everest.

All went well with the operation. Jan remained for two weeks in the clinic, enduring a great deal of pain. But she described herself, and the other patients whom she now met, as 'gloriously happy . . . We felt that we had achieved fulfilment.'

This seems to reflect the same feeling of excitement and satisfaction which James had experienced nineteen years earlier on hearing on his radio the BBC announcement of the climbing of Everest.

Jan was still in pain and moved with difficulty when she flew back to London; then followed two further sessions of surgery. But Elizabeth welcomed her home 'as though nothing in particular had happened'; and what Jan described as 'a grand sense of euphoria' overcame her 'in the fulfilment of my life's desire . . . I knew for certain that I had done the right thing.'

What would Jacky Fisher have made of it all? Impossible to be sure, but he admired courage and he loved women. For once perplexed, he might have silently reflected on Jan's determination and achievement and simply muttered to himself, 'Fear God and Dreadnought'.

So back to Fisher: why this link between us? I do not share Jan's obsession with his face; it is Fisher's creative mind, administrative vigour and panache of phrase which have captivated me. But Jan has written words about Fisher that may be the key: the 'greatest of his gifts was an ageless genius for delight' and he 'played life as an artist might play it'. Likewise Jan herself. That has been captivating for me, keeping alight the friendship lit some forty-five years ago.

As for Penny and me, in reply to a letter of mine about *Conundrum*, Jan wrote in spring 1974 that it was good to know that our long friendship was 'unaffected even by this bizarre climacteric', adding that:

> . . . what I myself feel now is that, having achieved some sort of inner unity . . . I am now liberated to look for something else – as though I am now equipped for a new kind of life altogether! In this sense I suppose it is at-one-ment that I have somewhere at the back of my mind . . .

It was, as always from Jan, a modest statement. I would like to think that somewhere the trumpets sounded for her triumph of courage.

28

One Week in Autumn, 1998

Another summer gone and we were into an autumn of turbulent weather. Penny and I living happily and comfortably at Yew Tree, Chilson; golden wedding celebrations with the family, now twenty-four-strong, recently over; on the face of it a couple in retirement: in reality both constantly engaged in a variety of commitments. No week is entirely free of them unless we have planned to be away on holiday. In 1998 the commitments for one October week happened to be of special interest.

Charlbury Church, Oxfordshire, Christmas card, 1982.

Sunday October 11

As on most Sundays, to Charlbury Church for the family communion service at 09:45. We had been in the church on the previous evening. A fundraising concert for the renovation of the small and ancient Shorthampton Church, which lies between Chilson and Charlbury: the Capricio Players – Daphne Clark (wife of a retired judge) and Katherine Ellis (an academic music teacher), whom I was asked to introduce to the audience, opening their programme with a brilliant performance of a Mozart piano and violin sonata.

My feeling on Sunday mornings usually reflects that of Evelyn Waugh, writing in his diary on 3 January 1954: 'Church again. My prayer is only: '"Here I am again. Show me what to do: help me to do it."'

But this morning's service was different. Penny was preaching; I could look forward to an interesting theme well delivered. She preached on the theme of remembering. She held the attention of the congregation (and certainly mine); but as we drove home she remarked that she had the impression that I did not think very highly of the sermon. How could she sense that?

'Oh, no . . . I thought that it was good. It came across well.' A pause. 'I do, I suppose, think more highly of some of your sermons than of others.'

Not an entirely satisfactory reply. I always want to think well of my latest watercolour, though I am often reluctantly conscious that it is not as good as some of my others. Penny may well take a similar view of some of her sermons. She invites my comments and accepts with modesty and good temper what must sometimes be an irritating response. I have no right whatever to be critical. She gives splendid service to the Church, to the Oxford Diocese, and to a number of 'distance learning' students. I could never have foreseen that I would be married to a woman who would conduct services, preach from pulpits and this year have a successful book published on pastoral care, *When I Needed a Neighbour.**

---

* Penny Nairne, *When I Needed a Neighbour: Enabling Pastoral Care in the Local Church*, Marshall Pickering, London, 1998.

Monday October 12

Feel uneasy on waking. I was due to go to London in the afternoon
to hear Chris Patten speaking at the Royal Geographical Society
about China, Hong Kong and developments in South East Asia.*
Few occasions could be more interesting at the present time – the
position in Hong Kong a year after it had been reunited with
China and now the sudden, severe setbacks in the Far East financial markets. But, in looking forward to the evening, my thoughts
were tiresomely clouded by my long-standing claustrophobic dislike of being trapped in the middle of a row of seats in what I
foresaw would be the strange and crowded RGS lecture theatre.

That irrational feeling on Monday morning, something more
than a normal fit of nerves, was aggravated by the prospect of two
other daunting occasions – a commitment to address, on Thursday,
the Association of Conservative Peers on the conduct of referendums, and the first 'Sir Patrick Nairne Lecture' to be held in my
honour at St Catherine's College on Friday. Hard to explain why
such a psychological anxiety – though somewhat diminished over
the years – has persisted for half a century as a kind of irksome
'resident in the house', caused, I believe, by a particular experience
of being shelled in the war and aggravated by a period of incar-
ceration in the Civil Service Sanatorium at Benenden. My cousin,
Dr Erasmus Barlow, at one time a consultant psychiatrist, provided
some encouragement when I visited him many years ago at St
Thomas's. A phobia can rarely be cured: one must learn to
'manage' it.

Our close neighbours in Chilson, Nigel and Shane Winser, had
invited me to the RGS evening as their guest; he deputy director,
she head of information. Slight embarrassment on my side: the
papers had mentioned the future Patten event and one Sunday
afternoon I had asked Nigel across his garden wall what the theme
of the lecture would be. He immediately invited me to come as his

---

* The Royal Geographical Society was founded in 1830 and granted a Royal
Charter in 1859. Its present headquarters in Kensington Gore were opened in 1913
and extended in the interwar period to provide a 750-seat theatre which is used for
lectures of wide public interest.

guest and join Shane and himself for the dinner afterwards. When
I arrived at the RGS a crowd of people was shuffling into the
entrance and it took me a few minutes to spot Nigel. He and Shane
most welcoming; took me up to the Director's office for a glass of
wine where I was introduced to the Director, Dr Rita Gardiner
(whom I had previously met when she was a guest at St Catherine's), to Chris Patten (whom I had met once before when he had
opened a Hong Kong exhibition in Edinburgh) and to the President, Lord Selborne, and his art historian wife, Joanna. Nigel and
Shane bustled about while I did my best to make casual conversation to people standing close to me whose names I did not catch.
Shane had reserved a gangway seat for me. But it soon became
obvious that many more RGS members had arrived than there
were seats available and Nigel and Shane quickly surrendered their
own seats to two schoolboys from Mill Hill school. There was a
delay of nearly fifteen minutes while latecomers were encouraged
to sit on the edge of the platform, on the floor, and down the aisles
– creating an impressive audience but also the tense atmosphere I
prefer to avoid.

Chris Patten did not deliver the address I had been expecting.
He touched on Hong Kong and China (while remarking that he
knew nothing about the latter) but he did so in the context of
talking about the increasing tensions created by the development
of capitalism in undemocratic states, notably China, politically
governed by an autocratic regime. He also referred to the current
situation in Malaysia where the Finance Minister and Deputy
Prime Minister, Anwar Ibrahim (well known to St Catherine's) was
now imprisoned. His theme was the essential need for the rule of
law, as we understand it, in a state evolving from a different and
less democratic political tradition.

His style was interesting. He spoke in a leisurely way, scarcely
referring to his notes and with light and personal touches. He
conveyed the impression that he was primarily aiming to present
his own political philosophy – in effect (as people say today) 're-
inventing' himself in the different political circumstances of 1998
from those at the beginning of the decade when he was chairman

of the Conservative Party. In making a short speech of thanks, Lord
Jellicoe spoke, to loud applause, of the great political future ahead
of Chris Patten. But what can that be?

As we stood around after the lecture, I had a word with Peter
and Iona Carrington (she looking pale and fragile). An agreeable
dinner in a candlelit room, which I had to leave early with my
mind set on the last train home; Shane came out with me and,
with no taxi in sight, she most kindly drove me to Paddington. A
long wearisome train journey to Charlbury but I was home by
23:20.

Tuesday October 13
On Monday morning I had telephoned Mr Len Pratley, our 'milk-
man' (in the same sense as the Royal Family has been said to
describe the Egyptian owner of Harrods as 'our grocer'), to say
that we had decided to buy his second-hand VW Golf (1989) to
replace our Bedford van (which Charlbury Garage thought that it
might be able to sell). I am quickly bored by the subject of cars,
but Penny and I had been compelled over the weekend to debate
the choice between two second-hand cars – the Golf and a Subaru.
Both had been mentioned to us by Sarah Potter, a parochial church
council colleague of Penny's and a reliable, and often valuable,
gossip about Charlbury affairs. We had been thinking about the
possibility of getting rid of the ageing van, and it would have been
foolish to have ignored Sarah's chance initiative. What particularly
appealed to me was that both the cars had automatic gears and
power steering and the Subaru also had four-wheel drive. We
inspected and took short drives in them both. We preferred the
Golf and Charlbury Garage recommended it. On Tuesday I collected and paid for it before leaving it with the garage for two new
tyres. Offer price £2850: price negotiated £2500. A feeling of
satisfaction and relief.

Preparation for Thursday absorbed much of the day. Baroness
Young (Janet Young, previously Leader of the House of Lords),
whom we had known for some years, approached me in early
August: would I be willing to address the Association of Conservative

Peers about the conduct of referendums one day in the early autumn? Speak for ten minutes, questions for twenty minutes: 2:30–3:00 p.m. Did not sound too formidable an undertaking; anyway could hardly refuse, though I am well aware that many proposed commitments tend to seem acceptable if the date is a good way off. The date of 15 October was fixed. But, as I set about preparing for the occasion, I had to resolve an exacting problem which I had foreseen at the outset: the need to keep what I wished to say to ten minutes and no longer. I practised several times in front of the kitchen timer, hacking away at my script between practices and tidying it up on the computer in the chalet in the garden.

Another priority was to have my hair trimmed in Chipping Norton. It must be due to my vanity or my army years that a haircut strengthens my morale before any occasion about which I am nervous (I used to notice that wearing his Guards Brigade tie appeared to have a similar effect on Lord Carrington). An elderly and skilful Sicilian runs a barber's shop in Chipping Norton with his son and grandson. I suspect that he may have come to England as a prisoner in the 1939–45 war; then settled in CN, which in some ways resembles, though in an English eighteenth-century style, a small Sicilian town, such as I came to know in the Sicily campaign of July–August 1943. SKY Television keeps him in touch with Sicily; that may partly explain why he still speaks such poor English, leaving me to respond to much of his limited conversation with, 'Oh, really' and 'Yes, I see . . .' when I cannot grasp what he has been saying.

Wednesday 14 October
A surprising turn of events – the publication of a major report by the committee, chaired by Lord Neill, on the financial aspect of elections and associated issues, which was recommending greater transparency and stricter rules of behaviour in party political affairs. The Neill Report, contrary to what had been expected, also included a chapter on the conduct of referendums. With my talk to the Conservative peers in mind, I urgently needed to know what

that chapter said. Into Oxford, lunched at St Catherine's and scanned the newspapers in the Senior Common Room. It suddenly occurred to me that the Internet might secure the text of the whole chapter for me. I consulted Margaret Simon in the development office and she and her assistant, Rachel, jumped at the challenge. They began to race each other while I stood by, throwing out suggestions which might help them to achieve access to a pro-gramme carrying the Neill Report even though it had been pub-lished only that morning. Rachel won by a short head and within a few minutes had printed out the referendum chapter for me.

In general, a most satisfactory chapter. The Report recommends the establishment of an Election Commission which would include among its functions the independent oversight of the conduct of referendums – as had been recommended in the report of the inde-pendent Commission on the Conduct of Referendums which I chaired in 1996.* The present government had received our report but in the 1997 referendums on devolution for Scotland and Wales had taken no account of our recommendations. How would the Government decide to react now? Difficult for it to ignore the Neill Report but there were indications that the Prime Minister wished to avoid any national referendums until after the next general election. On getting back home I turned again, rather wearily, to the text of my brief talk to the Tory peers, inserting references to the Neill Committee recommendations and testing once more the length and time – eleven minutes at the most. That would have to do.

Thursday 15 October
To London on the 09:40 train. A pause at the Oxford and Cam-bridge University Club – a quiet and invaluable oasis for some forty years – before walking in bright sunshine to the House of Lords. Here, thoughtfully arranged by Janet Young, Lord (Barney)

---

* The Electoral Commission, chaired in 2019 by Sir John Holmes, was established through the Political Parties, Elections and Referendums Act 2000, and was given wider supervisory and investigative powers through the Political Parties and Elections Act 2009.

Hayhoe was waiting at the entrance in order to look after me, give me lunch, and deliver me punctually to the right committee room by 2:30 p.m. – a delightful man whom I had never met. He had served in a wide range of departments, while never being promoted beyond Minister of State; a qualified engineer of modest background, a young Conservative during the post-war Labour years, a warm supporter of Ted Heath (whose more vigorous and attractive days he convincingly described). We got on well over an excellent lunch. I then followed him up many stairs and along narrow corridors until we reached the long and wide corridor outside the committee rooms. I sat on a seat to wait. Waiting in a passage outside a door invokes an inescapable feeling of 'outside the headmaster's study' and I vividly remembered many more nervous periods of waiting, some twenty years earlier, in the very same corridor outside the room of the Public Accounts Committee, before being cross-examined for about two hours as the Accounting Officer of the Department of Health and Social Security.

Time was short for the Conservative peers; Lord Hayhoe had warned me that they would be wanting to get away as soon as possible in order to get a good seat for the continuing debate that day on the reform of the House of Lords. Baroness Young wasted no time: a quick introduction and I was in play – with my carefully prepared text, while doing my best to keep my eyes on the three or four rows of peers a few feet away from me. Keeping close to my time, I had the feeling, in the way that a speaker can, that what I had to say was going down well – partly helped, I imagine, by my criticisms (also to be found in the Neill Report) of important aspects of the conduct of the Scottish and Welsh referendums. Questions followed with quick answers from me. A complex and shrewd question from Lord Tebbit relating to the practical difficulties of controlling the influence of expenditure, for or against a referendum question, during the months prior to the poll. I doubt if my reply satisfied him. Dead on 3 p.m. Janet Young brought the meeting to an end. Strong applause, and Patrick Jenkin (my last Secretary of State in the DHSS) and Lord Brabazon (family friend in Bembridge) came up to me for a friendly word. Janet, expressing warm thanks, saw me to the door of the Lords. A feeling of great relief as I walked away.

No taxi in sight and I walked, rather wearily, heavy bag of papers on my shoulder, to Cork Street. Richard Morgan, Warden of Radley, had telephoned a day or so earlier about the Robert Messum Gallery and said, 'I've been thinking about our commitment from the council to buy two or three pictures for the mansion walls. We haven't made much progress, and I've been wondering whether you happen to know the Robert Messum Gallery in Cork Street . . . ? Robert Messum has a boy here, and I think he might be ready to bring a few of his pictures for us to see here at Radley.'

The Messum suggestion would certainly be an option to discuss with Richard Morgan after the War Memorial Committee meeting on Saturday. A further feeling of relief as I secured a taxi outside the Burlington Arcade and caught the 17:12 train to Charlbury.

Friday 16 October
Final ordeal of the week: the Sir Patrick Nairne Lecture at St Catherine's. But, first, I had to collect the VW Golf, equipped with two new tyres, and also hand over the Bedford van at Charlbury Garage. Gerry, who owns the garage, hoped that he might be able to get me £1,000 for the van, though I suspect that, if he does, there will be some repair costs to offset against that. At first the Golf and I were not entirely at ease with each other but I liked the feel of it.

Penny had promised our son James (teaching at Bradfield College) that she would go and see Emma, the younger of his two daughters, at her new school . . . I caught an afternoon train at Charlbury and took a taxi to my room at the college. The Master, Raymond Plant, had invited me to say a few words in winding up the event – the kind of short 'impromptu' speech which has to be skilfully crafted and then memorised. I welcomed the invitation as an opportunity to thank the college but I was glad to have a final half an hour on my own in my room.

In characteristic Oxford fashion the 'Lecture' was not actually to be a lecture. It had been wisely transformed into an occasion which was intended to be more like a public seminar. A year earlier the Master and governing body had decided that, to mark the passage of ten years since I had retired from the Mastership, they would honour me by establishing an annual lecture – the Sir Patrick Nairne Lecture. I was taken by surprise – rather embarrassed and slightly amused. What were the implications of marking the decade? Still in touch with the college and not yet senile? A collective (though unmentionable) feeling that the Great Reaper could not be too far off? I expressed deep appreciation but, perhaps irritatingly, felt that I must mention to the Master my immediate concern that the honour to me might, in future years, prove a problem for the college. Might it not turn out to be rather difficult to find a lecture (or seminar) theme every year which would attract a respectable audience? Raymond shrugged off the reservation. He did not say so, but the college might be able to fall back on the old Oxford saying that a commitment to an annual lecture did not necessarily mean holding it every year.

Raymond went on to consult me about the choice of the inaugural lecturer in October 1998.

PLANT: What about Peter Mandelson?

NAIRNE: I rather think too soon and too directly political, but a good idea to have an alumnus. Perhaps John Birt might be right – on the BBC and future broadcasting developments? He must be nearing the end of his time. He should have plenty of issues to talk about but he might turn out to be a very dull lecturer . . .

The Master wrote to Birt. He replied that he did not like giving lectures: could he just answer questions? My reaction was negative. He would be likely to give somewhat dull and defensive answers to questions from the audience. Then, almost at the same moment, Raymond and I thought of Melvyn Bragg, perhaps the most skilful and experienced interviewer on cultural matters today. He was a friend of the college and a Domus Fellow so might be willing [to *interview Birt for the lecture*]. We were in luck. He was willing, and the date of 16 October was fixed.

We gathered in the Senior Common Room at 4:30 p.m. – a good tea on offer which few people, including myself, felt like eating. My guests arrived: Sir Denis Forman (former chairman of Granada, where both Birt and Bragg had worked in their younger days), whom I had met at Essex University and come to know better this year; Peter Way, close and long-standing friend from my Radley years; and Sandy and Lisa, who had driven from London. Just before 5 p.m. we walked across to the Bernard Sunley Lecture Theatre, which was full – though not over-full. At that moment Penny arrived having done well in the Friday evening traffic.

The Master stepped forward and, while I looked steadily at my feet, proceeded to explain the reason for the Sir Patrick Nairne Lecture in flattering and somewhat inaccurate terms. Then Bragg opened up with a short review of the media scene, speaking about the technological, global and multicultural aspects, before inviting Birt to say how he saw the current scene and the way ahead. John Birt smiled his somewhat awkward and owlish smile and proceeded to outline, at some length, the way in which the BBC was developing digital transmission and the wider ways in which the viewing public was being offered more and better programmes. It struck me as a kind of television commercial, his words bringing back my recollection of a newspaper interview he had given earlier in the year. It was interesting and informative but I was disappointed (though not, I suppose, surprised) that no new questions were raised for the audience to pursue.

Bragg followed up with two or perhaps three questions and, again, Birt replied with long factual answers. It became evident to Bragg that time was running out. He stopped Birt short and invited questions from the audience . . . When my turn came, would I remember the words I was intending to say? Would what I said strike the right note and refer in the right terms to those whom I needed to mention?

At last Melvyn Bragg caught my eye. I stood up in front of the audience with my arms folded. 'I am grateful to the Master for kindly inviting me to have the last word this evening, if only to enable me to provide living proof that this has not been the Sir Patrick Nairne Memorial Lecture.'

The audience responded to that opening as I had hoped, and the rest of my short speech of thanks to the Master and the college, and to John Birt and Melvyn Bragg, seemed to go well. It is a shrewd saying that 'impromptu speeches are often not worth the paper they are written on' and the shortest speeches need particularly careful preparation before delivery without notes; but, even so, it is surprisingly easy to be pushed off course by unexpected laughter (or its absence) or by a sudden blackout of memory.

Robin Butler remarked that the questions could have been sharper.* True, but no matter. It was a good occasion, even though it had not been spiced with the critical exchanges with Birt, as Director General of the BBC, for which I had hoped – and it was an all too generous recognition of my contribution to the college. I enjoyed seeing some friends from our years at Catz at the reception and talking at dinner to Denis Forman and with Melvyn Bragg and Richard Dawkins. Glad to be back home at Chilson by 11:30 p.m. – grateful, as always, that Penny was ready to drive.

Saturday 17 October
Michael Wigley, now chairman of the Radleian Society, drove over from Chadlington at 10 a.m. and gave me a lift to the Radley meeting of the War Memorial Committee. I may possibly be the oldest member now but I have not attended regularly over the years, feeling that I do enough for Radley as a member of the council. But this was an important meeting and, as the only council member able to attend, I was anxious to be there, partly because of the determined character of the chairman, Anthony West. The Charity Commissioners had ruled that some substantial funds, left in a will to the college and, for sound reasons, handed over to the War Memorial Committee to administer, should be taken away

---

* Robin, Lord Butler, a former Cabinet Secretary, had recently commenced his appointment as Master of University College, Oxford.

from the committee and administered by the college – that is, in effect, by the council.

After the meeting a brief chat with Richard Morgan about the task of choosing a few paintings, his ideas about the Robert Messum Gallery, and the implications of an approach from another gallery owner with a Radley connection. Michael Wigley dropped me back at Yew Tree for a late lunch. Radley had been looking lovely on what had turned out to be a beautiful autumn day, reminding me of how little the setting had changed since I had arrived as a new boy there sixty-three years ago.

The end of the week
Splendid to have the three major events over – commitments of the kind that I want to accept, which strain my nerves in advance but which I enjoy once I am engaged in them. Penny often, perhaps usually, appears to have a busier life than mine; but my days are always full and, with the week of 11–17 October behind me, I turned back to a long letter list, an agenda of tasks to be done or matters to be dealt with and an untidy study needing urgent attention. Both my memory and my arthritic spine are not as good as they were; but there may be comfort in the thought that, while it falls short of full retirement, a demanding life with too much to do may be as good a recipe as any for postponing the worst ravages of old age.

29

The Perfect Pastime of Painting, 2002

Lunched at Ditchley Park, home of the Ditchley Foundation, guests of the Director, Sir Nigel Broomfield, and his wife, Valerie. On arrival we stood around with a drink outside their house in the West Wing. Warm spring sunshine after a long spell of wet and cold weather, encouraging me to think that the 'open season' for watercolour landscape painting would soon begin. One of the other guests may have had the same thought: 'Do you still do much painting, Patrick?'

I was used to this question, often no more than a gambit in polite conversation. When I had said what little there was to say in reply – mainly to the effect that landscape painters *en plein air* hibernate in winter – I asked about my questioner's interest in art and painting. That proved to be a conversational cul-de-sac. It was someone I knew, a highly intelligent woman with academic interests but she did not spark at all on the subject of art. And for her, as perhaps for everyone standing round at Ditchley, I suspected that visual art meant only traditional painting and sculpture – more specifically paintings or drawings in frames hung on the walls of homes or galleries.

EARLY YEARS WITH MY FATHER

I grew up to think of art in that way. So, I think, did most of my contemporaries at home and at school. And yet, as long ago as my birth in 1921, the huge revolution in the visual arts throughout the twentieth century was already well under way. My father was aware of that. He would have recognised that there is usually a revolutionary, experimental fringe in many areas of human activity. But in the culture to which his generation, and to a significant extent my own, belonged it was 'paintings or drawings in frames on walls' which were dominant – in the Royal Academy, the Tate Gallery, the regional galleries, and the commercial galleries of central London. More experimental, non-figurative art had begun to flourish across the Channel since the early years of the twentieth century but only in the last forty years has there been in the United Kingdom a large and radical shift in a different and wider direction. It has now become usual to refer, not just to painting and sculpture, but, with broader implications, to the *visual arts*. 'The contemporary visual arts' is the current term, embracing painting, sculpture, drawings, pastels, installations, photography, film, video, and 'performance art'. This innovative and wide-ranging approach has become the dominant or defining feature of the visual arts today.

Watercolour landscape painting, however, has retained a position of its own, partly perhaps because most people have no difficulty in understanding, enjoying and occasionally buying it, but also because since the turn of the eighteenth century it has been recognised as an art form almost entirely unique to this country. Where else in the world is there a Royal Watercolour Society with its own gallery? What for me became a perfect pastime was, I grew up to learn, an essentially British pastime.

I have had a passion for painting for most of my life. It began with drawing, as it normally does for children. After lunch in September 2001, one of my grandchildren asked for paper and, armed with some crayons, boldly and rapidly set about drawing. He knew what he wanted to do. He had soon covered two or three pages in the traditional style of the very young artist – the most striking creation a drawing of a pirate with large round head, vertical fringe of hair, black eyepatch, and arms horizontal from the body in the shape of a toasting fork with three prongs for fingers. It might well have been a drawing of my own some seventy-five years earlier.

Drawing, with or without paint or crayons, was an essential test of a promising artist in the past. It may still be. Two letters in *The Times* of July 2002 asserted that drawing was still taught in at least some of the London art schools – though that may not mean that every student had to study it. William Dring RA RWS told me that one test of a candidate for the Royal Academy Schools was the ability to draw a circle well with one single sweep of the hand. I doubt if I could have passed. Even so, my introduction to the arts was largely due to the encouraging view in the family and at school that 'Pat can draw'.

I do not think that that can be said today. As a child I did draw and wanted to go on drawing. That was what mattered. I did not draw particularly well: another boy at my preparatory school drew better and his speciality of careful sketches of ocean liners was much admired in the classroom. But I doubt if his father, though a future air marshal, would have been able to give him the special advantage which I had: a father who had taken classes at the Slade School of Art and was constantly painting. I always had him as an influential role model at hand, painting in a home where good watercolour paintings hung on the walls. I suppose that I have been able to offer something of the same to our own family.

During my school years drawing and painting were on the fringe of general education. They were regarded as an 'extra' to be provided once a week, if at all, by a teacher from outside the school. Things are vastly different today. Pencils, crayons and paints are introduced to all children at an early age and the walls of primary schools are plastered with paintings and coloured drawings. However, there is still a cultural gap between the concepts and creative work of visual art in most schools and the character of the student work being done in the leading contemporary art schools. Under the age of ten to twelve, children want to draw and paint what they themselves can recognise as realistic representation: the scornful remark that 'That does not *look* like a house or a tree' can crush potential talent for ever.

St Catherine's Hill, Winchester, 1938, aged seventeen.

My father had talent and he was encouraged to develop it as a young officer in the Seaforth Highlanders. He strongly held the view that the ability to draw well was the essential basis for any success as a practising artist. But, oddly perhaps, he did not insist on my learning to draw well and there was never any suggestion that I might study at an art school.

It was chiefly his encouragement, however, which fostered what ability I had. He must have painted hundreds of watercolours in and around Compton, Shawford, Twyford, Silkstead and Hursley, and I was the son in the family who would usually go out painting with him. For example, one of my father's watercolours is of a threshing machine at work in a cornfield above Compton village – an old-fashioned harvesting scene. Beautifully drawn and lightly painted, it is a period piece as (what my father would call) a watercolour drawing. I think that, on that same occasion, I was sitting on a stool trying to paint the same scene myself. It would have been an afternoon gathering of the Compton and Shawford

Threshing machine by Charles Sylvester Nairne.

Painting Circle, established by my father and comprising a small group of amateur painters, including an architect, a retired army brigadier, three or four ladies, occasionally (in the years before the National Health Service) our local doctor, and in the summer holidays myself.

His sound teaching has remained with me – the importance in a painting of a balanced design, correct perspective and the crucial elements of light and tones.

For many years he was the honorary secretary – and, I think, the dominant member – of the Winchester Art Club, for which he organised an annual autumn exhibition at the Judges' Lodgings in the Cathedral Close. I can hear now my father's voice as he groaned about the agonies of selection, especially the complaints of one Winchester lady whose garish flower paintings were sometimes rejected. 'Flower paintings in oils are a curse among amateur painters,' he would declare after a trying afternoon of selection.

PAINTING AS RECREATION

Many developments in my life might have crowded out painting. For example, golf might well have done so for many years. But my devotion to watercolour painting came strongly to the fore after my appointment to the Civil Service led Penny and myself to rent a flat in Hammersmith. Only expensive London golf courses such as Wimbledon and Roehampton were reasonably near and, much more important, the arrival of our children put the family first. So painting became the recreation for what spare time I had.

Fortunately my enjoyment of sketching had remained alive during the war years. I kept a small sketchbook with me when I joined the Seaforth Highlanders in the north-east of Scotland and during my service with the 5th Battalion in North Africa and North-West Europe. I still have a rather special drawing of the Sferro Hills, where we fought our last battle in Sicily [*see Chapter 6: Sferro Hills, July 1943*]. But back after demobilisation at Plover Hill and Oxford in 1946–48, I was at home in the vacation, and, although golf had a high priority, I soon found myself out painting again with my father.

More significantly, perhaps, my painting was improving. I took to painting more regularly, and my confidence was greatly increased when a pale painting of Christ Church Meadow in the spring was hung in a special Oxford exhibition at the Ashmolean in 1947. That marked, I think, the start of my aiming rather higher over the next half century of watercolour painting.

Confidence was given a further boost in 1950. We had settled at Hammersmith Terrace where our small paved garden, crowded in the summer with hollyhocks, offered constantly changing views of the Thames which lapped our garden wall. A short walk beyond Chiswick Mall lay Chiswick Park where stood the Palladian villa of the first Lord Burlington. One early spring afternoon, with Penny nearby with Kathy in her pram, I painted a watercolour of some trees in the park. It turned out to be an attractive small painting and I boldly submitted it to the Royal Academy for the Summer Exhibition.

Looking towards Merton College, Christ Church Meadows,
Oxford, 15 June 1947.

WILLIAM DRING AND THE ROYAL ACADEMY

To my great surprise my painting was accepted, hung and sold. Perhaps it was William Dring who had encouraged me to submit a watercolour though he could not have seen the picture I had submitted. Known in his own family and in ours as 'John' rather than 'William', he and his wife, Gray, a painter herself, became almost as close friends of ours as of my parents.* He became a second and most valuable influence on my work though I have never been able to match his simple and skilful watercolour style.

William Dring owed a good deal to the encouragement of my father. As a young man from the Slade School in the early 1930s, he secured a post as a teacher of painting at the Southampton School of Art. He and Gray then found a flat above the garage of

---

* Grace Elizabeth Rothwell, William Dring's wife, also studied at the Slade School of Art.

a retired admiral and his wife at the top of Shawford Hill. The view from the flat towards Winchester and its cathedral inspired a painting given to us by John as a wedding present. It was likely to have been the admiral's wife who mentioned to my father the young couple of painters whom he might be interested to meet. My father gave him, I think, his first local commission – a pastel portrait of James and myself sitting together – and later commissions to do individual portraits of both of us. It was the start of a career of commissions for portraits all over the country, some in oils and many in pastel, and his work became widely known.

William Dring, portrait of Pat and James Nairne, pastel, 1934.

William Dring,
landscape sketch,
1930s.

William Dring,
pastel of Melissa
Dring, Christmas
card, 1956.

Dring himself would have resisted any attempt to classify him in some academic context. At, I imagine, his generous suggestion I was commissioned in 1947 to write an article on him and his work for one of the arts magazines.* I did my best to interview him but he had nothing to say about his work from a theoretical or philosophical aspect. He modestly saw himself as primarily a craftsman, painting what he had to paint, whether a portrait or a landscape, as well as he could in a workmanlike way. Setting aside the need to earn a living, he might well have described at least his watercolour landscapes – in the words of the painter [*Philip*] Wilson Steer – as 'something to do between meals'. I can recall him saying firmly to me: 'Be yourself and get on with it. Don't try and copy anyone else.'

INFLUENCE OF ENGLISH WATERCOLOURISTS

In my own approach to painting I have always been torn between the classical and romantic traditions – drawn to the simple classical form of John Sell Cotman's work, but also strongly influenced in practice by the romantic sensitivity of J. M. W. Turner. I have spent many hours of my life in galleries and museums and at painting and sculpture exhibitions. It is impossible not to be more attracted by some artists than by others and, so to speak, to 'inhale' their influence. By the time I left Radley I could recognise the works of the principal English watercolour painters of the late eighteenth and the nineteenth centuries – J. M. W. Turner, Thomas Girtin, John Sell Cotman, Peter De Wint, David Cox, and Richard Parkes Bonington. But I knew little about them until I was compelled to learn, after agreeing to present a paper on watercolour landscape painters to a University College society in 1947. I drew upon its text in a talk I gave forty-five years later at an anniversary luncheon of the New Forest Decorative and Fine Arts Society.

Watercolour landscape was not an invention by British painters: Dürer, Holbein and Van Dyck are notable examples of painters who

---

* Published in *The Studio*, July 1947.

used watercolour, though confined to minor sketches and portrait drawings. But the English alone made watercolour landscape a major artistic cult in its own right. It was a modest development at the start, as was landscape painting in this country. There was no market for it in its early years. That discriminating collector, George IV, never bought a Turner, a Constable, a Cotman or a Crome. The Queen's Collection contains few landscapes. The drawing rooms of the aristocracy and the landed gentry were filled with portraits of the family or of horses . . .

It was, I had learned, the impact of the Romantic movement in the arts which enriched and widened the culture of the visual arts. Girtin's delicate watercolour of Tintern Abbey, John Constable's dramatic Stonehenge, David Cox's windswept heaths, and Turner at work with his sketchbook in Venice – all illustrated, in their different ways a response to a romantic ideal. There exists a charming letter from the Suffolk portrait painter, Thomas Gainsborough: 'I am sick of portraits and wish very much to take my viol da gamba and walk off to some sweet village where I can paint landskips and enjoy the fag end of life in quietness and ease . . .'

I have often felt the same – sick of my desk and bureaucratic commitments, we have chosen to go on holiday to, in particular, Wales or Scotland or Italy, where I have painted 'landskips . . . in quietness and ease'. But Gainsborough's wish was not a practical option for him. Portrait painting provided a livelihood – 'picking pockets in the portrait way', as he put it. He found it difficult to sell his landscapes. One of the most famous of his paintings, *The Harvest Wagon*, was eventually given away to the carrier who took his paintings to London. Both Cotman and his son shared his experience. John Sell Cotman's notable landscape of *Greta Bridge* – which had pride of place in a Norwich Museum exhibition at Tate Britain in 2001 – was sold for a few shillings. He suffered bouts of depression and, in the middle of his life, wrote: 'My eldest son, who is following the same miserable profession with myself, feels the same hopelessness.'

But the shift to landscape painting and the taste for the romantic and picturesque in the visual arts had come to stay. In 1805
the Royal Watercolour Society was established of which Turner,
Girtin, Cox and De Wint – all young men at the time – were
notable among the early members. But there remained a need to
open up a market for landscape painting in both oil and watercolour. It may have been principally the success and fame of Turner
and the patronage he attracted which helped to achieve this.

This short slice of history has been important to my enjoyment
of painting and to my own amateur work. I have a handsome book
of Turner watercolours given to me in August 1967 and generously
inscribed by Denis Healey on leaving his private office in which I
had been the principal private secretary. Its introduction by Martin
Butlin of the Tate Gallery opens with the words: 'The watercolours
of J. M. W. Turner are one of the greatest achievements in the history
of English art . . . This achievement is all the more remarkable in
that Turner's main interest lay elsewhere, in his oil paintings.'

But was that so remarkable? It was Turner's oil paintings,
including some landscapes, which secured Turner's election to the
Royal Academy at the age of twenty-seven. The discouraging experiences of Constable and Cotman, which I have quoted, showed
that the founding of the Royal Watercolour Society did not quickly
reflect nor arouse a popular demand for watercolour landscapes,
though there was some demand for topographical studies. Turner
himself owed much to the enthusiasm of the young John Ruskin.
He was also fortunate in having as patrons Lord Egremont of Pet-
worth in Sussex and Walter Fawkes of Farnley Hall in Yorkshire.

MY OWN PAINTING

I am always thinking about watercolour technique. I start a painting by wetting the page with an old shaving brush or a large
paintbrush followed by a wash of colour, beginning with the sky,
and then making some marks on the paper to indicate the main
features of the composition I have in mind. My father had an
entirely different approach – a slow and deliberate method, creating

Watercolour, Mull, Scotland, 1995.

a painting on the basis of a careful preliminary drawing in pencil – in the style perhaps of John Sell Cotman whose work he particularly admired. He was a sound tutor for a young, unskilled pupil like myself. But other influences became more important, not only John Dring, but in later years the watercolours of Edward Seago. It has been their simplicity of subject and design and their bold and commanding brush work in the spirit of 'paint it and leave it' which I have tried to emulate.

I have not succeeded as I would wish. Perhaps I never shall. Every painting is an experiment, an organic process with an uncertain outcome at the outset. I paint *en plein air*, enjoying the task as a recreation which temporarily replaces all other concerns and of which the attractions of the landscape and the light are an essential part.

I first had a painting hung in a public exhibition in the then-new Southampton Art Gallery while I was still at Radley, and after 1945 I exhibited for several years in the Winchester Art Club. I have mentioned an exhibition in the Ashmolean and my first experience of the Royal Academy. When I have made the effort of

Painting Magdalen
Tower from Christ
Church Meadow,
Oxford, August 1990.

Patrick Nairne painting at Chilson; from Sandy Nairne's sketchbook, 1992 (detail).

submitting, I have also exhibited in the Royal Institution, Royal Society of British Artists, and the Oxford Art Society exhibitions.

Over the years I have also had six or seven exhibitions in London – on my own or shared with another painter – at the Clarges and Oliver Swann galleries and I sell locally up to ten watercolours a year. As I write this, in July 2002, what will probably be my final exhibition in London – forty-one paintings at the Clarges Gallery – has just closed with the sale of seventeen paintings, enough to leave me with a small net profit!

CONTEMPORARY VISUAL ART

My upbringing in that world, my family's commitment to watercolours and my own work over half a century have inescapably conditioned my view of contemporary visual art. How do I respond to the work of contemporary artists?

Not surprisingly I am more attracted to those outstanding artists of the last half-century who, whether figurative or abstract, have practised in a more traditional stream – to mention four distinctly different examples, John Piper, Edward Seago, Michael Andrews

Drawing of Brading Church, Isle of Wight, 1962.

Chilson, Oxfordshire, 2001.

and Howard Hodgkin. 'Modern art' has always been a relative, often misleading, term. It was not long before the modern French artists of, say, the impressionist period lost the power of providing 'the shock of the new'. Over the last thirty years (though that may be too sweeping) what had previously been regarded as avant-garde has been replaced by a new mainstream of contemporary visual art.

Such current work is devoted to exploring beyond the painting and sculpture of the past. Some of it I have found original and captivating; some of it derivative and dull; some of it shocking. I respond to the compulsion to go and see new work and then sometimes find that I have little to say about it beyond an acknow-ledgement that it is simply what a particular artist of the time chose to create and exhibit. I think that I can understand what Rachel Campbell-Johnston, art critic of *The Times*, had in mind when she wrote of the work of Martin Creed, winner of the Turner Prize in 2001: 'His flickering installation may mean everything or nothing. But at least it gives the viewer something to look at, some-thing more interesting than plotless movies and planks of wood. It gives the viewer a great opportunity to study the other viewers.'

I am reminded of a remark by Sir Hugh Casson, then President of the Royal Academy, when, as President of the Association of Civil Service Art Clubs, I presided at his opening of the Associ-ation's annual exhibition: 'The public has for the most part cut itself off from contemporary artists of today because contemporary artists of today have cut themselves off from the public.'

Casson said that some twenty-five years ago. It may be less true today, though I doubt it. The general public has had some years in which to catch up, to 'grow accustomed to the face' (to borrow the phrase from the musical, *My Fair Lady*) of the new avant-garde of contemporary art; but its reactions have always tended to be con-servative – quick to express shock at what is strikingly new and slow to welcome what is boldly experimental. But public reactions today go beyond a traditional outlook and cautious conservatism, notably when expressed in the sweeping, aggressive, and still fre-quent, statement that 'I simply can't be doing with modern art'.

THE SUBJECTIVE INDIVIDUALIST

There are several reasons for the above statement, and Hugh Casson was pointing straight at one of them – the self-centred, subjective approach of many contemporary artists. Artists have always been engaged in self-expression; and there must be a sub-jective element in all works of art. But, in general, most artists have also been concerned to create work to which the public can relate. Today, however, many of the more notable contemporary artists display work to which the general public cannot easily respond – reacting more often with querulous perplexity than with pleasure or enthusiastic interest.

I realise that I am looking for what is not on offer when I feel the lack of any objective aesthetic appeal through subject, colour or design. But I cannot readily recognise and acknowledge 'good art' when I am deeply puzzled about the what, why and wherefore of the artist's intention. The striking creations of, for example, Carl Andre, Damien Hirst or Sam Taylor-Johnson may open our eyes to new ways in which features or aspects of the world around us can be viewed but I am not alone in finding some expressions of their artistic vision boring or perverse and, above all, unappealing. I may not positively dislike what I see; I am always curious to see any new work by an artist of repute; I am ready to view it with respect; I may admire its skill. But what is too often true is that I rarely find myself as excited or as stimulated as I would wish to be or as curators or critics have sometimes claimed that I should be.

For many more members of the public the Turner Prize serves as a focus for their negative attitude towards the contemporary avant-garde. Tracey Emin's unmade bed and Chris Ofili's elephant dung have succeeded the bricks of Carl Andre and the works of Damien Hirst as the foremost objects of ridicule, disgust or contempt. I was impressed by the imaginative skill of the work in the Tate of both Emin and Ofili but the notorious bed interested me primarily as a classic example of self-centred, subjective contemporary work.

I was recently struck by some words of an artist and teacher, Jon Thompson, quoted in the context of information about the Middlesex University degree show of 2001.* It throws further light on the subjective character of the contemporary artist:

It is a compelling paradox perhaps that these are both the best of times and the worst of times in which to be a young practising artist in Britain. While it is certainly true that – in London at least – the doors into professional life seem to be tantalisingly ajar for the young and ambitious, the demand to conform to what is arguably an airless and shallow, some would say entirely outmoded, 'avant-gardism' colours the whole of the contemporary British art scene ... The

---

* In 2007 Jon Thompson published *How to Read a Modern Painting: Understanding and Enjoying the Modern Masters: Understanding and Enjoying 20th-Century Art*, Thames & Hudson, London.

demand to be original – a quality which may not be immediately visible – has quite given way to the requirement to be slick, stylish and contemporary; clever; sensational even.

That could not have been written about those French impressionists who provided my earliest experience of a public reaction to 'modern art', a reaction difficult to credit today. In 1945, after the end of the 1939–45 war, the first major exhibition of Picasso and Matisse – with a popular appeal today reflected in thousands of posters and postcards – was held in London. It provoked a predictable reaction then against 'modern art' from many of the public. Picasso and Matisse are, as it happens, being shown together again in Tate Modern [*Matisse Picasso, 11 May–18 August* 2002], attracting thousands of visitors who, whether or not they like their work, accept them as two of the greatest painters of the last century.

Shall we see the same kind of evolution – from dismay and dispute to acceptance and acclaim – in the public's reception in the years ahead of the more notable avant-garde artists of today? Perhaps a more relevant and sensible question is: what are the criteria by which to judge contemporary visual art and its continuing worth for the future? If definable, have they a permanent validity or must artistic criteria always remain open to revision?

WHAT IS GOOD ART?

The problem of the criteria by which to judge contemporary art – the difficult question today of 'What is good art?' – is, I believe, a second reason why the general public cannot always feel at ease with the work of contemporary artists.

Should we, for example, look to the annual selection of the shortlist for the Turner Prize as an authoritative guide to the best contemporary work and the qualities it displays? The answer to that should certainly be 'No'. There are many notable artists producing first-class work who are not regarded and would not regard themselves as in the field of the Turner Prize selectors. But the two earlier questions – relating to the definition of criteria and the continuing validity of criteria – must be carefully considered and are more difficult to answer. Can general criteria be formulated when the scope, range and character of visual art have so vastly changed? It is understandable – and to the good – that the younger artists today wish to move away from the more traditional subjects and techniques of the past. With the wider variety of techniques now available, they are naturally attracted to fresh and stimulating artistic options. But it seems to me to follow that, in judging the quality of an artist's work, the long-accepted criteria of, for example, aesthetic vision, design, colour tones, and draughtsmanship can no longer be generally applied.

Penny and I visited the Venice Biennale in 2001. The British pavilion was devoted to the work of Mark Wallinger – the statue, *Ecce Homo*, which had been previously displayed on the Fourth Plinth in Trafalgar Square, two films with music, and some sheets of drawings. We then crossed the lagoon to see an intriguing, rough and ready construction in the Giudecca which had been contrived by Mike Nelson. It was composed of a succession of small, wooden, occasionally empty, rooms or cabins, apparently designed to convey the circumstances and atmosphere of the strange story of the *Marie Celeste*, a ship found at sea with no sailors on board and no evidence at all of what had happened to the crew. By chance we were the only visitors to be walking round this intriguing, somewhat threatening, art installation, and the sound of an approaching thunderstorm made the experience distinctly sinister.

Neither of these major works in Venice by Wallinger and Nelson could be satisfactorily judged by the traditional criteria. Nor could the work each chose to show be readily compared. New criteria are needed to take account of their wholly different concepts of visual art. Their work could not be described as self-centred or subjective. On the contrary what both artists had in common was a primary concern to convey or communicate an 'impact' or an 'experience' – intellectual, emotional, and occasionally physical – presented to the public in a variety of forms outside the walls or floor of a gallery. Are there any criteria by which to judge objectively whether their work is good or bad – or is that now an irrelevant question? Do the art critics find themselves in a cul-de-sac, facing the blank wall of a wider and more baffling question: 'Is visual art today simply what the artist chooses to say it is – and that's all there is to it?'

THE WORDS OF CURATORS AND CRITICS

The problem of criteria may contribute to the cause of a third reason why the public can have difficulty with contemporary work in the galleries. This is the way in which some art correspondents, critics and curators choose to write about artists and their work. Their words and occasionally those of the artists themselves can often obscure, rather than clarify, the what, why and wherefore of works of art. There will often not be, and often need not be, any answer to the question 'what is it?' when, say, the artist's work is an 'installation', a creation in some form and material which cannot be recognised as a more traditional sculpture. But we usually look to curators and critics to offer some answer so I am inclined to be critical if it is blandly indicated that artists are concerned only with themselves and their own self-expression.

Almost all professions have their own jargon and gobbledygook. The bureaucratic language of the public services has an excessive share of it. But curatorial writing about contemporary artists should never obscure meaning. Sentences adorned with clichéd phrases and such fashionable words as 'resonate', 'evocative' and 'ironic' are an obstacle to the expression of clear thought; they have the effect of widening the gulf between artist and the public about which Hugh Casson spoke. Brought up, as I was, by the Whitehall counter doctrine of *Plain Words*, written over fifty years ago by Sir Ernest Gowers, I tease curators, when I can, about the self-inflicted wounds of galleries whose catalogues are heavy with pretentious and obscure paragraphs about their exhibitions.

Modern Art Oxford exhibited some years ago the highly regarded contemporary artist Howard Hodgkin, whose work has carried forward, rather than abandoned, the traditions of the past.

The Times weekend magazine [*31 March 2002*] published an interview between Sir Howard Hodgkin and the journalist Jonathan
Meades. I applaud much of what Hodgkin said:

MEADES: There's a good phrase of Dickens': 'the national dread
of colour'.

HODGKIN: My God, that's still alive. I mean I'm not thought of
as a serious artist because of that, because of colour. And also,
any visual artist who says, 'My work is about death, destruc-
tion', is immediately taken seriously in a different way, whatever the actual art is like.

MEADES: It's an English thing: there has to be a point, a meaning exterior to the work; there's got to be a text alongside the
work explaining what it's about.

HODGKIN: Yes, the primacy of the curator is what really matters.
When I had my big show at the Met in New York, I was
amazed that people came up to me and said, 'What an
extraordinarily courageous thing to do to paint pictures like
this.' It was this idea that it was such an extraordinary thing
that they didn't have any subtext, there was nothing that
could be added on to them.

That interesting dialogue is too dismissive of curators and their
essential role. But I warm to Hodgkin's view that the 'explanation'
of the curator or critic can sometimes achieve the opposite by
creating a barrier between the artist and the public.

THE VISUAL ARTS CULTURE

Professor Sir Christopher Frayling, rector of the Royal College of
Art, gave the Sir Patrick Nairne Lecture at St Catherine's in 1999.
He spoke about the teaching in art schools today, and I was par-
ticularly interested in what he was quoted as saying in another

weekend magazine of *The Times* in October 2001. It throws some further light on the visual arts culture and in particular, the subjective individualism of many contemporary artists and the difficulty of establishing objective artistic criteria.

> Something happened in the mid-Eighties. It was partly to do with the medium, with the advance of digitisation, which made the catching of images easier. It was also to do with a new emphasis on marketing, a richer culture in the high street and a radical inter-disciplinarity in art schools where all the old hierarchies between art and design and engineering broke down. Fine art students had to start learning business skills ... There was an idea that they ought to be more hip to the real world.

Another article of January 2002 from *The Times* magazine, entitled 'The Tastemakers', quoted the Chief Executive of Selfridges who had recently commissioned a major contemporary artist to create a giant installation for the Oxford Street store. His words carry echoes of those of Sir Christopher Frayling:

> A hundred years ago, we were a verbal culture. Words were used to sell everything. Then it became graphics. Now it is totally visual culture. The picture is everything. People are bombarded with visual communications. So of course art has become the medium of choice, because people understand it ... More people go shopping than go to museums, so why shouldn't shops borrow from museums and put art in them?

Even portrait painters are not immune to the desire to produce work which will catch the eye in the culture 'market' of today. To make a personal 'statement' in the form of a good painting – to be acclaimed perhaps as 'valuable and exciting' – can often be as important, if not more important, to the artist than the creation of a successful likeness of the sitter. The sitter will die and his face will be forgotten; an outstanding portrait painting can live on.

The stupendous success of the Tate Modern marks the widest

possible acceptance of 'modern' or 'contemporary' art. This is true but, to be fair to myself, it serves to underline that my difficulty (if insufficient enthusiasm can be called that) relates to quite a narrow, though certainly prominent, range of contemporary work.

BACK TO THE FAMILY

How would I sum up my view of the contemporary avant-garde? Put bluntly, I have unfailing interest but insufficient enthusiasm. I have tried to explain why I believe that many members of the public who care about the arts can feel alienated from the work of contemporary artists. I do not feel 'alienated' but nor do I feel, so to speak, a 'member of the club'. The curators at Modern Art Oxford (whom I greatly admire) tell me that they are 'very excited' by what is to be shown at a future exhibition. I look forward to the private view. When I see the show I am certainly interested, I am occasionally intrigued or puzzled, and I often admire the skill and ingenuity of the artist. But I rarely feel excited. On the contrary, in spite of all that the curator and critics may write, I am more often left disappointingly cold.

Painting for me has never been more than a pastime (whereas for our son James, it is his profession, as an artist and teacher) but I cannot do without it. In the introduction to his recent book on art history Professor Martin Kemp, Professor of Art History at Oxford University, made a teasing remark with a convincing ring: 'There is no reason for art. It does not feed us. It does not keep us at work. It does not stave off disease. But many of us cannot stop doing it, and it clearly meets fundamental human needs – visually, intellectually, psychologically.'* This is as relevant to the amateur painter as to the professional artist. It is certainly as true for me as for countless other artists.

My father, finally bedridden with arthritis, abandoned all drawing and painting in his last years. I intend to continue to paint for

---

* Martin Kemp, *The Oxford History of Western Art*, Oxford University Press, Oxford, 2000.

as long as I can and I received unexpected encouragement in a
letter from John Doyle, a past President of the Royal Watercolour
Society. I had sent him the card for my Clarges Gallery exhibition
and he generously wrote:

> I called into the Clarges Gallery and was most impressed by what you
> had done . . . Your pictures are delightfully fresh, some of the tones
> are a little cold; look for those wonderful dark warm tones to
> complement the cool ones. When two tones of the same value, one
> warm and one cool, are placed side by side, they act together and set
> up a wonderfully exciting resonance – try it . . .
>
> I am being very bossy! The blind leading the blind when up against
> nature – even Turner. All we can do is make marks on paper that
> remind people of the truth.

Good advice. I frequently reflect that I ought to make better use
of retirement, that there is nothing that I would like more than to
paint every day and to paint better. Painting is still for me the
perfect pastime. It used to be on family picnics when the children
were young ('Paint a helicopter in the sky, Daddy' . . . 'You'll have
to stop now: it's high time we went home'). It is today when we
are on holiday or out for the day (with Penny reading aloud on
the grass beside me and the occasional stranger boldly looking over
my shoulder and whispering to a companion). So, I still respond
to the wistful spirit of Thomas Gainsborough and his engaging
wish to:

> . . . walk off to some sweet village where I can paint landskips and
> enjoy the fag end of life in quietness and ease . . .

Pat at the DHSS offices, 1977; reproduced in *The Times*, 28 June 2013.

APPENDICES

Appendix 1

Denis Healey, Letter to Patrick Nairne, on his appointment as Assistant Undersecretary of State (Logistics), after working together on the extensive Defence Review reductions.

Ministry of Defence, Whitehall, London SW1
August 10th 1967

My dear Pat

One of the many things you taught me over the last three years is on no account to allow any official to leave his employment under one without the appropriate letter of thanks. I do not know whether it is more to your credit or my shame that this is the first such letter I have written myself – just one more example of how much I have owed you in small things as well as large!

It did not take me long in office to learn that my Private Secretary was the most important man in the department – a mixture of Leporello & Mephistopheles, the fulcrum or axle of the whole operation, responsible for lubricating himself! I have no expectation of coming across anyone in the rest of my career who combines all the desirable qualities even half as well.

In the diplomatic function, as go-between, you were an infallible source of intelligence not only for me but also I hope about me to the others. Considering how much of your time I monopolised I have never understood how you were able to see so much of everyone else who mattered in the department.

In the advisory function, your wisdom, experience, and imagination, were invaluable. Most of all, perhaps, in retrospect I value the indefatigable stamina which enabled you to force me to think things through when my own energies were flagging.

Management has always been uniquely a Nairne forte – here again you showed extraordinary ability to follow through a decision and programme the handling of a problem so that the solution was achieved on time. What little I have learnt about administration – a closed book to me in 1964 – I owe overwhelmingly to you.

This combination of qualities would have made another most dauntingly superhuman. But you have the saving graces of humanity, courtesy and tact in the face of the Hill-Nortons and Bunburys of this world. – as well as a zest for life, and an enjoyment of the arts which I have always found refreshing.*

I hope that we shall continue to meet as colleagues and to work together in the future, but I hope shall always count one another as friends.

Meanwhile with luck you should find the pace of life less furious and the problems you meet at work, if no less complicated, at least less wearing on the emotions. I hope this will give you more time with your family – I was all too conscious of what Penny lost through my gain. If you have one failing, it is being over-conscientious – you must now

---

* A reference to the Admiral of the Fleet, Sir Peter Hill-Norton, and to Oscar Wilde's famous character, Bunbury, in *The Importance of Being Earnest*, 1895.

recharge your batteries. You have only one failure on record, which must have made reading this epistle a penance. You never taught me to write properly!

With gratitude, affection and warmest good wishes for the future.

Yours ever

Denis

Appendix 2

Revd Sydney Smith, Letter to Lady Georgiana Morpeth, 16 February 1820. The text of this letter was inserted in my father's common-place book and he regarded Sydney Smith's outlook on life as particularly sympathetic. The letter was printed in the service sheet for the Service of Thanksgiving for my father at the University Church of St Mary the Virgin, Oxford, on 17 October 2013.

Dear Lady Georgiana

Nobody has suffered more from low spirits than I have done — so I feel for you. 1st. Live as well as you dare. 2nd. Go into the shower-bath with a small quantity of water at a temperature low enough to give you a slight sensation of cold, 75° or 80°. 3rd. Amusing books. 4th. Short views of human life — not further than dinner or tea. 5th. Be as busy as you can. 6th. See as much as you can of those friends who respect and like you. 7th. And of those acquaintances who amuse you. 8th. Make no secret of low spirits to your friends, but talk of them freely — they are always worse for dignified concealment. 9th. Attend to the effects tea and coffee produce upon you. 10th. Compare your lot with that of other people. 11th. Don't expect too much from human life — a sorry business at the best. 12th. Avoid poetry, dramatic representations (except comedy), music, serious novels, melancholy, sentimental people, and everything likely to excite feeling or emotion, not ending in active benevolence. 13th. *Do good*, and endeavour to please everybody of every degree. 14th. Be as much as you can in the open air without fatigue. 15th. Make the room where you commonly sit, gay and pleasant. 16th. Struggle by little and little against idleness. 17th. Don't be too severe upon yourself, or underrate yourself, but do yourself justice. 18th. Keep good blazing fires. 19th. Be firm and constant in the exercise of rational religion. 20th. Believe me, dear Lady Georgiana,

Very truly yours,

Sydney Smith

Foston, 16 February 1820

Appendix 3: Chronology
Rt Hon. Patrick Dalmahoy Nairne, GCB, MC, PC

CHRONOLOGY
15 August 1921–3 June 2015

Much of this chronology is drawn from Patrick Nairne's own text, titled 'Course of My Life', drafted in 1998.

YEAR	EVENT
1921	15 August. Born, 3 Courtfield Gardens, SW5; second son to Lieutenant Colonel Charles Sylvester Nairne (1880–1966) and Edith Dalmahoy Kemp (1889–1975)
	• 29 September. Baptised St Luke's, Chelsea; performed by Rev. J. D. Nairne
1923	7 December. Birth of brother James Kemp Nairne
1927	November. Nairne family move into Plover Hill, Shawford, Winchester
1929	23 August. Birth of brother David Colin Nairne (d. 1998)
1930–35	September. After Miss Taylor's private day school in Shawford, joins elder brother, Sandy (b. 1920), at Hordle House Prep school, Milford-on-Sea
1934	7 December. Confirmed in Hordle House Chapel
1935–38	September. Starts at Radley College, Abingdon; Scholarship; Boyd's / Morgan's Social
1937	15 July. Death of elder brother Sandy from appendicitis and peritonitis, while at Dauntsey's School
1939	See Radley's 150th Anniversary and *The Radley Register 1847–1962* for record at Radley; edits *The Emergency Ration*, informal Radley magazine
	• December. Awarded Exhibition to University College, Oxford
1940	May. Left Radley, then to University College, Oxford, to read Classics
	• May, Oxford Trinity Term, arrived at University College (Master: Sir William Beveridge), reading Classical Mods (Tutor: Mr Levens,

Merton). Member Oxford University Officer Training Corps
(Certificate B). June 1940 received permission from the Master
Sir William Beveridge to leave the college to join the army. Worked
briefly on Herefordshire farm with Duncan Raikes. July–November
at Plover Hill. Member of the (newly formed) Home Guard during
the Battle of Britain.

1941–44   Spring 1941. Commissioned in Seaforth Highlanders, part of
            51st Division
            • November 1940: called up to 166 Officer Cadets Training
            Unit, Douglas, Isle of Man. March 1941: successfully passed
            out of OCTU. Commissioned as second lieutenant in the
            Seaforth Highlanders. 14 March 1941: reported to Seaforth
            Highlanders Depot, Fort George (Adjutant: John Sym; Assistant
            Adjutant: Douglas Law). Platoon Commander in Jack Walford's
            C Company. Attended Junior Leaders Course, Dick Place,
            Edinburgh. Posted temporarily to Stornoway, Isle of Lewis, to
            train RAF Regiment Platoon at Coastal Air Station. Posted
            temporarily to Home Guard, 1st Moray Bn, as acting adjutant
            (the permanent adjutant had fallen down when drunk and
            broken his arm). Autumn 1941: posted temporarily to Island of
            Lewis again to train the Island Home Guard. November 1941:
            finally left Fort George on posting to the 5th (Caithness and
            Sutherland) Battalion, the Seaforth Highlanders, in 152 Brigade,
            51st Highland Division, stationed at Stonehaven, Aberdeenshire,
            under the command of Lieut. Colonel J. E. Stirling.
            • November 1941–December 1945: in 5th Seaforths, 152 Bde,
            51st Highland Division – Scotland – England – Western Desert
            – Tripolitania – Algeria – Sicily – Scotland – NW Europe –
            Germany. [See *Sans Peur* (or *Battalion*) by Alastair Borthwick.]
            • November 1941–November 1942: Highland Division in
            Scotland and Hampshire, preparing for war service overseas.
            Spring 1942: attended Battle School in the Cotswolds.
            • 18 June 1942: Highland Division embarked on the Clyde.
            Convoy called at Cape Town. 15 August 1942: (twenty-first
            birthday) landed at Suez. El Tahag Camp in Canal Area. Moved
            (whole Division driving in convoy through Cairo to strengthen
            Egyptian morale) to West of the Pyramids and then to Western
            Desert. In reserve during Rommel's unsuccessful September
            attack at Alam el Halfa.
            • 23 October–3/4 November: took part in Battle of Alamein.

1/2 November: 152 Bde attack. Pursuit of retreating Germans and Italians through Cyrenaica, West of Benghazi – El Agheila. Germans retreat again. Christmas and New Year in the Desert.

• January 1943–January 1944: advance into Tripolitania. 21 January: Battle of the Hills at Homs, wounded in leg, evacuated to Egypt Canal Area. Sick leave, in hospital with jaundice in Cairo. 1 April: returned to 5th Seaforths as intelligence officer, before Battle of Akarit. 6/7 April: capture of Roumana Ridge. Moved west towards Tunisia to join up with 1st Army. Went sick with form of glandular fever. Evacuated again to Egypt Canal Area. In June returned to Battalion at Djidjelli in Algeria, training in landing craft for an invasion. Sailed along coast to Sousse in Tunisia. 5 July: sailed from Sousse in LSIs (landing ship infantry) for Malta. July 10: invaded Sicily, landing Cape Pachino. Marched inland. 13/14 July: halted by German parachutists. Battle of Francofonte. Advanced NE towards Catanian Plain. 31 July–1 August: attacked Germans in Battle of Sferro Hills. Moved to slopes of Mt Etna on German withdrawal from Sicily. Developed pleural effusion of lung and malaria. Evacuated to hospital in North Africa. Medically downgraded and evacuated to Meanwood Park Hospital, Leeds.

1943	July. Awarded Military Cross
1943–45	Letters arrived from parents with 'MC' tacked on to my name – awarded, it emerged, for performance at Battle of Francofonte in July.

• On leave at home for Christmas. January 1944 (medical category B) posted to be adjutant, Infantry Training Centre (Seaforth and Cameron Highlanders), Pinefield Camp, Elgin.

• January 1944–January 1945: Adjutant ITC (Commanding Officer: Lieut. Colonel Pat Hannay, Cameron Hldrs) until September 1944, when graded medical A again and posted back to 5th Battalion as adjutant (Commanding Officer: still Jack Walford) stationed at Olland near Eindhoven in Holland. [*Following Pat Nairne's return from Sicily to England, the Highland Division had fought in Normandy Campaign and battle at Le Havre and moved eastward to Holland, where 1st Airborne Division's landing at Arnhem had just failed.*] James (brother) also serving in 152 Brigade (2nd Battalion). 5th Bn moved to 'the Island' between Nijmegen and Arnhem. Two minor night attacks across canals, clearing the Germans from SW

Holland. Early December: major German counter-attack against US Army, through Ardennes. Highland Division rapidly moved south-east of Liege. Christmas and New Year at Les Cours. January 10: Battle at Mierchamps, north of salient created by German offensive, wounded in neck and hand. Evacuated to UK and, once again, to Meanwood Park Hospital, Leeds.

• January 1945: moved from Meanwood Park Hospital to Park Prewett Hospital near Basingstoke. Then to Winchester Hospital. Medically graded B or C. On leave at Plover Hill.

• May: end of War against Germany. In Winchester for VE Day celebrations. Posted to Seaforth training battalion (Commanding Officer: once again, Jack Walford) near Annan, Dumfriesshire, 2 i/c infantry company. August: posted back to 5th Seaforth.

• Once again adjutant, with John Sym as Commanding Officer, at Altenbruch near Cuxhaven.

• End of War against Japan. December: War Office letter conveying release from the army under Class B (priority return to university education). Finally left 5th Battalion. To Strathpeffer for demobilisation routine. Home for Christmas at Plover Hill.

1946–47   January. Return to Oxford for shortened degree in modern history; awarded First

• 17 January '46: Returned to Oxford. Back in University College: modern history, shortened Honours (instead of Classical Hon. Mods) Principal tutor: Giles Alington, with Lawrence Stone in autumn term '46. Tutor in special subject of modern English government: Norman Chester at Nuffield. Lived January–June '46 in college (Staircase 10.3); October '46–June '47 at 15 Merton Street. Main concerns: academic work and future employment. Played hockey for college; helped to start Shelley Club (papers read – cultural discussions); *ISIS* magazine correspondent for OU Conservative Association; failed – after three re-counts – to be elected as President of the Junior Common Room.

• Mid-April 1947: took preliminary exam for Administrative Class of Civil Service, emerging as borderline candidate. May: after a visit to Eastbourne College was offered post as junior master by the headmaster, John Nugee (previously Sub-Warden of Radley). Shortly afterwards offered teaching post at Radley,

to be combined with secretaryship of Old Radleian Society.
Father inclined to advise acceptance, but refused both offers.

• 16 May 1947 met Penelope Bridges at LMH Dance.

• Oxford Finals of shortened Honours Course in modern
history: on 23 July, after tough 'viva', emerged with a 'First'.
Special individual Civil Service interview in the summer;
that interview went well with the result (to which degree result
must have contributed) that I was invited to next stage of
Administrative Class entry exam, the two-day selection board
'house party' of tests at Stoke D'Abernon Manor House in
September. Final Civil Service interview on 24 September at
Civil Service Commission behind Burlington House. Letter
on 16 October conveying news of acceptance for Administrative
Class of Civil Service (second on list of seventy-four entrants in
1947). Posting to the Admiralty arrived in November.

• Sunday 23 November to Charlbury with Penny Bridges by
train; lunched at The Bell; climbed the tower of the church;
walked into Cornbury Park, where it suddenly seemed the right
moment at which to ask Penny to become engaged and marry.

• December. Enters Home Civil Service – Admiralty and then
Ministry of Defence

• 2 December reported to the Admiralty – as recorded in diary:
'FIRST day's work.' Assistant principal in the Admiralty (Secretary
of the Admiralty, Sir John Lang). The service departments
had employed a number of good academics during the war
and they had returned to their universities, so in theory there
were vacancies and good prospects. During probation period
of two years, served in establishments (CE Branch), fleet and
shore policy (M Branch), general finance (GF Branch), Vickers
Armstrong at Barrow-in-Furness, training visits to Admiralty Bath,
Portsmouth Dockyard, the Fleet (one of the last battleships, KG.
V). In 1950 made secretary of a naval personnel committee: the
Re-engagement Committee under Admiral Hawkins.

1948   Berlin Airlift and fear of war with the Russians, and temporary
              fear of having to postpone wedding arranged for September.

              • 18 September. Marries Penelope Chauncey Bridges, St
                Andrew's Church, Linton Road, Oxford

              • 18 September: Wedding at St Andrew's, Linton Road, close
                to 24 Charlbury Road, where P's parents, Robert and Lucy
                Bridges (though she wished me to call her Charlotte) then

lived. Honeymoon in Isle of Eriska and Edinburgh. Moved into 2 Hammersmith Terrace, ground floor and basement flat, as tenants of Sir George and Lady Bull.

1949   6 September. Birth of Katharine Davina

1950   At end of Re-engagement Committee appointed Private Secretary to James Callaghan, (who was then Parliamentary Secretary and became prime minister some twenty-five years later) but, after one day in his office, doctors diagnosed mild TB. Laid up at Hammersmith Terrace, Plover Hill and Acacia Cottage, Appleford (to which P's parents had moved).

1951   Easter: holiday in Lerici and Florence, during which news came of sudden death of P's Father. Returned to the Admiralty as principal in O & M.

• 7 December. Birth of Fiona Penelope

1951–52   September 1951. Honorary Secretary of Hampshire House Youth Club, Hog Lane, Hammersmith W6

1953   February: bought South Lodge, between Cobham and Oxshott, for £4,650. Learned in March that TB had returned. On 8 April to Benenden Sanatorium. P moved with K and F to Plover Hill while South Lodge was being put in order (with Radley friend, Peter Cleverly, as architect).

• 8 June. Birth of Alexander [Sandy] Robert

• 10 November: released from Benenden and rejoined family at South Lodge. TB never returned.

1954   1st February: returned to the Admiralty. Employed to write 'A Newcomer's Guide to the Admiralty'. In CE 4 (Civil Service manpower); Military Branch (Middle East, Far East, South Atlantic and International Law, to which I had devoted some study in Benenden).

1956   Suez Crisis. Much involved with Foreign Office links with Admiralty (especially re international law of the sea) and with Operation Muskateer (Invasion of Suez Canal Area).

1957–58   In Military Branch. Closure of dockyards, transfer of Malta Dockyard to Welsh ship-repairing firm of Baileys.

1958–60   20 November. Appointed private secretary to the First Sea Lord, Lord Selkirk

• December 1958: started work as principal private secretary to the First Lord, Earl of Selkirk, in succession to Philip Moore, later Private Secretary to the Queen, and, in autumn 1959, to Lord Carrington, who became First Lord (after Tory election victory under Harold Macmillan) and later Defence Secretary.

1960   10 February. Birth of James Patrick and Andrew Colin
• Summer: promoted to assistant secretary and appointed head of Naval Personnel Branch 2 (officers entry, training, specialisation etc.)

1961   10 May. Birth of Margaret Caroline Susan

1963   Appointed head of Military Branch 1 (future size and shape of navy).

1963–64   • Reorganisation of service departments into one Ministry of Defence. Left Admiralty building for Horse Guards Avenue; M1 became DS4.

1965–67   January. Private secretary to Denis Healey, Secretary of State for Defence
• January 1965: appointed private secretary to Denis Healey, in new Labour government under Harold Wilson. Major defence review: round the world tour. (See Denis Healey *Autobiography*.)

1967–70   Assistant Undersecretary of State (Logistics)

1970   March. Deputy Undersecretary of State (Policy and Programmes), working with Lord Carrington
• Spring: promoted to deputy secretary (DUS [Policy and Programmes]). May 1970: Tory election victory under Edward Heath. Lord Carrington Secretary of State for Defence; five Power Defence Arrangements in SE Asia; Malta crisis and negotiations with Mr Mintoff; defence discussions in Australia, NZ, Washington, Japan, Hong Kong and Persian Gulf. (See Peter Carrington *Autobiography*.)

1971   June. Appointed CB

1973   July. Second permanent secretary at Cabinet Office, head of Civil Contingencies Unit

• July, promoted to second permanent secretary in Cabinet Office, head of the European Unit and official chairman of the Civil Contingencies Unit, under Sir John Hunt (who had succeeded Sir Burke Trend). Policy issues relating to UK's recent entry into the EEC (Common Market); Miners' Strike; CCU in action; introduction of three-day industrial week to save power.

1974   February. General election: Labour government returned to power with Harold Wilson as PM. Miners' strike settled, broadly on their terms; government's commitment to renegotiate terms of entry into the EEC.

• October 1974: further general election. Commitment to complete renegotiation and then 'consult the British people' by holding a national referendum. Double task of coordinating progress in renegotiation at official level and of organising the UK's first national referendum. EEC summit meetings in Paris and Dublin. Cabinet divided on outcome of renegotiation: 'formal agreement to differ' with majority for remaining in EEC.

1975   June referendum: 65 per cent of voters supported EEC membership.

• November. Permanent secretary (to 1981), Department of Health and Social Security (two ministries combined in 1968)

• December. Appointed KCB

1975–99   Governor of Radley College (to 1999); chairman of Radleian Society; President 1980–83

• November 1975: promoted to first permanent secretary at the Department of Health and Social Security under Barbara Castle, later David Ennals and, after Tory election victory in May 1979, Patrick Jenkin. During DHSS years confronted with problems of inflation of over 20 per cent; industrial action among doctors, NHS trade unions and pay-beds, a reorganisation of the NHS which, in effect, transformed a hospital service into a health service but which was over-elaborate in structure and led to the complaint of 'tears about tiers', and new hospitals which had been too slow and too costly in building (notably the Royal Liverpool Hospital, specially visited by the Public Accounts Committee). Royal Commission on the NHS, chaired by Sir Alec Merrison.

1976   President, Association of Civil Service Art Clubs (to 1989)

1977   Letter to Sir Douglas Allen (Lord Croham), head of Home Civil
               Service, expressing 'concern at impact on civil servants' morale
               of media attacks blaming them for Ministers' mistakes'.
               • 12 June. Elected Fellow of the Royal Society of Arts

1978–79   'The Winter of Discontent', with the Government (under James
               Callaghan) overwhelmed by industrial action.

1979   May. Tory election victory under Margaret Thatcher: Patrick
               Jenkin Secretary of State at the DHSS. Introduction of a fresh
               reorganisation of the NHS with general blessing from the Royal
               Commission. The Black Report on the health of the nation.
               Ministerial guidance to delegate more to the local level (though
               soon to be followed by greater centralisation).

1980   Honorary Degree, University of Leicester
               • September. Exhibition of watercolours, The Sewell Arts Centre,
               Radley College

1981   August. Retired from Civil Service.
               • Appointed GCB
               • Appointed Master, St Catherine's College, Oxford (to 1988)
               • Summer 1981: sold South Lodge, Cobham. In October
               installed as Master of St Catherine's at Stated General Meeting
               – late holiday near Uzes, west of Avignon. Early November:
               moved out of South Lodge. P and I took up a new life at the
               college. Snow and first family Christmas in the lodgings.
               • Appointed Honorary Fellow University College, Oxford
               • Council of the Royal College of Art (to 1986)
               • Executive Committee of VSO [Voluntary Service Overseas] (to
                 1987)
               • Trustee Modern Art Oxford; Chair of Advisory Board from
               1988; then President from 1998
               • Oxford Art Society Member (to 2009)
               • Trustee, then chairman 1982–87 Society for Italic Handwriting

1982   Bought Yew Tree, Chilson, near Charlbury, Oxfordshire, and in
               March 1983 established home there while continuing to live in
               the Lodgings during term.
               • In retirement joined campaign towards repeal of Section 2 of

Official Secrets Act and for FOI
• Appointed to Franks Committee: The Falkland Islands
Review; made a Privy Council member
• Committee Member Seafarers' Hospital Society; then
President, 1986–2002
• Trustee, National Maritime Museum (to 1992)
• Trustee, Joseph Rowntree Memorial Trust (to 1996)

1983   October. Exhibition of watercolours, Clarges Gallery
              • Appointed Chancellor of the University of Essex (to 1997);
              awarded Honorary Degree

1984   Appointed as government monitor in Hong Kong, autumn 1984
              (with Mr Justice Simon Li Fook-sean) with responsibility for
              supervising, and reporting on, the consultation of the Hong
              Kong people about the draft treaty in respect of unification
              with China in 1997
              • Honorary Degree, St Andrew's University
              • Called on civil servants to let five years elapse before taking
              jobs with firms with which they had had dealings

1985   Non-executive director of two investment trusts – Finsbury
              Group and Scottish Cities Investment Trust
              • Non-executive director, West Midlands Board, Central TV (to
              1992)

1987   Chairman, Institute of Medical Ethics, Working Party on HIV/
              AIDS
              • Chairman, Media Resource Service Steering Committee, CIBA
              Foundation
              • President, National Television Rental Association
              • Member, Government Security Panel relating to the
              Immigration Act
              • Sponsor, The Helwel Trust (Zululand) –
              http://www.helweltrust.co.uk/archives.htm – connection through
              Anthony and Maggie Barker, founders, and italic handwriting
              • Chairman, Oxford University Appointments Committee
              • Elector to the Bampton Lectureship
              • Senior Member, Oxford University Gilbert & Sullivan Society
              • Trustee, National Aids Trust (to 1995)

1988   October: retired from Mastership of St Catherine's College (on

reaching age of sixty-seven). Elected Honorary Fellow.
- Moved permanently to Yew Tree, Chilson, Oxfordshire
- Chair, Irene Wellington Educational Trust
- Elected Honorary Fellow, St Catherine's College
- Council and Governor, Ditchley Foundation (to 1996)

1989	April. Exhibition of watercolours, Oliver Swann Galleries
1991	Founding chairman, Nuffield Council on Bioethics (to 1996)
1992	Appointed to Archbishop of Canterbury's Advisory Group on Medical Ethics - November. Exhibition of watercolours, Oliver Swann Galleries
1993	President, Oxfordshire Craft Guild (to 1997) - Appointed Church Commissioner (for Oxford University) (to 1998)
1994	Council Member, Oxford University Society (to 2004)
1996	Chairman, Commission on the Conduct of Referendums
1997	June. Exhibition of watercolours, Clarges Gallery
1998	Discussions and correspondence with Sir Christopher Foster about good government continue to 2010 - Trustee, Oxford School of Drama (to 2011)
1999	November. Contributes to exhibition, 'Private painters in public life', London School of Economics
2002	15 May. Installed as Knight Grand Cross of the Most Honourable Order of the Bath, Lady Chapel of Henry VII, Westminster Abbey; stall plate, banner and crest
2013	3 June. Dies in Banbury Hospital - 13 June. Funeral, St Mary's Charlbury - June. Principal obituaries: see Appendix 4 - 7 September. Patrick Nairne's ashes interred in Garden of Remembrance, St Mary's Charlbury - 17 October. Service of Thanksgiving, University Church of St Mary the Virgin, Oxford; reception in University College Hall

Appendix 4: Bibliography

A. Published articles, letters and reviews by Patrick Nairne

'William Dring', *The Studio*, July 1947

Review of T. A Critchley, *The Civil Service Today*, with introduction by Lord Beveridge (Gollanz, 1951), *Public Administration*, 1951

'Management and the Administrative Class', *Public Administration*, Summer 1964, vol. 42, pp. 113–122

'A Day in the Life of the Master of St Catherine's', St Catherine's magazine, [n.d.]; 1980s

'Reflections on Retiring', *New Window* (Staff magazine DHSS), 5 August 1981, vol. 34, p. 4

'Fewer mandarins in Whitehall', letter to *The Times*, 28 May 1982

'Science graduates in the Civil Service', letter to *The Times*, 28 June 1982

'Some Reflections on Change', *Management in Government*, 1982, vol. 37(2), pp. 71–82

'Remembering Alfred Fairbank', obituary for *The Society for Italic Handwriting*, 1982, website: http://www.italic-handwriting.org/magazine/articles/members/in-memoriam-alfred-fairbank/patrick-nairne

'Is radio demystifying the Whitehall Mandarins?' *The Listener*, 12 May 1983

'The Think Tank', letter to *The Times*, 24 June 1983

'Managing the DHSS Elephant: Reflections on a Giant Department', *The Political Quarterly*, 1983, vol. 54, pp. 243–256

'Inside Number Ten', letter to *The Times*, 3 May 1984

Report of the Assessment Office, Independent Monitoring Team, Hong Kong, with Simon Li Fook-sean, Government White Paper Cmd. 9407, December 1984

Review of Clive Ponting, *The Right to Know* (Sphere, 1985), and Judith Cook, *The Price of Freedom* (Hodder & Stoughton, 1985), *The Times Educational Supplement*, 5 April 1985

'Managing the National Health Service', *British Medical Journal*, 13 July 1985, vol. 291, pp. 121–124; based on a lecture at St Catherine's, 4 February 1985

'Running the NHS', letter to *The Times*, 30 October 1985

'Putting hospital patients in context', letter to *The Times*, 1 November 1985

Foreword, in *Challenges to Social Policy*, ed. Richard Berthoud (Policy Studies Institute, 1985)

'Myths and Management', *Oxford Magazine*, 4th week, Michaelmas Term, 1985

'Essential skills for jobs at the top', letter to *The Times*, 4 April 1986; relating to Clive Ponting, *Whitehall: Tragedy & Farce* (Hamish Hamilton, 1986)

'Call for reform of Secrets Acts', letter to *The Times*, 13 February 1987

'Medical records for all to see', letter to *The Times*, 24 April 1987

'Changes in the NHS', letter to *The Times*, 26 June 1987

Review of Charles Webster, *The Health Services Since the War* – *vol. 1* (Her Majesty's Stationery Office, 1988), *British Medical Journal*, April 1988

'The National Health Service: reflections on a changing service', *British Medical Journal*, 28 May 1988, vol. 296, pp. 1518–1520; from lecture given at Green College, Oxford

'Splitting the Elephant', *Guardian*, 2 August 1988

Review of Peter Hennessy, *Whitehall* (Secker and Warburg, 1989), *Public Policy and Administration*, Winter 1989, vol. 4, no. 3, pp. 48–50

'The National Health Service – a Grand Design in distress', *Journal of the Royal Society of Medicine*, 1989, vol. 82, pp. 6–11; from the Jephcott Lecture, Royal Society of Medicine, 17 April 1988

'Yes Minister, please tell us more', *The Times*, 8 May 1990; relating to Freedom of Information and *Hypotheticals* programme on BBC2

'The Civil Service – "Mandarins and Ministers"', *Papers in Politics* (Wroxton College, 1990)

'Hong Kong's Future', letter to *The Times*, 22 July 1991

Introduction, Belinda Banham, *Snapshots in Time: Some Experiences in Healthcare, 1936–91* (Patten Press, 1991), 1991

'Rum Ration in the 5th Seaforth; Alamein to Sfax 1942–43', *The Queen's Own Highlander* (50 Years after Alamein edition), Winter 1992, pp. 156–157

Introduction, Jane Matthews, *Welcome Aboard: The Story of the Seamen's Hospital Society and the Dreadnought* (Quotes, 1992); 1992

'Civil service relations', letter to *The Times*, 25 January 1993

'Demystifying Bioethics: A Lay Perspective' (guest editorial) *Journal of Medical Ethics*, 4 December 1993, vol. 19, pp. 197–199

'Complexity of EU Referendum', letter to *The Times*, May 1994

'Health care into the next century', letter to *The Times*, 4 August 1994

Review of 'Reflections on Retirement' by Sir Michael Quinlan and Sir Terry Heiser, in *Public Policy and Administration*, Spring 1994, vol 9, no. 1, pp. 3–6

Foreword, in Janet Walker, 'Cost of communication breakdown', research report, British Telecom publication, London, January 1995

Foreword, in 'Report of the Commission on the Conduct of Referendums', Electoral Reform Society, The Constitution Unit, University College, London, 1996

'The Civil Service "Mandarins and Ministers"', Wroxton Papers, in *Politics, Series A*. Paper A6, pp. 4–11, Philip Charles Media: Barnstable; reproduced in Peter Barberis (ed.), *The Whitehall Reader* (Open University Press, 1996)

'The Next Government – Agenda for the Civil Service' (editorial), *Public Policy and Administration*, Spring 1997, vol. 12, no. 1, pp. 1–7

'The State Under Stress', *Public Policy and Administration*, Spring 1997, vol 12, no. 1, pp. 69–70

'The End of the Thirties – A Radley Rite of Passage', *The Radleian*, Summer 1997

'Last Exit', letter to the *London Review of Books*, 22 January 1998, vol. 20(2)

'Conduct of referendums and the Neill Committee', letter to *The Times*, 20 October 1998

Letter to *The Times*, 15 November 2001; correcting Michael Gove, 'Franks and the Falklands', 2001

Deborah Cassidi, *Favourite Wisdom* (Bloomsbury, 2003); quotations offered by Patrick Nairne for the anthology

Alzheimer's Society, text for 25th Anniversary Booklet, 2004; Patrick Nairne was a patron of the Oxfordshire branch

'Charles Snell, writing master' (*bap.* 1667, *d.* 1733)', 389 words; entry for *Dictionary of National Biography*, 2004, available at www.oxforddnb.com/index/37/101037989/

'Handwriting for Life', *Society for Italic Handwriting* website (added 17 July 2009) www.italic-handwriting.org/magazine/articles/history/handwriting-for-life

Short contribution in Mike Cast and Michelle Abadie (eds), *8,000 Years of Wisdom: 100 Octogenarians share their lessons learned from life* (Accent Press, 2010)

B. Broadcasts: radio and tv

'No Minister', BBC radio, Hugo Young and Anne Sloman, July 1981

'Are We Over-Governed?' sound recording, [n.d.]; 1981

'Thinking Aloud', Brian Magee, BBC TV, 19 January 1986

'People and Politics', sound recording, [n.d.] 1987

'Edgeways', BBC Radio, recorded 9 December 1987

'Talking Politics', BBC Radio 4, 10 August 1991 and [n.d.] 2003

'Open Mind', Radio, 15 March 1992

'The Number Ten Show – If I Were Prime Minister', series from 12 January 1995, Executive Producer Jeremy Bugler, Fulmar Productions for Channel 4

'Back to the Future', presented by Liz Forgan, Channel Four, December 1997

Sound recording, BBC Radio 4, [n.d.] 1998

Advising Brook Lapping TV for *Hypotheticals*, BBC2, 31 July 1998

C. Obituaries – Patrick Nairne

Daily Telegraph, 4 June 2013: http://www.telegraph.co.uk/news/obituaries/10098955/Sir-Patrick-Nairne.html

The Times, 5 June 2013: http://www.thetimes.co.uk/tto/opinion/obituaries/article3782548.ece

Guardian, 5 June 2013: http://www.theguardian.com/politics/2013/jun/05/sir-patrick-nairne

Essex University, 5 June 2013, tributes: http://www.essex.ac.uk/events/event.aspx?e_id=5263

Independent, 9 June 2013: http://www.independent.co.uk/news/obituaries/sir-patrick-nairne-civil-servant-who-had-key-roles-in-the-dhss-and-the-ministry-of-defence-8651275.html

Oxford Mail, 13 June 2013: http://www.oxfordmail.co.uk/news/community/obituaries/obits/10480104.Obituary__Sir_Patrick_Nairne__top_civil_servant_who_fought_at_El_Alamein/

The Times Higher Education Supplement, 20 June 2013: https://www.timeshighereducation.com/obituary-sir-patrick-nairne/2004913.article

The Radleian, tributes published from Service of Thanksgiving by Sandy Nairne, Andrew Motion, Richard Wilson, 17 October 2013, St Mary the Virgin, Oxford, *The Old Radleian*, 2014, pp. 24–29: https://issuu.com/radleycollege/docs/old_radleian_2014

Journal of Medical Ethics, 2013, vol. 39: http://jme.bmj.com/content/39/10/660.extract

Acknowledgements

First thanks go to my family who encouraged me to edit a selection of my father's writings. His surviving brother, Major James Nairne, has been an insightful source of information about childhood and their service in the Seaforth Highlanders. I have appreciated his support, as also from my sisters and brothers – Kathy, Fiona, James, Andrew and Margaret – each of whom offered advice and practical help throughout the preparation of the book: editing and gathering images for it. I also appreciate the invaluable help of my wife, Lisa Tickner, and the interest and encouragement of our children, Kit and Eleanor Nairne.

In considering my father's papers and writings I was guided by conversations with Sir David Cannadine and Lord Hennessy, and by Andrew Riley at the Churchill Archive Centre, Cambridge, where his papers are now housed. I am delighted that Peter Hennessy accepted my invitation to write a short foreword, which situates my father as part of the post-war generation of civil servants whose ideals and determination to make a better world were formed through their experience of conflict in the Second World War.

I wish to record my very considerable gratitude to the many supporters of the book, who expressed their interest through advance subscription. Some have been especially generous. They are listed here, and their words of encouragement have been as valuable as their financial support. They have made the project possible.

My thanks go to all the institutions in which my father worked or with which he was associated, including Radley College, the Seaforth Highlanders, the Civil Service, University College Oxford,

St Catherine's College Oxford, University of Essex, the Ditchley, Nuffield and Joseph Rowntree Foundations; and many others to which he contributed as an advisor or trustee.

I gratefully acknowledge permission to quote from letters and writings, including from Tim Healey (Appendix 1), Jan Morris (Chapter 27), *New Window*, the Department of Health and Social Security Staff Magazine, the Royal College of Defence Studies, the Royal Society of Medicine, *The Queen's Own Highlander*, the Commission on the Conduct of Referendums, the *Society for Italic Handwriting Journal*, Alastair Borthwick's *Sans Peur* (1946, republished as *Battalion* 1994) and the University Church of St Mary the Virgin, Oxford. The line on p. xxiv is from *My Fathers Son* by Dom Moraes published by Vintage, and reproduced by kind permission of The Random House Group Ltd. © 1900. I am also grateful for permission to reproduce images, including from Melissa Dring for works by her father John Dring; The University of Essex and Andrew Festing (p. 177); the Squire Archive at Radley College (p. 59); the *Daily Mirror* (p. 140); Press Association Images (p. 197), and *The Times* through News Licensing (p. 314). The 1898 Colonial Office List map of the Falkland Islands (p. 200) is reproduced by kind permission © National Library of Scotland.

My publishers, Unbound, have been helpful and creative at all stages, from refining the original idea, setting up web pages to help solicit support, through to the various intricacies of editing, designing and producing the volume. I am very grateful to all Unbound's staff, in particular to Mathew Clayton, Georgia Odd and – especially – Imogen Denny, who has patiently answered all my queries and made excellent suggestions at all stages of editing and production.

The Coincidence of Novembers is dedicated to the memory of my parents and their sixty-five-year marriage: to my father Pat, whose book this is, and to my mother Penny, who has been equally in my heart and mind as the project progressed.

Sandy Nairne
London, January 2020

Index

Unbound is the world's first crowdfunding publisher, established in 2011.

We believe that wonderful things can happen when you clear a path for people who share a passion. That's why we've built a platform that brings together readers and authors to crowdfund books they believe in – and give fresh ideas that don't fit the traditional mould the chance they deserve.

This book is in your hands because readers made it possible. Everyone who pledged their support, except those who wished to remain anonymous, is listed below. Join them by visiting unbound. com and supporting a book today.

Hamish Aird
Charles Alexander
Robert Armstrong
Peter Avis
Richard Gerald James Ball
Lisa Barber
Anthony Barker
Hussein Barma
Pim Baxter OBE
Chris & Jo Bell
David Bell
Christopher Bellew
Francis Bennett
John Birch
Paul Bird
Rosalind P. Blakesley
Lucy Blythe
Nicholas Boles

Nicholas Bradbury
Jeremy Bradshaw
Jonny Briggs
Christopher Brown
Stephanie Browner
Felicity Bryan
Robin Butler
Jane and Euan Cameron
David Cannadine and Linda
     Colley
Augustus Casely-Hayford
Glena Chadwick
Sonia Coode-Adams MBE
Mike & Rosie Corlett
Patrick Crawford
Ivor Crewe
Geoffrey Crossick
Nicola Dandridge

Fabian Davis
Lucy Davis
Michael Day
David Dell
Jennifer Dowding
Melissa Dring
Geoffrey Alex Dunbar
Sam Fisher
Christopher Foster
Flora Fricker
David Fursdon
Tom Galloway
Christopher Goodhart
James Gowans
Fiona and George Greenwood
Melissa Greenwood
Peter and Davinia Grimaldi
Kathleen Grover
Robert Hazell
Alexa Ann Hechle
Tony Henfrey
Peter Hennessy
Phillip & Sheila Herbert
Joshua A Hill
Charles Hoare Nairne
Michael Hodgson
Alan Hollinghurst
Mary Horlock
Clodagh Houldsworth
Caro Howell
Peter Howell
Sue Hoyle
Perdita Hunt
Philippa Hunt
The Irene Wellington
    Educational Trust
Nichola Johnson
Ron Johnston

Mark Jones
Ludmilla Jordanova
Magdalene Keaney
Dan Kieran
George Laurence
Andrew Lawson
Peter LeRoy
Paul Levy and Penny Marcus
Richard Lloyd Jones
Patrick Lunt
Anthony and Tessa Lydekker
Fiona MacCarthy
Sarah Maitland-Jones
William Makower
Nico Mann
Eliza Manningham-Buller
Theodore R Marmor
Dr Tania Mathias
Anthony Maxwell
Jane Maxwell
Katie & Peter McCurrach
Gemma Mcgeehan
Robert Mckenzie
Roy McMillan
Rupert McNeil
Sunil S Mehta
Joanna Merz
David Mills
John Mitchinson
Richard Morgan
Peter Mortimer
Andrew Motion
Jock Mullard
Andrew Nairne
Christopher Nairne
Eleanor Nairne
James and Angela Nairne
Katharine Nairne

Louisa Nairne
Major J K Nairne
Margaret Nairne
Matthew Nairne
Patrick Nairne
The Estate of Patrick and
    Penny Nairne
Carlo Navato
David Nicholls
Onora O'Neill
Richard Ormond
Michael Partridge
John Pattisson
Suzette Peake (née Mitchell)
George Peck
Tom Phillips
Trevor Phillips
Joseph Pilling
Julian Platt
Justin Pollard
Stephen and Nicola Pulman
Christopher Purvis
Jo and Tom Railton
Nick and John Rawlins
Lois Refkin
Mike Richards
Paul and Vanessa Richards
Emma Ridgway
Jill Ritblat
Simon and Virginia Robertson
Anthony Robinson
Hugo Rogers
Jeremy Ross
Peter Ryan
Anna Nicola Sansom
Abhilash Sarhadi
Marian Schmidt
Michael Scholar

David Scholey
Nicholas Serota
Linda Shoare
Jan Simpson
Lucy Slater
Anne Sloman
Carole Souter
Ann Spokes Symonds
Mike Summers
Hugh Taylor
Lisa Tickner
Andrew Townsend
Jamie Townsend
Rosemary Tucker
Petia Tzanova
The Library, University College
    Oxford
Anthony Vernon
Charles Vincent
William and Caroline
    Waldegrave
Sir Harold Walker
Marina Warner
Merlin Waterson
Ed Way
Elizabeth Way
Michael Way
Pippa Way
Margaret Weston
Sir John Weston
Jonathan Wheatley
Amy Whitaker
Graham White
Richard Wilson
Peter Wilson-Smith
David Wright
Duncan Wu